The RIF Guide to Encouraging Young Readers

The RIF Guide to Encouraging Young Readers

A fun-filled sourcebook of over 200 favorite reading activities of kids and parents from across the country, *plus* an annotated list of books and resources

By Reading Is Fundamental®

EDITED BY RUTH GRAVES

Doubleday

NEW YORK   LONDON   TORONTO   SYDNEY   AUCKLAND

Published by Doubleday, a division of
Bantam Doubleday Dell Publishing Group, Inc.,
666 Fifth Avenue, New York, New York 10103.

Doubleday and the portrayal of an anchor with a
dolphin are trademarks of Doubleday, a division of
Bantam Doubleday Dell Publishing Group, Inc.

Library of Congress Cataloging-in-Publication Data

The R.I.F.* guide to encouraging young readers.

"A fun-filled sourcebook of over 200 favorite reading activities of kids and parents from across the country, *plus* an annotated list of books and resources"
    Includes bibliographies.
        1. Reading—United States—Parent participation—
Handbooks, manuals, etc.   2. Children—United States—
Books and reading—Handbooks, manuals, etc.   3. Activity
programs in education—United States—Handbooks, manuals,
etc.   I. Graves, Ruth.   II. Reading is Fundamental, inc.
LB1050.2.R33 1987   649'.58   86-24055
ISBN 0-385-24110-0
ISBN 0-385-23632-8 (pbk)

2   4   6   8   9   7   5   3

BG

To families of readers everywhere

Contents

Preface

For more than twenty years, Reading Is Fundamental (RIF) has brought books and children together all across the country, in all kinds of settings. Whether in schools, libraries, parks, or community centers, children are reading because RIF has shown them how much fun reading can be. With this guide, RIF can now encourage young readers *in the home*—where their love for reading is first nurtured, and where parents can have such lasting influence.

Since 1966, when the organization was founded by Margaret McNamara, RIF and its board of directors have had a strong commitment to parents and their role in encouraging their children to read. Parents have responded many times over with their own commitment to RIF and children's reading. Today, of the nearly 100,000 people volunteering their time to RIF, some 40 percent are parents. In all fifty states, the District of Columbia, and the offshore territories, parents are working with RIF to encourage young people to read and to aspire through reading.

The RIF Guide was made possible by the creative contributions of parents and the many others who work with us. We are delighted that their ideas, which have worked so well for them, can now be shared with a wider audience. We invite you to use the guide in the same spirit in which it was created—a spirit of fun.

Mrs. Elliot Richardson
Chairman of the Board

At Home with Reading

Where can you get expert help on nurturing your children's love of reading, gain access to the very best learning tools and resources, and have a good laugh besides?

Right in your own home! That's where Reading Is Fundamental is convinced you'll find all of the necessary ingredients: naturally curious children, bountiful resources masquerading as everyday household objects, and your own wise sense of what delights and challenges your youngsters.

Sometimes, though, we parents question just how expert we really are. Because we love and aspire for our youngsters, we want to do our best to help them learn and grow. But then there are *those* days: when sticky fingers cry for cleaning and compete with a pile of beckoning work; when hours are consumed at an outside job; or when the weather turns foul and the children grow restless. On such days, anxiety can quickly supplant assurance and even the most dedicated among us ask ourselves the gloomy question: "Am I really teaching these kids anything?"

Of course we are! Just think of the impressive record we have amassed by the time our children are toddlers. With our assistance, they have learned to walk, to talk, and to do a host of other things. They are constantly learning from us, imitating us, absorbing ideas, values, and information, learning from everything we say and do. Children learn from everyone they encounter and from the environment around them, especially the one we create at home.

This book about reading is centered around the home and family life. Its method, and message, can be summed up quite simply: *Relax, trust your instincts, and enjoy your children.* In doing so, consider the many reassuring advantages we parents have in guiding our children.

To begin with, we know our children as no one else does. We have observed their rhythms, habits, preferences, and distinctive personalities every day they have been with us. We have the luxury of adapting to those individual needs, pacings, and interests without the constraints imposed, say, by a formal curriculum. Our everyday routines offer countless opportunities for learning, opportunities that allow us to be relaxed, playful, and spontaneous.

And let us not forget that special status we hold with our children: We are, to them, the most important people in their universe. Our time, our attention, our approval are precious to them. Above all, we love our children more than anyone else does.

We are often called the role models, and the primary teachers of our children. These we may be, but first and foremost, we are parents.

This book, then, is for parents. It can be shared with grandparents, baby-sitters, and others who spend time with your children. It is about words, written and spoken—about sharing words, enjoying words, relaxing with words, becoming comfortable with words. It is about incorporating words and reading as natural parts of everyday family life. It is also about creating a home environment in which books are friends, reading is a welcome pastime, and the atmosphere is one in which curiosity and imagination flourish.

The activities described in this book are designed to help create that kind of environment, to help turn even the most mundane (and sometimes disagreeable) household routines into reading opportunities—and to have fun doing so.

How to Use the Guide

This book contains hundreds of activities to engage children in the fun of words and reading, a list of more than two hundred books recommended by people who know children and books, and lists of helpful publications, organizations, and other resources. It is not a "how-to" book so much as a "we too"—a book that shares with you the experiences and ideas of thousands of others who want to spark and sustain children's interest in reading.

In the chapters that follow, we have tried to respond to needs and preferences that parents have most often expressed to us. We have drawn on the experience of RIF volunteers from around the country working with children of various backgrounds; from the body of knowledge on getting youngsters to read accumulated since RIF began in 1966; from the generous advice and assistance of parents, librarians, writers, and teachers; and from our own experiences as parents.

And finally, we have tried to remain true to the dual principles embodied in our name: Reading is both fun and fundamental. We urge you to keep fun front and center as you use this book. If you do, you are more likely to achieve the serious purpose of getting your children to read—because they want to.

About the Activities. Some of the activities suggest ways to have simple, spontaneous, giggly fun with children. Others require some advance planning and take the form of games, outings, and crafts. Nearly all the ideas presented here call for spending time with your children. When appropriate, you may wish to build special occasions around some of these activities. Others are designed to weave the fun of reading into the fabric of everyday life.

Some of the suggestions are probably things you have already done with your children. Others may be new. All are geared to helping children discover—and experience—the wonderful world of words. Beyond this, what they have in common is the belief that play promotes learning.

In format, the activities are presented recipe-style. But unlike conventional recipes, where substitution of 3 tablespoons of sugar for 3 tablespoons of flour can lead to a culinary disaster, your personal and spontaneous substitutions and embellishments can create gourmet reading delights.

Age ranges are suggested for each activity. Don't worry if your child doesn't care for an activity in his or her age range or prefers an activity for older or younger children. The age ranges are merely intended as convenient signposts for you to consider as you select ideas.

We suggest that you sample the activities one at a time over a period of weeks and months, perhaps even years. The book is not meant to be read or used page by page, from front to back. Rather, open it up, scan the pages for interesting games, choose one, and give it a try.

You may want to stay with an activity for two minutes, or two hours. It all depends on your child's interest and your own. A word of caution: If you try an activity and find your child growing restive or yourself growing irritable, it's time to do something else.

Children have different tastes, just as adults do. No matter how good the reading "recipe" seems, don't force-feed your child. Grim determination is the one ingredient likely to spoil a youngster's appetite for reading.

The same principles apply to "Books to Grow On," the annotated book list. There is no cause for alarm if your child prefers books in a lower or higher age range. The age ranges listed are general guides and no more. The important thing is that your children enjoy the books they read. Nor is this list to be considered the last word in books for children. There are literally thousands of them available at your local library or bookstore.

SOME TIPS FOR ENCOURAGING YOUNG READERS

In addition to the activities and books themselves, there are other ways to make the home a happy reading place. We offer here a few basic suggestions growing out of RIF's experience. We include them to help you make connections, to give you ideas, to remind you of things you probably already know but may not have used or thought of for a while.

Have fun with reading. Most children who go to school will learn the mechanics of reading. They will be better equipped to do so— and to continue reading and honing the skill—if they enjoy it, if they have developed an affection for books and the desire to read. Reading is not, after all, just a skill. It's a grand adventure. Look for ways to link reading with pleasure, for children just naturally like to do what is fun and will keep coming back for more. The more children read, and enjoy reading, the more they will develop the skill, and avoid the pressure and frustration an overemphasis on the skill itself can bring.

Read aloud. Begin when your children are infants, and never stop. Aside from what it does for a child's ability in reading, time spent reading aloud—from books, articles, stories, or even the cereal box—is a precious experience that draws reader and listener closer together.

Have lots of reading materials around. Books, magazines, and newspapers are all important household furnishings that invite reading. It doesn't much matter whether you purchase them, whether you get them from the library, or whether they are new or used. The important thing is that reading materials be there where you live and where your children can see them, touch them, and read them.

Let your children see you reading. Many a parent settles into a good book or magazine after the children are safely tucked in bed, never realizing that in consequence the children don't even know that Mom and Dad are avid readers. Children who are used to seeing opened books lying around, hearing you read aloud an interesting passage or a newspaper article, and seeing you curled up with a good book will learn by your example.

Visit the library regularly. The library has a wealth and variety of reading materials we couldn't hope to duplicate at home. Youngsters can browse and sample a feast of ideas there. As soon as the library will permit it, let your children have library cards of their own . . . and give them plenty of opportunities to use them.

Let them know you value reading. If your children see you getting books from the library, buying books, and giving and requesting books as gifts, they will soon grasp that you place a high value on reading.

Add excitement to reading activities. Enthusiasm, curiosity, and imagination can rub off on youngsters. Simply labeling a reading game an "adventure" gives the act of reading a special air of excitement and status.

Allow children some choices. We parents will sooner or later see our kids absorbed in something we consider mental junk food. Curb the impulse to thrust *War and Peace* into a child's hands! Instead, gently lead a child to better books with the books you give and read aloud, and with other ideas you'll find in this guide.

In our RIF programs we find repeatedly that the more children read, the more sophisticated their choices become. And they cherish the opportunity to choose for themselves.

A scene I observed illustrates the point: A mother and child were seated in a library before a shelf of children's books. One by one, the mother handed books to her little girl, who neatly placed them in three stacks: the first of books she liked, the second of books she rejected, and the third of books (face down) that she seemed to hate. When the stack of chosen favorites got high enough, they replaced the rejects and the mother, trusting the child's choices, helped her check them out without a second guess. Based on RIF's experiences with children, and my own as a mother, I wouldn't hesitate to say that this child will grow up reading.

Talk to your children. Not only does talking to your children help them to understand words and word patterns, but it shows them a measure of respect they will appreciate. It helps them learn the art of conversing, thinking, and exchanging ideas.

Listen to your children. By listening we pick up many clues about our children's interests and needs that help us encourage their reading.

Listen to yourself. And finally, while we're on the subject of conversation, take time to listen to *yourself.* Don't we all have those days when it seems the sum total of our vocabulary adds up to "Don't"? It takes a little extra concentration sometimes to turn our words into a real conversation, to have a genuine chat with our youngsters. In the long run it's worth the effort. Not only does conversation encourage reading, but it helps to get parent and child alike through some of the rockier aspects of child rearing.

Make room for laughter. Laughter is not only a good antidote to the blahs and a notable relaxer, it can also lead to reading. Sharing jokes, playing silly games, repeating nonsense rhymes, posting or reading aloud funny clippings—these can give kids a good laugh and make them comfortable with words. A shared laugh draws parent and child closer, and when associated with reading, makes the reading more enticing.

Give time and attention. In this busy world, time and attention may be the most precious of commodities. But if we want to help our children to grow up reading, thinking, and imagining, there is no way around giving the time and the attention. It comes down to making choices—sometimes hard ones. Some parents have told us they sat down and figured out how they spent their time and then simply decided which activities they would give up in order to devote the time to the children. (In my own case, it was easy—I gave up housework. You could write in our furniture dust, but everyone in the household would read it, along with everything else they could find.)

Give the gift of approval. Although we may sometimes doubt it, our children really *do* want to please us. When your child proudly displays tempera-laden fingers and a mess of green and brown smears on a paper, announcing that it is Jack climbing the beanstalk, forget the fingers. Try hard to see the intrepid Jack, applaud the young artist, and post the work on the refrigerator door. Your child's imagination and interest in reading will thrive on your praise and encouragement.

A Word of Thanks and an Invitation

The activities and book list were generated by hundreds of people who share their love of children and books through RIF. We are grateful to all contributors, and we are pleased to be able to acknowledge many of them by name in the Acknowledgments section of the guide.

We invite *you* to share with us your own ideas and experiences in helping your children enjoy reading so that we may pass them on to other parents. Send your ideas to the following address:

> Ruth Graves, President
> Reading Is Fundamental, Inc.
> 600 Maryland Avenue, S.W.
> Suite 500
> Washington, D.C. 20560

All of us at Reading Is Fundamental hope that you and your children enjoy this guide and the wonderful world of reading.

Activities to Encourage Young Readers

Read It Aloud

Nursery Rhymes
An Appreciative Audience
Chorus Lines
Word Bank
Reading Partners
Play It Again, Sam!
Shake, Rattle, and Read!
Hats on for Reading
Flannel Board Stories
Draw and Tell
Sound Effects
Ghost Stories
Read Along with Mom or Dad
Finding Out Whodunit
Talking Books

Bedtime stories are only one example of reading aloud. This intimate experience with your children begins the very first time you recite a nursery rhyme to them as infants, and continues through their school years whenever, for example, you read aloud a newspaper tidbit you think will interest them.

You can read aloud to your children most anywhere—on a bed, in a comfortable chair large enough for two, under a shade tree, or inside a makeshift tent. Or you can go beyond the "basics" by adding hats or costumes, an audience of dolls, or a homemade recording of sound effects. You can also make up your own stories.

Continue to read aloud when your children learn to read—challenge their imaginations with pictureless books, and bolster their vocabulary with stories above their reading level. Encourage *them* to read aloud to *you* from whatever written material is at hand—road signs, a restaurant menu, the cereal box, or captions in the family photo album.

Just as you share the pleasure of reading by reading aloud to a child, he or she may in turn share it with a younger brother or sister who can't yet read, or with someone whose ability to read has been physically impaired. At any age, reading aloud whets the appetite for reading experiences of all kinds.

Nursery Rhymes

AGES: Toddlers, prereaders, beginning readers

Children pick up sound patterns very quickly. After you recite a nursery rhyme to your children two or three times, they may be able to fill in the end rhymes if you pause. Even if you don't, they may beat you to the punch.

Read a nursery rhyme aloud to your children. Then read it again, but this time have your children repeat each line after you. Once they're familiar with a rhyme, pause to let them supply the rhyming word at the end of a line. For example: "Jack and Jill went up the . . ." Before long, they'll be able to recite most or all of the rhyme without a cue from you.

Besides nursery rhymes, your children may enjoy rhyming books (see Chorus Lines in this section) and longer poems from a children's anthology. See if your library has an appealing collection, but don't hesitate to share some of your own favorite verse. Rhyming poets such as Robert Frost, Carl Sandburg, and Langston Hughes often appeal to both children and adults. You may even learn to recite "Who Has Seen the Wind?" by heart—with your young readers.

An Appreciative Audience

AGES: Prereaders, beginning readers
MATERIALS: Dolls and stuffed animals

Since you can't always drop what you're doing every time your enthusiastic young reader feels like opening a book, help your child find another audience. If an older child is unavailable, suggest that a few favorite dolls or stuffed animals listen to your child read instead.

Seat this quiet audience at the foot of your child's bed or reading chair. Or if a stuffed animal is large enough, your child might enjoy sitting on its lap. When the reading gets under way, slip out of the room and go back to what you were doing.

Dolls and animals may like to join your regular read-aloud sessions. Bunnies will be all ears when you read *The Tale of Peter Rabbit*, and no teddy bear will want to miss an episode in the *Little Bear* series. When you can, find the appropriate animal or doll. Following the reading, you might help the "guest expert" answer all your child's questions.

Chorus Lines

AGES: Toddlers, prereaders, beginning readers

Encourage audience participation during read-aloud time by choosing books that have lots of rhymes and repetition. Your children won't be able to resist chiming in at the appropriate places, and the younger ones will enjoy the idea that they are helping you read.

Good candidates for this category include *Brown Bear, Brown Bear, What Do You See?; The Little Engine That Could; Millions of Cats; Tikki Tikki Tembo; The House That Jack Built; Too Much Noise; A Fly Went By;* and *At Mary Bloom's.*

In many such stories, there is a growing list of items your children have to remember as they recite the refrains with you. For example, in *A Fly Went By,* "The fly ran away, in fear of the frog, who ran from the cat, who ran from the dog . . ." and on and on until the list includes a pig, cow, fox, man, and the poor lame sheep who started it all.

Word Bank

AGES: Prereaders, beginning readers
MATERIALS: File box for 4" × 6" file cards, pack of alphabet dividers, file cards, small picture cutouts or stickers, white glue

Here's a new savings plan for your children: The children savor a new word every day, then save it in a personal bank. Day after day, they draw on these savings for reading fun and reinforcement.

Let each child decorate a file box with colorful pictures or stickers. Inside go the pack of dividers (in alphabetical order), and behind them enough file cards to fill the box.

Each morning take a card from the back of the box and ask for a new word your child would like you to write. Any word is okay. If Grandma is planning to visit that day, the grandchild may want you to write *Grandma*. If the dog has jumped on the sofa, the desired word might be *couch, sofa, down,* or even *naughty.* Write in large upper- and lowercase letters while your child watches and repeats the word.

Hand your child the new card to do with as he or she pleases for a while. Your child may want to draw a picture on it, mail it in a toy mailbox, read it to a friend or baby sister, tack it up on a bulletin board, or tape it to the refrigerator. When your child has finished with the word, help file it in the bank behind the appropriate letter divider.

Each morning (or whatever time you wish) your child can take out the old word cards, read or repeat the words, redeposit the cards, and receive a new word. When a child has saved for a while, rather than remove all the words for review each day, draw one word from each letter of the alphabet or draw all the words filed under one letter.

Reading Partners

AGES: Beginning readers

Form a partnership with your beginning reader by setting aside fifteen or twenty minutes a day to read *with* rather than *to* your child. (That's what makes you a partner rather than story reader.) If you can't spare the time, an older brother or sister or a daytime sitter might be willing.

Here are a couple of techniques that reading partners can try together:

- *Reading Echo.* First you read a line, then your child reads the line back to you. This technique encourages children to read with expression and without hesitation.
- *Buddy System.* You read a sentence, paragraph, or page, then your child reads the next sentence, paragraph, or page. Move from picture books with minimal text to books with short chapters, like the *Little Bear* series, the *Frog and Toad* series, or books by Beverly Cleary. You read one chapter, your child reads the next. Keep a homemade bookmark in the page where you leave off.

Play It Again, Sam!

AGES: Beginning readers, older readers
MATERIALS: Cassette recorder, cassette tape

"How do I sound?" your child asks. "Better this time," you'll say, after you play back a recording of your child reading the same page for the umpteenth time. Sure enough, your child's performance has improved dramatically.

Don't worry if your child reads aloud in a monotone, hesitates, mispronounces words, or skips them altogether—it's all part of learning to read. Rather than point out these problems, bring out the cassette recorder and let your child listen.

Children are delighted to hear their own voices, but they are also chagrined to hear themselves make mistakes. Without your prompting, your child will probably ask to "do it again" until the reading meets young standards.

If your child reads smoothly, but in a monotone, record yourself reading aloud the same passage. Read with expression, and don't spare the dramatics. Your child can try modeling performances on yours, reading with the same expression and inflections.

Shake, Rattle, and Read!

AGES: Prereaders, beginning readers
MATERIALS: Rhythm instruments or any of the following—noise-makers, baby rattles, pots and pans, cereal boxes (with cereal still inside), chopsticks, silverware

If you can stand the noise, strike up a rhythm band to accompany your read-aloud sessions.

Many good read-aloud books have repeating lines that children enjoy reciting with you (see Chorus Lines in this section). What makes these lines easy to remember is their rhyme and rhythm. Next time you plan to read a book with a refrain, pass out some rhythm instruments first—real instruments, like maracas and rhythm sticks, or household substitutes, like baby rattles and chopsticks.

Then while you all recite "Tikki-tikki-tembo, no-sa-rembo, chari-bari-ruchi, pip-peri-pembo," one child shakes a cereal box, another rattles the vitamin jar, and you beat a pot with a spoon.

Have your rhythm band rehearse syllables, too. Say a word, then have everybody beat and shout out the syllables with you. Your children can accompany the syllables of their own names and the names of other family members ("Grand-ma San-dy") and friends.

Hats on for Reading

AGES: Prereaders, beginning readers
MATERIALS: All kinds of hats, a box or other container to hold the
   hats

Add some drama to your read-aloud time with the simplest of props
—a hat.

While you read about Mike Mulligan, wear your child's toy hard
hat; better yet, let your young one wear it! Crown your own princess
to inaugurate *The Little Princess*, or don the witch's hat she wore on
Halloween to deliver *Strega Nona*. When you tell the story of Johnny
Appleseed, stick a pot on your head!

Help your kids start a hat collection if they don't already have one.
Dig into the costume bag, check the attic (and ask grandparents to
check theirs), or rummage at thrift stores and yard sales. Save your
children's cardboard crowns and Dad's painting visor. Put them all
in a bag or "hat box" that you can drag out for dressing up or
putting on plays as well as reading aloud.

You may not have hats to suit every story, but even a party hat will
add a festive spirit to your reading, and just the act of putting on
your baseball cap may become a signal that read-aloud time is about
to begin.

You might pull out the whole collection to read a book like *Caps for
Sale* or *500 Hats of Bartholomew Cubbins*. Stack a bunch of hats and
stick them on top of your child's head to put your reader in just the
right mood for these silly stories.

Flannel Board Stories

AGES: Toddlers, prereaders, beginning readers
MATERIALS: Shirt box or other shallow box with lid, flannel cloth, glue, felt, scissors

Flannel boards are backdrops against which felt characters perform. They are great storytelling props and simple to make. A flannel board can even go on a long trip; the felt pieces adhere to the board and won't get lost between the car seats.

To make a flannel board, remove the lid from a shirt box. Cut a piece of flannel to fit the inside of the lid and glue it down. Then cut out a set of felt figures. Conventional animals and people figures are fine and encourage children to use their imagination, so don't spend a lot of time making your bear look like Winnie-the-Pooh or your girl look like Goldilocks. Also cut out a few felt props (trees, furniture, a glass slipper, and so forth) for your child's favorite stories.

As you or your child narrates a story or fairy tale, bring out a different felt figure as each character is introduced and press it against the flannel board, adding felt props to help show what is happening. Give Winnie-the-Pooh a honey pot; let Goldilocks try sitting on the Three Bears' chairs.

Your children might enjoy using the flannel board during quiet times to tell themselves a story—a familiar tale or one they create, inspired by the felt characters. When the board is not in use, the felt pieces go inside the box and the flannel board lid goes back on top.

Like an ordinary flannel board, the variations that follow encourage storytelling and retelling, and enhance imaginative play:

- *Flannel Box Theater.* Line the inside of a cigar or shoe box with flannel or felt. Cut out felt figures and props, or cut them out of paper and glue a piece of felt on the back of each cutout.
  Your children position the felt figures upright along the walls of

the box where they will stick to the flannel. They can manipulate the figures to perform in the box stage as they make up an original story or retell an old favorite.

- *Tear and Tell.* Your children make the props in this variation. Give them several pieces of construction paper. As you introduce new story characters, pause to let them tear or cut representative figures out of the paper. Lay these figures out on your lap or on your flannel board. Tearing or cutting will help children's fine motor development as well as busy their hands if they're restless listeners.

Draw and Tell

AGES: Toddlers, prereaders, beginning readers
MATERIALS: Drawing paper, crayons

This activity is like a chalk talk, but with crayons. Crayon drawings help children visualize the story you're telling and inspire them to make up new ones.

If your library has a copy of *Harold and the Purple Crayon,* check it out and read it aloud with your children. Then hand them their favorite color crayons and pieces of paper. As they begin to draw (or scribble), coax them to talk about what they're drawing. The more they talk, the more they'll draw. Questions such as, "And then what happened?" and "Now what is she doing?" will encourage children to put their ideas in sequence. "Why" questions will encourage them to think and to express ideas.

Use the same idea to hold your children's attention while you tell a story. Illustrate this one yourself, perhaps writing a few key words on the drawings if your children are prereaders or beginning readers. Children love watching a story unfold in pictures. Don't worry about drawing well; stick figure characters can be distinguished from one another with an interesting detail—curly hair, moustache, shopping bag, red shoes, and so forth. You can make a quick succession of drawings or one large scene to which you keep adding details.

If your children are active, giving them paper and crayons will help keep their hands busy while you read a story aloud. Chances are the drawings will have something to do with the story, representing a character or action. Encourage your youngsters to look up at the book illustrations before you turn the pages. Then, like Harold, they can return to their own visual wanderings.

Sound Effects

AGES: Babies, toddlers, prereaders

Here's a technique that will keep restless children more involved during read-aloud time. Ask your children to help you provide sound effects in the appropriate places.

Use your voices and hands to make the bed creak, the floor squeak, the leaves swish, and the tea kettle hiss (to accompany *Too Much Noise*). Children who actively participate in a reading listen with rapt attention and rarely miss a cue.

A great book to introduce sound effects is *Crash! Boom! Bang!* You and your children can explore a whole encyclopedia of onomatopoeic sounds, or words that imitate natural sounds, like *gurgle, chirp,* and *hiccup.*

Hold the attention of babies and toddlers by making animal sounds to accompany their storybooks. Don't just say "moo"; drop the register of your voice and low like a cow! When your ten-month-old points to a picture of a dog, do the whole routine: drop down on all fours, sniff your squealing baby's fingers, and playfully growl and bark—then resume reading. How can your child help but be amazed at the effects books have on *you?*

Ghost Stories

AGES: Beginning readers, older readers
MATERIALS: Flashlight, cassette or record player (optional), scary mask (optional), sheet, cord

Remember the voice that moaned, "Who took my bo-o-o-ne?" as the campfire crackled and you nearly jumped out of your skin? If your children also delight in spooky stories, your whole family can now enjoy those spine-tingling sensations right in the comfort of your home.

- *Striking Fear with a Flashlight.* This idea is for older children who find scary things fascinating. Turn off the lights. Don a ski mask or a Halloween mask, or make an ugly face. If you have a cassette or record player, turn on some eerie background music (*Danse Macabre* and *Moonlight Sonata* are good choices), or the children's own prerecorded spooky soundtrack. If you don't have a cassette player, do a little moaning and groaning. Then suddenly, shine a flashlight on your own masked face!

  When the screams and giggles subside, you can begin telling your favorite ghost story. You might also offer to do your best Bela Lugosi imitation. When you're finished, turn off the flashlight and pass it and the mask to the next ghost storyteller.

- *Tales in the Tepee.* This idea is for children who don't like their rooms too dark or their stories too scary.

  Stretch a cord between a doorknob and a chair. Throw a sheet over the top and stake it out on both sides with small piles of books. Crawl in beside your children. Then snuggle together and read a few not-too-spooky supernatural stories by flashlight. Try *Four Scary Stories* for starters, in which three endearing creatures—a scalawag, an imp, and a goblin—scare the living daylights out of

themselves by telling each other . . . BOY stories (what else!).
Maybe you and your children can make up some of these.

Read Along with Mom or Dad

AGES: Prereaders, beginning readers
MATERIALS: Cassette recorder, blank cassette

If you have access to a cassette recorder, you can give your children
cassette tapes of their favorite stories recorded by their favorite
voice—yours!

Choose books that you and your children have enjoyed reading
aloud together. In fact, you can record during your regular read-
aloud sessions. Read slowly and with expression, pausing to give the
children time to look at the pictures. Include turn-the-page signals
in your recording ("Turn the page, Paul"). Mark the tape or cassette
case with the full title of the book.

Present recordings on a rainy day when you want your children to
amuse themselves, or leave them with a sitter so that the children
can listen to your familiar renditions when you can't deliver them in
person.

If you are giving a child a new book, wrap it up with a homemade
read-along cassette that begins, "This is for Katie on her fourth
birthday . . ."

Finding Out Whodunit

AGES: Older readers
MATERIALS: Small notebook or file cards for each participant, pens or pencils, hats (optional)

Detective novels make great read-aloud fare for you and your older children, and much of the fun is in out-detecting the detectives. Every family member is a suspect in this effort to beat Miss Marple, Ellery Queen, or the great Sherlock Holmes in discovering whodunit.

Each family member assumes the role of a suspect for the duration of the novel. Wearing hats will help everybody remember who's who, and add some suspenseful drama to the reading. So will making appropriate faces—you don't need hats for that.

As the story progresses, perhaps a chapter a night, the participants take notes on their own characters' movements and motives. Before reading the final chapter and epilogue, each suspect prepares both an alibi and a confession based on his or her notes and presents it to the group. (The performances are all the more effective if they include tears, recriminations, and other emotional displays.)

After all the suspects have proved their innocence and confessed their guilt, the players turn detective. Each person reviews the information, discards any red herrings (meaningless clues the author plants in the story to mislead the reader), and votes on who he or she believes is the guilty party.

Read the last chapter and epilogue. Were you right? Right or wrong, when it came to paying close attention to the plot and character development, everyone picked up on some important clues to reading comprehension.

Talking Books

AGES: Older readers
MATERIALS: Cassette recorder, blank cassette

Here's an idea for older readers who would like to share their best reading asset—their eyes.

National organizations like Recording for the Blind audition adults to narrate books on tape, or "talking books," for people who are visually impaired. Your children may be able to do the same thing on a local level, or for a friend or a member of the family.

- *Library Special Services.* Encourage your children to phone the main branch of the local library to inquire whether the library system offers recording services for people in the community who are visually impaired. If so, can they volunteer to narrate a book for a younger reader? Even if there is no precedent, the director of services may be interested in your children's proposal.

  Narrating books is not as simple as it sounds. A recording must be clear, have interest and expression, and be error-free.
- *Reading to Grandma or Grandpa.* Does a grandparent or other family member have cataracts or some other visual handicap that prevents him or her from reading? Your child's offer to read aloud on a regular basis—books, newspapers, letters—will represent a priceless gift as well as an opportunity to spend more time together.

  Your children might also be willing to help a grandparent find out about services available for people with visual impairments, or help order talking books from a local library or organization.
Community Efforts. Your children's scout troop, youth group, or class can organize a read-aloud program for visually impaired children in the community, or for classmates. Volunteers take

turns recording stories or reading aloud to the child at the child's home. Adults should help develop and supervise such an activity.

Your children's youth group or troop can also inquire about the local library's regular read-aloud programs, then pass on the information to visually impaired children and arrange to help them participate.

Signs of Progress

A Book Tie-In
Cookie Monster Bites for Books
Parking Lot Attendant
Read Around the Clock
Calendar Keeper
Readometers
Bookworm
Climb the Beanstalk
A Penny for Your Books
Sticker Books
Book Chain
Story Objects
Puzzle Grab Bag
Outbatting Pete Rose
Around the World in Eighty Books
Reading Passport
Category Bingo
Reading Quilt
Reading Time Line

Westward Ho!
Slalom Course
State Lines
Reading Raffle
Family Card Catalog

Creative record-keeping activities can be such fun that they may provide your children with incentives to read on. Included in this section are ideas for helping kids keep track of the time they spend reading or being read to, and the number of books they read or have read to them.

If your children enjoy visualizing their progress, try activities that involve adding elements (leaves on a beanstalk, segments on a bookworm, miles on a map) or filling in charts (degrees on a readometer, hours on a clock). For adventurous readers, issue reading passports. For less enthusiastic readers, try a theme that will hold their interest: For example, challenge your young readers to beat the records of their favorite baseball player (books and home runs being equal).

For prereaders and beginning readers—perhaps the most eager to show off their accomplishments—bring on raffles, miniature cars and trucks, bright stickers, and the like as incentives.

Ideally, keeping track of progress will be its own reward, providing that special satisfaction that comes with achieving a goal—whether it be completing a picture or a puzzle. For younger or more reluctant readers, however, you may want to provide more tangible rewards. Some possibilities:

- A new book or gift certificate from a local bookstore
- New art supplies
- Tickets to a community playhouse, movie theater, concert, skating rink, or ball game
- Chore relief
- A trip to the zoo, a museum, or historical landmark
- An opportunity to stay up past the usual bedtime to read

A Book Tie-In

AGES: Prereaders, beginning readers
MATERIALS: Necktie, scissors

Here's a way to get rid of the loud necktie Dad received from someone *other* than his children on Father's Day and to get kids excited about read-aloud time.

Have Dad wear the necktie during read-aloud time. Every time a certain number of books are read from cover to cover, say five, Dad cuts an inch off the bottom of his tie.

When the last inch goes, let your children rummage in your closet or at a thrift store for another goofy-looking tie and start again. They may want to wear their own ties next time.

Another neckwear variation—this one a little more constructive— is to string beads onto a long ribbon. Add a bead every time you read a book aloud, until the necklace is complete. Let your child wear the necklace during read-aloud time.

Cookie Monster Bites for Books

AGES: Prereaders, beginning readers
MATERIALS: Brown paper bag, eraser-tipped pencil, black ink pad,
hole puncher

Here's an idea that will appeal to young fans of Sesame Street. Children with big appetites for reading help the insatiable Cookie Monster munch away his cookie bite by bite.

Let your children cut a big round cookie out of the brown bag. (It doesn't have to be perfectly round.) Next, they ink the pencil eraser and stamp on lots of chocolate chips.

For every book you read aloud to your children (or your children read alone or together with you), they can nibble away at the paper cookie with a hole puncher. For a cookie three inches in diameter, five nibbles for every book would be about right. (You might have to help small hands give the hole puncher a hard enough squeeze.)

The bites should be close together, but you can tear away the "crumbs"—the narrow fragments remaining between the holes. See how many books it takes before your Cookie Monster polishes off the cookie.

Parking Lot Attendant

AGES: Prereaders, beginning readers, older readers
MATERIALS: Shirt box, ruler, felt pen, collection of miniature cars

Do your children have a collection of miniature cars and trucks? If so, here's a new game: They can play parking lot attendant and fill their lot with vehicles that represent the books they read.

Draw a grid inside the bottom of a shirt box. The spaces should be the right size for the little cars. Cut off one end of the box so the cars can drive in. Your children can decorate the parking lot with signs if they like: Jacob's Parking Lot, Exit, Compact Cars Only, and so on.

Every time they finish a book or you finish reading one to them, your children pick a car from the collection and park it in the lot. When all the spaces are taken, reverse the activity. Now your children remove a car for every book read.

Read Around the Clock

AGES: Beginning readers
**MATERIALS: Plain paper plate or construction paper, round object
  to trace, ruler or protractor, felt pen, crayons**

For beginning readers, an hour's worth of reading under their belts is quite an accomplishment. To acknowledge this, create a paper clockface. Your children can watch the minutes add up as they color in a segment of the clock each time *they* read aloud to *you*.

Use a paper plate or trace a round object on a sheet of construction paper and cut it out. (Your children might like to do this themselves.) Use a protractor or ruler to divide the clockface into five-minute segments, then write in the twelve points (hours) around the perimeter with a black felt pen (the ink will show through the crayon). Your children can write their own names in the center. Each child in your family might want a clock to call his or her own.

Every evening, or whatever time you designate, your children choose their books and read aloud to you for five minutes. Observe a real clock to keep track of the time. When they have finished reading, let each child color in a segment on the dial, moving clockwise. The youngsters may want to use their favorite color crayon every time, or they may prefer to use different crayons to make their charts more colorful.

If you'd like, reward your children when they have read an hour, perhaps with a few stickers, a new beginning reading book, or wristwatches with which they can keep track of their reading time. If you decide to make new clockfaces, hold on to the ones they have already filled in so they can see how many they can accumulate. When they seem ready, extend the reading periods to ten-minute segments.

If you have a tape recorder, you can record your children's first reading segment (at "twelve noon") and the last segment ("twelve midnight"), allowing them to listen to their own progress as well as watch it. With enough practice, they'll soon be reading like clockwork!

Calendar Keeper

AGES: Prereaders, beginning readers
MATERIALS: Calendars, pen, crayons or stickers

Your youngsters can make sure they get in their ten or fifteen minutes of daily read-aloud time (either they read to you or you read to them) by keeping a reading calendar.

At the beginning of the month, hang a calendar grid where your children can reach it, or give them a desk calendar. Ask each child to read for a certain amount of time each day. After each read-aloud session, they can color in one block on the calendar or put in a sticker or star.

Your children continue filling in the calendar until they have a month full of colorful accomplishment, then another month, and so on. Before long, reading will become a habit and they won't need a calendar to remind them.

Readometers

AGES: Prereaders, beginning readers, older readers
MATERIALS: Construction paper, scissors, black and red crayons or markers, tape

When children warm up to reading, the temperature on their readometers rises at a feverish pace!

Cut out a readometer—a long paper thermometer with a bulb at the bottom—for each book fan in the family, parents included. Divide the stem of the readometer into a dozen or so blocks, or degrees. Tape the readometers on the refrigerator, where you can watch each other's progress.

Participants color a block red for each book they read alone or have read to them, beginning at the bottom of the readometer. They then proceed to read their way up.

Bookworm

AGES: Prereaders, beginning readers, older readers
MATERIALS: Construction paper, round object, scissors, felt pens, cellophane tape, thumbtack or masking tape

Your children turn into bookworms themselves to make this bookworm grow. If it grows long enough, its tail may meet its head as it stretches around the children's room!

For every book they read, your children add a segment to a bookworm's body. Tack or tape up the bookworm's head on a wall, then attach segments to make the worm grow in one direction (left or right). Establish a goal: for example, to make the bookworm go around the room, or from one child's room into another's, or wind its way around the bookshelves. If two children are cooperating, one can begin at the bookworm's head and the other at the end of the bookworm's body, adding circles until the two sections meet.

Give your kids a pack of colored construction paper, a drinking glass or other round object to trace, and scissors to cut out lots of colored paper circles (at least a dozen to get started). One child draws the bookworm's face on a circle, and maybe attaches some paper antennae.

After finishing a book, the child chooses a paper circle, writes in the book's title and author, then adds the segment to the bookworm's lengthening body. The bookworm displays not only the number of books, but which books the children have read.

Climb the Beanstalk

AGES: Prereaders, beginning readers, older readers
MATERIALS: Roll of green crepe paper, long green ribbon (or long strand of green yarn), masking tape, green construction paper, scissors, envelope, cellophane tape

Show your children how they can achieve great heights by reading: Give them a beanstalk to climb, just like Jack's.

Tape a strip of green crepe paper from the floor to the ceiling in your children's bedroom or playroom. Have the kids cut lots of green leaves out of construction paper—maybe while they're watching television or listening to some music. Store the leaves in an envelope in an easy to reach place.

For every book your children read (or books you read aloud to them), they write the book title and author's name on a leaf and add it to their beanstalk, beginning a few inches above the floor and working their way toward the ceiling. By the time they're halfway to the top, they may need a stepladder and your supervision to tape on their leaves. Establish a distance between leaves, a few inches or shorter if there are several children involved.

How long does it take your kids to reach the top? You might want to write dates on the bottom and top leaves, or on each leaf.

A Penny for Your Books

AGES: Prereaders, beginning readers, older readers
MATERIALS: Posterboard, crayons or felt pens, pennies, cellophane tape

Pennies are the stepping stones to a special place on this homemade map, but it takes reading, not walking, to get there.

With your children, draw a rough map of your neighborhood, town, city block, or other area that includes both your home and one or more "reward destinations," such as a movie theater or an amusement park. Draw in a few landmarks along the way, but don't worry about placing them exactly.

For each book a child reads alone or you read aloud together, tape a penny on the map on the direct route from your home to a reward destination (head for one at a time). When your child reaches the destination, make good on the reward. Set up a date for a matinee, or hand your child a ticket for the carousel.

The pennies, meanwhile, can go into a piggy bank to help purchase the next children's book.

Sticker Books

AGES: Prereaders, beginning readers, older readers
**MATERIALS: Standard 8½" × 11" paper, ruler, pen, assortment of
    stickers (large ones for younger children, small ones for older
    children; glue and picture cutouts from magazines and greeting
    cards can be substituted)**

Reward children's reading with an array of colorful stickers—one
for short books, two for longer ones if you like. The children collect
their stickers in booklets they can later redeem for prizes.

Fold a standard 8½" × 11" piece of paper in half from top to
bottom, then in half across to make a booklet like the ones supermarkets provide for trading stamps. Cut the pages apart at the
bottom. With ruler and pen, divide each page of the booklet into six
boxes. A sticker should fit in each section.

After your children read or have read to them enough books to fill
their booklets with bright stickers, they can redeem them for a still
bigger reward—a new book, another big bunch of stickers if a child
is really crazy about them, or a special privilege, like having a sleep-
over party or going on an outing.

Book Chain

AGES: Prereaders, beginning readers, older readers
MATERIALS: Colored construction paper, felt pen, cellophane tape, thumbtacks or masking tape

After they read a book, your children add a link on a paper chain. Can one child make the chain reach from the ceiling to the floor? Can two or three readers cooperate and make the chain go all around the room—twice?

The children cut pieces of colored construction paper into 1″ × 6″ strips and store them in a handy container—a rinsed frozen juice can will do.

After finishing a book, the reader writes the book title on a paper strip, then overlaps and tapes the ends to form a link. The first link is anchored with a tack or masking tape to a starting point: a corner of the ceiling, a bedpost, the top bookshelf. The second paper strip is linked through the first, the third through the second, and so on as the chain lengthens.

Keep the chain going until your children reach a goal or lose interest. Perhaps you can save a long chain for a party decoration or put it around a Christmas tree that has *no electric lights* (or the paper will be a fire hazard).

Story Objects

AGES: Prereaders, beginning readers, older readers
MATERIALS: Paper, small pictures (magazine cutouts, stickers, drawings), crayon or marker

A book scavenger hunt will offer reluctant readers an incentive to finish a book and speed readers an incentive to slow down and pay attention to details.

Read a younger child's book first, making a list of objects mentioned in the story as you go. Be sure to include objects referred to on the first and last pages. Collect small pictures of these objects to paste on a piece of paper in the order they turn up in the story. You can draw the pictures rather than collect and paste them, or you can write the names of the objects for children who can recognize the words.

Give your children the picture list. As they read, they circle each object as they encounter it in the book. When they circle the last object, they will have finished the hunt and read the book cover to cover.

For older readers, make a list of interesting words (ones you think they will have to look up) and short descriptive phrases from the book. Your children will then have to read carefully or risk missing some of the literary fragments on your list.

Puzzle Grab Bag

AGES: Prereaders, beginning readers, older readers
MATERIALS: Magazine, cardboard, glue, paper lunch bag

Every time your children finish a book or read for a specified number of minutes, let them reach into a bag and pull out a piece of a jigsaw puzzle. How long before they complete the puzzle?

Cut a large full-color picture out of a magazine—something you think will interest them. Brush glue on both the back of the picture and the piece of cardboard, and glue the two together. Trim if necessary, then cut the picture into jigsaw-puzzle pieces. Make the puzzle pieces larger for younger children, smaller for older readers.

Following a certain amount of reading, let your children reach into the bag and pull out a puzzle piece. Before long, they will have enough pieces to begin interlocking them, and eventually will complete the puzzle.

Outbatting Pete Rose

AGES: Beginning readers, older readers
MATERIALS: Sports magazine or almanac, paper and pencil

Can the ball players in your family use a little reading incentive? If books equal home runs, touchdowns, goals, or baskets, your kids can try to match or break the records of their favorite sports figures.

You might challenge fans of Pete Rose to break his record for the number of career hits (more than 4,200) by reading more than that number of book pages. Or if that much reading is out of their league, two kids can cooperate to break Roger Maris's record for the number of home runs hit in a single season—61—by reading 31 books apiece. A younger child might try to read as many pages as Hank Aaron hit home runs (755).

Suggest that your children set up their own goals using whatever sports trivia they like. A sports magazine or current almanac can provide up-to-date statistics. Here are a few more possibilities:

- Record number of touchdowns in a season by a running back (a book equals a touchdown).
- Total yards gained in a season by a favorite team (a page equals a yard). Can your readers keep up with the team?
- Record number of points scored by a basketball player in a single game (a book equals a point) or by a team in a single season (a page equals a point).
- If visual incentives work better with your children, suggest a track and field event. Do your children like the pole vault? Help them draw a scaled-down diagram of a pole vault (an inch equals a foot) with each inch equal to a book. A child will have to read twenty books to break the world record for the highest vault. Your kids can measure the pole and mark their own ascent. They can make similar record-breaking and record-keeping charts for the high jump, the long jump, or the hundred-yard dash (a book for every second).

Around the World in Eighty Books

AGES: Beginning readers, older readers
MATERIALS: World map or map of the United States, map tacks or
   thumbtacks with colored heads, felt-tip pen

Reading can make globe-trotters of your children or send them on a
cross-country trek. Charting their travels on a real map will help
them visualize where stories actually take place and help them understand how geography influences people and cultures.

Ask the librarian at your public library to recommend an age-
appropriate reading "itinerary." The list of recommendations may
take readers to the Scottish Highlands (*Lassie Come Home*), Australia
(*Storm Boy*), and the South Seas (*Call It Courage*) as they zigzag
around the globe. Or your children may tour the United States,
starting on the East Coast (*A Tree Grows in Brooklyn*) and working
their way west (*The Long Journey*).

Hang a world map or a map of the United States on the wall in
your children's room. After finishing a book, the child pinpoints the
location (the main setting) on the map with a map tack or thumbtack, and draws a line from the pin out to the margin, where the
child writes in the title and author of the book.

Keep the map hanging as long as your children are interested in
logging their book travels. They can travel together by reading the
same books, or each reader can venture on his or her own.

Your children can send postcards requesting more information
about their international destinations to the embassies (in Washington, D.C.) of the countries they're reading about. For information
about various cities and towns in the United States, they can write to
the local Chamber of Commerce. Most organizations are happy to
send free materials.

Reading Passport

AGES: **Beginning readers, older readers**
MATERIALS: **Spiral-bound deck of index cards or small spiral-bound notebook, child's photo, glue, novelty rubber stamp, stamp pad, clear contact paper**

Before your children take off on a round-the-world reading odyssey, issue them each a passport so they can keep track of the places they visit. This kind of record-keeping activity is great for the long summer break.

To make a passport, tear the front cover off the spiral-bound cards. On the first card, glue your child's photograph. Write Passport in large letters, and your child's name. Laminate the card with clear contact paper for protection.

After finishing a book, your child opens the passport to the next blank card and writes in the title of the book, the author's name, the place where most of the story took place, and the date. Your child brings the passport to you—the border guard—and you stamp the page to validate that your child has traveled there.

Category Bingo

AGES: Beginning readers, older readers
MATERIALS: Paper, pen, ruler

Children read books covering all kinds of subjects before they can cover a row of squares on this special bingo card—a fun way to broaden their reading interests.

For each player, make a five-by-five-square grid on a piece of paper. Mark the center square with an *X*, or write something clever on this free space, like Already Booked. In the other squares, write a subject category—mystery, sports, animal story, biography, science, fantasy or science fiction, history, and so forth. You can repeat categories.

A child reads a book in one of the categories, then marks an *X* on the appropriate square. To get bingo—five in a row down, across, or on a diagonal—your child will have to read books in several categories. Encourage your kids to get bingo in several directions. Bingo prizes might include a new book or some new art supplies.

Reading Quilt

AGES: Beginning readers, older readers (requires adult assistance)
MATERIALS: Two or more yards of plain fabric (cotton blend or muslin—an old bedsheet will do), scissors, fabric crayons (available at craft or sewing stores), batting, needle and thread or sewing machine

Patchwork picture quilts will keep your children warm with memories of the books they have enjoyed over a period of time. They'll need fabric and fabric crayons to get started.

Cut half the fabric into eight- or ten-inch squares. Save the other half for backing the quilt. After finishing a book (*The Patchwork Quilt* by Valerie Flournoy and *Sam Johnson and the Blue Ribbon Quilt* by Lisa Campbell Ernst are nice ones to start this project), your child draws on a fabric square a picture inspired by the story setting or one of the story's characters. Let your child also print the title of the book and the author's name somewhere on the square.

When there are enough squares for a good-size quilt, an adult (you, a grandparent, or daycare sitter, perhaps) volunteers to sew the squares together, add batting and a backing, and quilt the corners of each square. An older child may be able to help with the quilting. If a younger reader begins to lose patience, you might opt for a quilted pillow instead—only eight book squares may be needed.

Drape the quilt over a favorite reading chair or display it on the wall in your child's room. If your child has made a quilted pillow, you can put it in your young reader's favorite reading nook.

Reading Time Line

AGES: Older readers
**MATERIALS: Roll of adding machine or calculator tape, ruler, pen, a
copy of a time line from an encyclopedia or history book, crayons or colored pencils**

Beginning with Columbus's voyage, your children can read their
way through the centuries of American history, charting events on a
time line as they live through them in books. This is a good activity
for encouraging children stuck on contemporary fiction to try some
historical novels and biographies.

Help your children decide on a historic period to cover in their
reading. They may want to read about the Revolutionary War period, beginning with *Johnny Tremain*, or about the period from slavery to emancipation with such books as *Jump Ship to Freedom*, *Roll of
Thunder, Hear My Cry*, and *Listen Children*. An advanced reader can
take on the whole world in twentieth-century fiction with books like
All Quiet on the Western Front, *Hiroshima No Pika*, and *North to Freedom*.

Each child first draws a time line along a strip of adding machine
tape, dividing the line by years, decades, or whatever time segment
makes the most sense. With each book, a child fills in the time line
with various dates and information; for example:

- The title of the novel being read at the point on the time line when
  the story took place.
- The title of the biography being read at the points spanning the
  lifetime of the person about whom the book was written.
- Important historical events mentioned in the books.
- Small pictures illustrating a story episode or historical event. (An
  illustrated time line is an interesting project in itself.)

Noting events along a time line will help give your children's
reading a historical perspective they might otherwise have ignored.

For a younger reader, a time line can serve as a fun introduction to research and note taking.

Westward Ho!

AGES: Older readers
MATERIALS: Historic map in an encyclopedia or history book, thumbtacks or masking tape, small picture of a covered wagon

Your children can read their way along the historic Oregon Trail or any other well-traveled path and clock a lot of reading miles. An encyclopedia or history book will provide maps and mileage. This activity is especially interesting when it parallels what your children are learning in a social studies class.

Your children can trace a historical map, make a photocopy, or order one from the National Geographic Society (inquire about the National Geographic Society's *The Making of America* series by writing to this address: P.O. Box 2806, Washington, D.C. 20013). After they mark the beginning and end of the trail they plan to follow, tack the map to a bulletin board or tape it on a wall.

For every book they read, your children move small symbolic paper figures or vehicles along the trail a certain number of miles. For example, they might advance a covered wagon one hundred miles along the Oregon Trail, finishing the trek twenty books later. Here are some other possibilities:

• *The Iditarod Trail.* Your children can read to advance a miniature dogsled along a map of the famous Iditarod Trail from Nome to Anchorage. Your children might be interested in reading about Eskimos before they set out on this Arctic adventure.
• *Pony Express.* Your children can trot a pony between St. Joseph, Missouri, and Sacramento, California, along the same path the first western mail carriers took in 1860.
• *The Royal Road.* California kids might enjoy following the original

El Camino Real, the trail along which Father Junipero Serra and his fellow monks set up the California missions from San Diego to San Francisco. A monk figure can lead the way.

The historical trail your kids decide to follow may inspire them to read historical novels that take place during the same period. For example, heading west on the Oregon Trail, they would find Laura Ingalls in *The Little House* series a good companion. For advanced readers, you might also suggest some published journals by famous trailblazers—*The Journals of Lewis & Clark*, for example.

Slalom Course

AGES: Beginning readers, older readers
MATERIALS: Large piece of Styrofoam (packaging material from an appliance or stereo box, for instance), toothpicks, construction paper, scissors, glue, small figurine or doll, scrap of cardboard

Here's a just-for-fun trail your children might like to blaze this winter—down a ski slope. A miniature skier follows a slalom course, passing flags as your children read books.

Your children can simply draw a slalom course, or they might have more fun constructing a three-dimensional course. Here's how: Get hold of a large piece of Styrofoam (save the packaging from a new appliance or TV, or ask for a piece of packaging at a store). Make flags by gluing small paper triangles on toothpicks. Your kids stick the flags wherever they like into the Styrofoam course. To make a skier, they cut out a couple of cardboard skis and glue them under a doll.

The figure is stationed at the top of the course until your children give the signal—a finished book! Then the skier descends past the first flag. Will the skier finish the course in record time? Or at least before the snow season is over?

If your children have drawn a course, they can color in flags as they "read" past them, or they can write in the book titles.

State Lines

AGES: Beginning readers, older readers
MATERIALS: State road map, highlighter or marker

Do you know the most direct route across your state? Your children can help you figure that out as they read from one state line to another, and maybe back again along a different route.

Your kids can plan their routes ahead of time. Spread out a state road map and let them choose a place to start—at the interstate line of a major highway, at the northern- or eastern-most point, at a border town, and so forth.

After they read a book, they trace along the route with a highlighter or marker a certain number of miles for every book or a mile for every page, depending on the distance they have to travel and the time in which they hope to complete the trip. Texans will get more mileage for their reading than Rhode Islanders, but they'll have a lot farther to go.

If your children enjoy the map reading involved in this activity, they may want to try one of these variations:

- Take another route back across the state, making it a round trip.
- Be a hobo. Travel as long as you like, taking whatever roads you like.
- Flip a coin at each junction to see where chance takes you.
- See how many towns and cities you can travel through. Write to Chambers of Commerce for information about the places you've been.

Reading Raffle

AGES: Prereaders, beginning readers, older readers
MATERIALS: Index cards, shoe box or other container, pencil or pen,
  prizes (see suggestions below)

The more your children read, the better their chances of winning a
reading raffle!

Cut a small stack of index cards in half lengthwise for raffle tickets.
For every book they read or you read to them, your children can fill
out a raffle ticket (an older family member can fill out a ticket for a
younger child). All the adults in the household participate, too. The
ticket must include the reader's name and the title of the book.
Collect the tickets in a shoe box with the lid off so everyone can
watch them pile up.

Once a month, or some other designated period, have the family
assemble for the drawing. Stir the contents of the raffle box and let
one of the children stick in a hand and draw the winning ticket.
Prizes (announced beforehand) might include a gift certificate to a
local bookstore, a favorite dinner or dessert dish, or chore relief.

All but the winning ticket remain in the box for the next drawing.
When the box begins to get too full, dump the contents and let the
raffle tickets start accumulating again.

Family Card Catalog

AGES: Prereaders, beginning readers, older readers
MATERIALS: File box, pack of dividers with blank tabs, file cards, small pencil

Make reading a legacy in your family. Set up a card catalog so older brothers and sisters can keep track of the good books they read through the years and then pass their recommendations on to the younger readers in the family.

Stock a file box with file cards, dividers, and one or two small pencils. Label the dividers very generally to reflect your children's advancing skills. For example: picture books, read-aloud books, stories for beginning readers, short novels or chapter books, books for older readers, poetry, plays, and so forth.

As your children read books they enjoy (don't bother with the ones they don't like), have them fill out a file card with the title of the book, the author's name, where the book came from (home or public library), and any personal comments. Assist younger children by writing down the sentences they dictate to you about their picture books or first read-alone stories.

You may want to fill out cards yourself for read-aloud books so you can make a few notes about the techniques that worked for a particular story. For example: "Tony and Rosa recited the refrain with me," or "Mark liked to say 'good night' to all the things in his *own* room after we finished reading."

File the cards under the appropriate headings. Now when your children come to you for a recommendation, play librarian and point them toward the family card catalog.

Recipes for Reading

Like cookies, reading of the homemade variety is often the very best. For the following activities, you won't have to look any farther than the kitchen to find all the ingredients you need. For example, if you open the cupboard you will find a lively selection of words and graphics all over food packages, jars, soup cans, and the like. Your children cannot fail to be stimulated!

Your cooking assistants will need to read if they want to find the flour, measure the sugar, or read aloud the next step on the recipe card. If they can't read yet, they'll need to know the jargon when you tell them to stir, beat, or sift.

For small children, there are gooey pleasures for fingers to explore. Those pudding designs will become your children's first O's and T's, and will help them learn to recognize and write letters. Prereaders can pretend to do what you do—that includes pretending to read labels and directions. Beginning readers can follow simple directions and eat the rewards.

For older readers, kitchen ideas may come from the books they read. They may want to replicate a dish enjoyed by a favorite story character, or make glue or even paper by using a recipe in a crafts book.

For you, the kitchen offers activities that keep your children busy while you do what you have to do—make dinner!

Kitchen Sandbox

AGES: Toddlers, prereaders
MATERIALS: Cornmeal, plastic containers, measuring spoons, funnel or sifter, chopstick or unsharpened pencil, shallow roasting pan

Children will play as happily with a pan full of cornmeal set on the floor of your kitchen as they do in an outdoor sandbox. After a little scooping and pouring, help your kids discover another way to play with the pan: Put it on a child's lap like a lap desk and draw some letters inside with a stick or a finger.

Spread a thin layer of meal over the bottom of the pan and form a letter by plowing through the meal with your finger. Say the letter and its associated sound for a child who doesn't recognize letters yet; ask a child who can recognize letters to identify the one you have drawn. Children may want to trace your letter, try one of their own, or just draw designs.

Some children may prefer a tool such as a chopstick or unsharpened pencil to a finger because that's how they see older people write. It doesn't matter how they grasp the tool now; they can learn the proper way when they are ready to learn how to form, rather than recognize, letters.

Cleaning up is no big deal: When your kids are finished playing, just dust off clothes and sweep the floor.

Squirt a Message

AGES: **Toddlers, prereaders**
MATERIALS: **Cannisters of whipped cream or cheese spread (pudding and food coloring for variation), cookie sheet or tray**

This activity will especially appeal to younger children who love to get their hands into something messy.

Set your children up with cannisters that dispense whipped cream or cheese spread when you depress the nozzle, and a washable surface (a shallow pan, cookie sheet, or even the kitchen table). Toddlers can sit in a high chair and use the tray.

Demonstrate by squirting out a familiar letter or a child's own name. After admiring and tasting your calligraphy, the kids can try the squirting themselves. A very young child won't have the control to squirt letters, but will be able to squirt and spread out enough cream or cheese for fingerpainting letters. Or you can squirt and say the letters, and your child can smoosh them.

For a tasty variation, let your children fingerpaint with pudding. If you spoon a dollop of vanilla pudding on a play surface and add a few drops of food coloring, they can swirl in the color, making O's and S's. Of course, the best part is licking those gooey fingers!

Edible Alphabet

AGES: Toddlers, prereaders
MATERIALS: Ingredients and cooking utensils called for in a recipe (see suggestions below), alphabet chart or letter cards (optional)

Learning to recognize letters of the alphabet is not only fun, it tastes good! That is, if you shape the ABCs out of things your children like to eat. Try one of these ideas for breakfast or a snack:

• *Pretzel Letters.* Let your children help mix a batch of pretzel dough, then roll and twist pieces of dough into letter shapes. Bake as you ordinarily would.

• *Pancake Letters.* Make pancake batter, but instead of pouring the batter onto the griddle in spreading circles, use a baster or squeeze bottle to squeeze out batter in the shapes of letters. These skinny pancakes cook quickly. Let your children help flip and serve.

For more substantial pancakes, use a baster as described, but after flipping, pour batter over the letter, wait till the pancake bubbles, and flip again. The pancake letter will have cooked more than the rest of the pancake, so it will stand out a little darker.

• *Cookie Letters.* Make your favorite stiff dough for cutting out cookies. Roll out the dough and cut out letters with alphabet cookie cutters or a knife. Your children can work with the cookie cutters, but of course you'll use the knife.

• *Cracker Letters.* Buy a package of oriental egg roll wrappers from the supermarket. Cut letter shapes out of the skins with cookie cutters or a knife. Sprinkle on grated cheese or a mixture of cinnamon and sugar, then bake until crisp.

• *Mouse Letters.* Give your children each a slice of American cheese. Let the little "mice" nibble away at the cheese to form letters and shapes (let them tell you what they have made). You can do the same with a piece of bread or a sandwich.

Toss the Salad

AGES: Prereaders, beginning readers
MATERIALS: Salad ingredients, salad bowl

Turn salad making into a game with your youngsters. They can help by handing you the ingredients you need according to their beginning sounds. You can do the same with soups, stews, fruit salads, and other dishes that start out with lots of raw ingredients.

Place the salad items on the table—the more items, the better. The game goes like this: "I need something for the salad that begins like *lamp.*" A child may hand you the lettuce. Continue to call out words that begin with the same sounds as other ingredients you need for the salad, or take turns so that an older child can think of words with certain beginning sounds.

When the salad is finished, let your children dress it and toss it. Even if they're not big vegetable eaters, they may enjoy eating a dish you made together.

Pretend Cooking

AGES: Toddlers, prereaders
MATERIALS: Chairs, bowls and cooking implements (wooden spoon, spatula, hand beater, measuring cups and spoons), flour or meal, sprinkles and colored sugars in shaker jars

While you prepare dinner, your toddler or preschooler can keep busy by pretending to do the same—with the same tools and a few of the same ingredients. Talk about everything you do and everything you use; your young ones will pick up lots of cooking vocabulary.

Have your children draw chairs up to the counter to work beside you if there's room; if not, they can work at the table. Give them small amounts of flour for starters, then samples of what you're using (a pinch of herbs, a shake of salt). They may want to add water and beat everything with a spoon or hand beater, or they may want to sift things from one bowl into another.

Name the ingredients as you hand them to your children, and encourage them to smell or taste. Keep a few jars of cake decorations on hand, such as sprinkles and colored sugars, that they can shake into their bowls for extra excitement.

When your youngsters have become accomplished pretend cooks, let them tell you what they're making and ask you for the ingredients. Don't be surprised if their pretend batter begins to resemble the real thing. In fact, you might apportion the ingredients so that after sticking the "cake" or whatever into the oven, it turns out to be something you can really eat.

Picture Menu

AGES: Prereaders, beginning readers
MATERIALS: Paper, magazines, scissors, glue, color markers

I think of a restaurant menu as just another opportunity for reading aloud to your children. At fast-food restaurants, you can point out words on the overhead board; at sit-down restaurants where the menus have pictures of some dishes, you can read the choices under each category and point to the corresponding pictures. Once familiar with a real menu, your children might like to make their own for a pretend restaurant.

Talk about the different food categories on a menu—sandwiches, side dishes, drinks, desserts, and so forth. Then give your kids a collection of magazines that generally have food features, like *McCall's* or *Good Housekeeping*. Help cut out pictures of foods that look appetizing, then have your youngsters sort the items into the categories you talked about.

Write each category on a piece of paper and let your children glue the appropriate pictures underneath. If necessary, tape two pieces of paper together to make a larger menu. Ask your children to name the restaurant and write that, too, on top of the menu.

Now your kids can play restaurant. They can set a place for you with toy dishes while you go over the menu, they can take your order, and they can serve an imaginary full-course meal. Bon appétit!

Fine Dining at Wilbur's Trough

AGES: Beginning readers, older readers
MATERIALS: Paper, pencil, fine-line markers, clear contact paper
   (optional)

Sometimes children finish a book but want to spend more time with
the characters. You'll know this to be the case if your kids read, or
ask you to read, the same book over and over again. If sequels are
available, you can encourage your children to read them. You can
also suggest an imaginary extension of the story: Imagine Wilbur
the Pig from *Charlotte's Web* in the restaurant business! That's what
happens when your children create a menu that will appeal particularly to the characters in a story.

Mr. Toad from *The Wind in the Willows* might open an elegant
tearoom, while Wilbur the Pig might prefer to convert a large barn
into an inn that serves country-style food. Of course, the restaurant
needs a name—something that corresponds to the story's theme
and, at the same time, indicates the kind of ambiance and fare a
customer can expect.

Help your child list various menu categories, such as appetizers,
salads, soups, main courses, sandwiches, side dishes, drinks, and
desserts. Come up with dishes for each category, keeping in mind
the unusual palates of your customers-to-be.

The original story may provide some ideas; for example, Charlotte the Spider describes her diet as "flies, bugs, grasshoppers,
choice beetles, moths, butterflies, tasty cockroaches, gnats, midges,
daddy longlegs, centipedes, mosquitoes, crickets—anything that is
careless enough to get caught in my web." Hence, a dish called the
Crawling Cobbler might be featured under "Desserts" on Wilbur's
menu. For pigs like himself, Wilbur might cook up some Slops Stew,
containing scraps "fresh from the trough."

When your children have finished planning the menu, they can make a neat copy on a fresh sheet of paper or cardboard. This may turn into a project in itself. They might want to draw boxes around the specials, add a decorative border, or paste on food pictures cut out of magazines.

Offer to laminate the menu with clear contact paper, if you have it. Your child can display the menu as interesting kitchen art. Or play restaurant—you be the customer and your kids can be the chefs and waiters.

Assistant Cook

AGES: Beginning readers, older readers

When you feel you have the time to spend, it can be fun to have help in planning and preparing a meal. In fact, you can establish a certain day every week when your children share the responsibilities for making dinner.

Let your children choose a recipe from a package or cookbook a day or two ahead and help you list all the required ingredients. Shop together for anything you don't already have.

Measuring the ingredients and following the directions in a recipe are excellent reading activities. After a few experiences *with* supervision, your children may be able to manage these tasks alone. Then you'll have real help in the kitchen.

The Udder Side of the Story

AGES: Beginning readers, older readers
MATERIALS: Ingredients and cooking utensils called for in a recipe (see suggestions below), pencil and paper, book about food origins (see suggestions below)

Cookies are made from flour, milk, eggs, sugar, and vanilla—but where do *they* all come from? The next time you go over a list of ingredients with your children, talk a little about the items before you transform them into something yet another step removed from their raw state.

Have your children copy lists of ingredients from their favorite recipes. See if they can tell you where each item came from or what it was in its raw state, for example:

• Milk—from a cow
• Flour—from wheat
• Sugar—from sugarcane
• Vanilla flavoring—from vanilla beans

This kind of discussion can follow a reading or telling of *The Little Red Hen, Pancakes! Pancakes!,* or, for older readers, *The Milk Story.*

Read It and Eat

AGES: Prereaders, beginning readers, older readers
MATERIALS: Recipe for food featured in book, ingredients, cooking utensils

Does *The Popcorn Book* leave your kids craving a hot buttered snack? Have some ready to eat while you read (it makes reading like going to the movies), or suggest that you pop some together afterward.

Some books actually provide the reader with a pivotal recipe; for example, there's a recipe for Grandmother's cranberry bread in *Cranberry Thanksgiving,* and for freckle juice in *Freckle Juice.* Encourage an older child to try out such recipes, or prepare them ahead of time along with a younger child for a surprise afterreading treat.

If you are reading a book that mentions a special food but offers no recipe, your children can try to find an appropriate recipe in a cookbook at home or the library. It may take a while, but they'll probably succeed in finding a recipe for a pioneer dish mentioned in *The Little House on the Prairie* in a cookbook like *The Settlement Cookbook.*

Once your children find and copy the recipe, they then figure out what ingredients need to be added to your shopping list. They can help measure out the ingredients and read aloud the directions as you cook, or they can do the cooking themselves.

Younger children will enjoy helping you cut out and bake a gingerbread man or animal cookies after you finish telling a folktale or reading an animal story. If the storybook involves eating, they may want to do likewise. For example, they might like to spread jam on bread for a snack after you read aloud *Bread and Jam for Frances* or *The Giant Jam Sandwich.*

Most parents will find that when there's a tie-in to eating, there's motivation for reading.

Found Recipes

AGES: **Beginning readers, older readers**
MATERIALS: **Recipe cards, scissors, cellophane tape or pen, recipe box**

Did your mother let you make marshmallow squares from the recipe on the panel of a Rice Krispies box when you were a kid? Or mock apple pie out of Ritz crackers? The recipes are still there, and your children may be just as tempted to try them out as you were. Encourage them to clip the recipe and make the treat; after one try, they may also be tempted to read and find more recipes that appeal to them.

There are a number of good cookbooks for children, including *The Betty Crocker Cookbook for Children.* Your children can check cookbooks out of the library and look through them for interesting recipes. If you're willing, they can copy the recipes onto cards and file them in your recipe box, or you can give them a file box of their own. On occasion, let your children choose a recipe, buy the ingredients, and follow the directions for making the dish or snack.

Your young readers are also likely to come across recipes in places other than books, such as on the panels of packaged foods and in magazines and newspapers. You may find your kids scanning the food section of the weekend newspaper, or reading empty boxes and bags of food before discarding them.

Arts and Crafts Recipes

AGES: Beginning readers, older readers
MATERIALS: Vary, according to recipe

Are your children running out of paste? They can make their own! The same goes for playdough, fingerpaint, ink—even soap.

Many a how-to book offers children no-cook or simple-to-cook recipes for various arts and crafts materials and nonedible household items. For example, *Kits for Kids* offers such kitchen concoctions as colored sugar for sandpainting, invisible ink, fingerpaint, "best clay recipe," and flame color mix to sprinkle on fireplace logs. In *Steve Caney's Kids' America*, your kids will find traditional recipes for making soap, nut or berry ink, natural fabric dyes, and colored candle wax.

A younger child can help you knead the playdough for the whole play group, or make up some bubble solution to bring on a picnic—both recipes are featured in *Making Things*. This book, and many others like it on library shelves, require only kitchen ingredients and utensils to make homemade craft materials that are just as good as the ones you buy at the store. The only difference may be that your children will do some reading or practice a little hand-eye coordination to help make it themselves.

Bittersweet Words

AGES: Prereaders, beginning readers, older readers
MATERIALS: Paper, pencils

You have just served the densest, creamiest cheesecake of your kitchen career, and what do your children say? "Good, Mom," or more enthusiastically, "Tastes great, Dad." Is their choice of words a little bland for *your* taste? Help your children, even the younger ones, spice up their vocabularies—at least around the kitchen.

On a large piece of paper, make a list of words to describe the taste or texture of foods: *sweet, sour, bitter, tart, salty, hard, soft, dry, moist, creamy, lumpy, crisp, smooth, round, flat,* and so forth. (If one child is playing, limit the list to five or six words.) Give the list and pencils to your children, set a time limit (say, ten minutes), and have the children list as many foods as they can that fit in each category. The same food item may be used in more than one category; for example, potato chips might appear under both *salty* and *crisp.*

Extend the activity by having the children alphabetize the items in each category. If more than one child is playing, each child can choose a category or two to put in order.

Play a similar game with children who can't yet read and write. Say one of the food categories, and both you and your child think aloud of as many appropriate items as possible that would fit in the category. When you have exhausted one category, try another.

Don't hesitate to use a new word with your child. Define the word and give one or two examples—"*Crisp* means that it is a little hard and that it makes a crunching sound when you bite into it, like a cracker or dry cereal." Play this game in the kitchen, where you can open a few cabinets or look on the pantry shelves to keep your brainstorm going.

Alphabet Noodles

AGES: Prereaders, beginning readers, older readers
MATERIALS: Alphabet noodles or cereal, pie pan for sorting, dark construction paper. *For place cards and gift tags:* Colored construction paper, hole punch, ribbon. *For spill-and-spell game:* Empty alphabet soup can, kitchen timer

How can your children use alphabet noodles or cereal to have fun and play reading games? Let them count the ways! Here is a batch of ideas to get them started.

• *Picky, Picky!* Young children will love sorting through a pan of dry alphabet noodles or cereal and picking out letters they recognize, the letters in their own names, or short words they know how to spell. By placing the words on a piece of dark-colored construction paper, the letters will stand out and therefore be easier to read.

Children also love to pick out letters in a spoonful of noodle soup or alphabet cereal and milk. These letters are too soggy to save, but your children may want to see how many different letters they can recognize before swallowing.

• *Place cards.* Alphabet noodles add an extra dimension to holiday or party place cards. Sit down with your children and make a list of the birthday party guests or guests who are expected to join the family for a holiday dinner.

To make place cards, your children cut out squares of paper, fold them in half, and place them open end down, like pup tents. Pour a bag of alphabet noodles into a pie pan so they can sort out the letters for each name on the list. Then they glue the name on a place card.

Prereaders will need your help sorting out the letters and sequencing them properly. Your list should be written out in all capital letters so your children can match the noodle letters, which are also all capitals, to the printed letters.

- *Gift Tags.* Your children can glue names made out of noodles on colorful paper tags for birthday or holiday gift boxes. Punch a hole in the tag and tie on a ribbon, then attach it to the present.
- *Party Cupcakes.* Make personalized cupcakes for a child's birthday party. Set each guest's name in alphabet cereal letters on top of a frosted cupcake. The birthday child can help pick out the letters and arrange them.
- *Spill and Spell.* Rinse out the can after you make store-bought alphabet soup, but leave the label on. Remove any burrs on the rim and wrap the rim with cloth tape. Pour in a half cup of dry alphabet noodles. Now you have a spill-and-spell game to give your children.

To play, your children spill out the letters, in the soup can, on a table. Reposition letters that are upside down or backward. Set a kitchen timer for a certain amount of time (say, five minutes), then see how many words they can make before the timer rings. They can write down the words if you're keeping score. Next time, you take a turn.

Cereal-Box Bonanza

AGES: Prereaders, beginning readers, older readers
MATERIALS: Cereal box, paper, pencils

Almost every day, kids and adults alike read and reread the cereal boxes sitting on the breakfast table. Why not take advantage of this cardboard kiosk? The bold graphics, hyped-up language, free offerings, and nutrition chart can all be the focus of educational fun.

Here are several activities that require nothing more than a cereal box (full or empty), paper, and pencils.

- *Early Word Recognition.* "Snap, crackle, pop!" may be among the first words your children recognize. Point out the words individually as they recite a cereal jingle, a slogan ("They're gr-e-a-t!"), or the name of a cereal to help them make the association between spoken and written words. Write the words one by one on a piece of paper and ask your kids to point to the matching word on the box so that they begin to recognize the same words out of context.
- *Nutrition Research.* Along one narrow side panel of the cereal box, in fine print, is a nutrition chart and list of ingredients. Here are some of the longest and most obscure words your children may encounter.

  Go through the list and write down all the unfamiliar words, then help your children look them up in a dictionary. You'll be reassured, for example, to learn that folic acid is a natural substance that comes from green leaves.

  Compare the nutritional information on two boxes of cereal. Is the cereal Dad likes more or less nutritious than the one your child prefers? Which has more sugar? Which has more fiber? More protein?
- *Alphabetical Ingredients.* Ingredients are listed according to what percentage of the cereal they comprise, from most to least. Your children can write down the ingredients in a new order—from A to Z.
- *Good Taste in Words.* As your children read the description of the cereal, ask what words the copywriter used to make the cereal sound good to eat. Go on to suggest that they replace each of these words with a word that means the opposite (a thesaurus might help). The new copy will sound like something Oscar the Grouch might have written.
- *New Package.* Perhaps your children would like to invent a new cereal. What shape will it be? What color and flavor? Suggest that they design a wrapper for the new cereal that you can paste over the old cereal box. They can draw pictures of the cereal, describe it, and include nutritional information, a recipe, and a free sendaway offer.
- *Story Starters.* Cut out the characters and pictures that appear on the front and back of your children's favorite cereal box. Staple or glue them onto ice cream sticks so they can use them as stick puppets to tell a story.
- *Recipes.* Some cereal boxes feature a snack or dessert recipe. If the

recipe appeals to your children, help them assemble the ingredients and follow the directions. If there is no recipe, they can substitute the cereal for some of the flour or oats called for in another recipe (many cookie recipes work well with such substitutions).

Fortune Cookies

AGES: Beginning readers, older readers
MATERIALS: Homemade fortune cookies (or brand-name tubular cookies, such as Pepperidge Farm Pirouettes), paper, pencil or typewriter, scissors

Fortune cookies are fun for reading as well as eating. You don't have to go out to a Chinese restaurant to have them; your kids can make 'em and bake 'em right in your own oven, or poke paper fortunes into packaged cookies.

Before they get to the baking part of the activity, the children have to write or type fortunes or other messages on small slips of paper. These slips are wrapped or poked inside the cookies for the eaters to discover and read.

Confucius doesn't have anything to say about what goes inside the fortune cookies. It's up to your children, in all their wisdom, to come up with the wit and the words. Here are a few ideas to get them started:

• *Maxims.* Write your own word to the wise, such as "The child who does the homework, passes the test" or "He who bakes the cookies gets to lick the bowl."
• *Book Fortunes.* Write fortunes that are meant for the characters in a book. For example, if you are reading *Tuck Everlasting,* you might write, "Beware of the man in the yellow suit," or Tuck's own words, "You can't have living without dying."
• *Predictions.* Serve fortune cookies while you stay up on New Year's

Eve. The cookies hold your predictions for the new year: "Joe will grow two inches." "Daddy will shave off his beard." "Jenny will finish *Gone with the Wind.*"

- *Fantasy Fortunes.* Let your imagination run wild! Create out-of-this-world fortunes that will amaze your friends and family: "The rainbow will have an eighth color—ablot—before red." "Next month there will be two moons in the sky." "Your true love will come to you on a winged dragon."
- *Unfortunate Fortunes.* Tease family members with fortunes that read like Murphy's Law or that bode bad luck: "You will be caught in a rainstorm without an umbrella." "You will lose a winning lottery ticket."

Remind the children to leave space between the fortunes as they print or type them on a sheet of paper so they can cut them apart into strips narrow enough to wrap or poke inside a cookie. If your general cookbook doesn't have a recipe for making fortune cookies or cigarette rousses (like Pirouettes), two kids' activity books do: *Steve Caney's Kids' America* and *Gifts of Writing.* Or have your children check the index in a children's cookbook.

Wish Upon a Cupcake

AGES: All ages
MATERIALS: Paper, pencil or typewriter, homemade cupcakes, frosting, knife, birthday candles and holders, matches

The birthday child doesn't make all the wishes when you bake these cupcakes—the rest of the family make them, too.

Each member of the household (except the person celebrating the birthday) writes a special birthday wish on a small slip of paper. Young children can tell you a wish and you can write it for them. Wishes may be fond ("May you stay as sweet as you are now") or facetious ("May you receive twice as many presents as you did on your last birthday!").

Make the cupcakes yourself, or recruit a brother or sister. To stuff the wishes, first use a knife to make a hole in each cupcake. Poke a wish slip in each hole, then spread on frosting to cover the holes.

Light candles on the birthday child's cupcake and let the child make the first wish. Then, as other family members bite into their own cupcakes, they remove the wish slip and read it aloud.

Kooky Cooking

AGES: Prereaders, beginning readers, older readers
MATERIALS: File cards or recipe cards, pen or pencil

Cooking, like any other creative activity, *should* get out of hand. That's what may happen with the following ideas that encourage original thinking and wordplay.

• *Preposterous Pies.* Little Jack Horner would be shocked to pull his thumb out of these pies if your children were to add all the ingredients called for in the recipes!

Make a set of flashcards with a different ingredient on each one, some realistic and some outlandish or fanciful. As your children read through the deck, they decide which ingredients will go into the pie. They can also decide what kind of pie—cherry, apple-apricot, or mustard mint.

Here are some possible ingredients: 2 cups of flour, 20 cups of flower, 2 teaspoons of surprise, 3 cans of chickens, 7 tablespoons witch's potion, 1 teaspoon baking soda, 1 tablespoon ice cream soda, 1/2 cup mustard seed, 3/4 bucket of ketchup, a pinch of baby powder, 2 sliced apples, 1/2 hive of honey, grated horn of a unicorn.

• *Gross Gourmet Delights.* How do you make fried worms? Roll them in beaten egg, dredge in flour, and fry in butter—how else!

Have a child who is familiar with cooking terms and techniques come up with other unappetizing appetizers (slugs on the half shell), sickening soups (beetle bouillon), and disgusting dinners (monkey stew)—and the straightforward steps for their preparation. Supply recipe cards on which the children can write the list of ingredients, step-by-step directions, heating time, and temperature.

- *Monster Meals.* Have your kids ever tried Ghoulish Goulash? What ingredients do they imagine a monster would use? In this creative brainstorming activity (no reading required), the recipes are as horrifying as the "monsterpieces" they produce.

While you're preparing a less interesting meal, writing out your shopping list, or setting the table, you and your children can also be planning a monster meal. Let them name the dish, then take turns calling out the ingredients. Stews and salads are best because the list of ingredients is limited only by their imaginations.

Family Cookbook

AGES: Older readers
MATERIALS: File cards, file box, pens, paper, black pen, stapler

Keep recipes in your family forever by publishing a family cookbook. An upcoming holiday meal would be an appropriate occasion to propose the project to your children and enlist their help.

First have your children solicit their favorite family recipes. When they ask Grandma to pass the cornbread stuffing, they also ask her if she's willing to share the recipe. The same request is made for Dad's giblet gravy and Aunt Margie's cranberry bread.

Hand out the file cards and pens after the meal. If necessary, affix a stamp on the cards so that those cooks who need to refer to their recipe cards at home can send back the ingredients and directions. Do the same at the next family barbecue. Ask Uncle Bob for the recipe for his molten chili or Mom for her tangy lemon marinade.

Offer your children the recipes for their favorite dishes and birthday cake.

Meanwhile, the children file the cards by menu categories: appetizers, soups, main dishes, side dishes, desserts, snacks, and so on. After organizing the recipes, they will need to check spellings on the ingredients lists, clarify any confusing directions, and credit the contributors.

There are many ways to assemble the recipes into a book:

- A parent or older child can volunteer to type up the collection. If you have access to a photocopier, make enough copies so that your children can collate and staple a booklet for each person who contributed a recipe.
- Do you have a home computer? Your children can use a word processing program to organize and edit the recipes, then print out copies for everyone in the extended family.
- The child with the best handwriting can copy the recipes neatly on sheets of notebook paper. Insert the pages in a binder behind subject dividers labeled with the different menu categories.
- The recipes can be copied into a spiral-bound deck of index cards. Your children can design a paper cover to paste over the original cover. Suggest that they number or alphabetize the recipes and include a contents card listing the names and corresponding numbers.

Perhaps next year your children can fry the latkes for the family's annual Hanukkah party or bake the hot cross buns for Easter brunch!

Ashopping We Will Go

Coupon Card Games
Stock the Shelves
Holiday Wish List
Coupon Clipper
Supermarket Scavenger Hunt
Personal Shopping List
Intergalactic Shopping List
Household Yellow Pages
Price Problems
Bargain Hunter

How do you fit reading into your busy schedule? Wherever and whenever you can! You can discover many opportunities for reading or reading-related activities during the family's daily routine. A case in point: grocery shopping.

From the moment you enter the supermarket, your children are bombarded with new words on a multitude of signs and labels. The aisles list food categories (young children know by what's on the shelf even if they can't read the signs), and the spice jars are organized alphabetically.

The next time you go shopping, invite your children to lend a "helping" hand. The readers can go down the aisles with their own lists; prereaders can match items on the shelf with picture cards they hold in their hands. An older child can help clip and keep coupons; a younger child can use them to play a version of Go Fish.

Many other routine shopping trips can give rise to games and activities. Whenever your children want to shop for a gift or personal item, encourage them to do a little comparison shopping first in the newspaper, in mail-order catalogs, or by phone using the Yellow Pages. Besides saving money, there's another educational payoff—they'll have done some extra reading and critical thinking.

Coupon Card Games

AGES: Prereaders, beginning readers
MATERIALS: Coupons, index cards, cellophane tape, clear contact paper

Here's a way to make good use of all those expired coupons that are cluttering up your drawers. Coupons make colorful faces for a deck of playing cards. Your children can use the cards to play matching games like Go Fish or Concentration.

Collect fifteen or more pairs of coupons. Coupons match if they are for the same generic product; they don't have to be for the same brand. In other words, a Heinz ketchup coupon matches a Delmonte ketchup coupon. You can collect product labels as well as coupons if they show pictures of the items.

Tape each coupon on an index card. Wrap clear contact paper around each card so the edges won't lift and tear after lots of play. Gather all the cards and shuffle them.

- *Go Shop.* Play with two, three, or four players. Deal three or four cards to each child and yourself. Place the rest in a draw pile. If players have been dealt matching pairs, they place them faceup on the table in a personal pile and draw cards to replace them.

  Player 1 asks the person on the left if that person has a card to match one in his or her own hand. "Do you have a coupon for cheese?" player 1 might ask. (Prereaders will be able to identify the item on the card by the picture.) If player 2 has the card, it is given to player 1, who removes the matching card from his or her own hand and places the pair in a personal pile. If player 2 doesn't have a match, player 3 (to the left) also checks his or her hand. If that person does not have the card, he or she says "Go shop." Then player 1 draws a card and it's player 2's turn to ask. Continue until there are no more cards. The player with the most matches wins.

• *Shopping Concentration.* Lay out the cards facedown in neat rows of four or five cards across. Then play Concentration. One player turns over any two cards. If the cards match, the player gets to keep them and takes another turn. If they don't match, he or she turns the cards back over and it's somebody else's turn.

The object of the game is to remember the position of previous cards so that after you turn over a new card, you can locate its match readily. Play until you run out of cards. The player with the most cards at the end of the game wins.

Stock the Shelves

AGES: **Prereaders, beginning readers**
MATERIALS: **Canned goods and packaged foods, spice jars**

When your children want to play store, suggest that they stock soup cans or spices on make-believe grocery store shelves using the same system they do in many real stores—alphabetical order.

Empty a pantry shelf of all but the soup cans. Suggest that your stock clerks make a long train by putting the cans in alphabetical order according to the first word on each label (cream of mushroom soup under *C*). You may have to show them how to alphabetize by the second letter if your stock of soup includes chicken noodle and clam chowder.

Next have the clerks replace all the spice jars and cannisters on their shelves in alphabetical order. They may have to alphabetize all the way to the fourth letter if you spice your foods with chili powder and chives.

Holiday Wish List

AGES: Prereaders, beginning readers, older readers
MATERIALS: Pad, pencil, mail-order catalogs, gift catalogs sent from department stores

'Tis the season when gift catalogs abound in the mail. Don't throw them out! They will provide your children with hours of reading and wishful thinking and call into play many reading skills.

As your children browse through these extravagant publications, they can be thinking about what they'd like to give as well as what they'd like to receive for Christmas or Hanukkah. Keep a pad and pencil near the catalogs so readers can take notes.

Encourage your children to look past the glossy photos of items that interest them and read the descriptions carefully and critically, especially the fine print. Is the winter sweater you want to buy for Grandpa made of an acrylic blend, or 100 percent wool? Does the dollhouse come assembled, or do you have to build it yourself? Does the spin-art machine come with batteries, or do you have to buy them separately? How much does the same item cost in a different catalog? Does the price include shipping charges?

Young children who don't know how to write can cut out pictures from the catalog and paste them on a piece of paper. Go over this picture list with your child and discuss the choices. Read aloud descriptions so your youngster can make comparisons and draw conclusions.

After the holidays, save the gift catalogs for a variety of classification games and art projects.

Coupon Clipper

AGES: Beginning readers, older readers
MATERIALS: File box or accordion-fold file pocket, dividers, felt pen, scissors

Give your children the responsibility of clipping and keeping food coupons. Perhaps half or all of the savings can go into your children's piggy banks or into a household kitty reserved for special trips or family purchases.

Have your children regularly clip coupons from the food section of the newspaper and the weekend inserts. Add to the collection any coupons that arrive in the mail, those you come across in magazines, and those you save from empty packages of food.

Help set up a system for sorting and filing the coupons. A file box or accordion-fold pocket file with dividers will hold a tidy collection; coupon fanatics can stuff individually marked envelopes and store them in a shoe box. Suggest useful categories to label the dividers or envelopes—baby products, paper goods, frozen foods, dairy, desserts, drinks, and so on.

Your children sort and file away the coupons. Before your next shopping trip, go over the shopping list together. Ask them to pull any coupons from the file for items on your list.

Supermarket Scavenger Hunt

AGES: Prereaders, beginning readers, older readers
MATERIALS: Labels or paper lists, pencils

Send your children on a scavenger hunt in the supermarket. Heading down the aisles with you, they try to find the various food and household items on their lists—a fun way to let them help you do the shopping.

After you write out your shopping list, divide up the list into smaller lists—one for each child. Be sure each list includes items in different categories so a player won't complete his or her list down one aisle. For prereaders, provide an envelope of labels so that they can find items by matching.

Let your children see their lists well ahead of time so they can plan where to look; otherwise, the game will hold up your shopping. As they find the items, they drop them into your cart and cross them off their lists. Cross them off your big shopping list, too.

After you have gone down all the aisles once, take stock of your stock. Are there missing items? Suggest where they might be found, and head back to those aisles to help find them on the shelves. The hunt is over when shopping is finished.

Personal Shopping List

AGES: **Beginning readers, older readers**
MATERIALS: **Pencil and paper, access to a photocopier, stapler or glue, clear contact paper and crayon (optional)**

Is the children's toothpaste running low in the bathroom, or is the kids' pencil collection beginning to look a little stubby? Here's a way to remedy the situation that involves reading and writing.

Have your children sit down and list all the day-to-day items that occasionally run out: bathroom supplies, school supplies, clothing, and maybe some of their favorite foods. Look over the list to make sure it's reasonable.

If you have access to a photocopy machine, make lots of copies of the list and form a pad by gluing or stapling at the top (a copy shop can do this for you). Or you can make the original list reusable by covering it with clear contact paper. After your children mark what they need with a crayon or grease pencil, they can rub off the marks with a tissue.

Prior to a shopping trip, or as the need arises, your children go over the list and mark those items they need. They can then give you their list or help transfer those items to your household shopping list.

Intergalactic Shopping List

AGES: Prereaders, beginning readers, older readers
MATERIALS: Paper and pencil

What would a Martian put on his shopping list? A triplet of shoes for his three feet? A green hat to match his skin? Decorations for his antennae? A book about life on earth?

Your children will love helping you make up an imaginary shopping list like this anytime you need a quick and creative diversion—while you're making dinner, driving to the supermarket, or making up your real shopping list.

For variations, ask the children to make a list for Oscar the Grouch, the man in the moon, an octopus, or any other creature with wants and needs that are out of the ordinary.

Household Yellow Pages

AGES: Beginning readers, older readers
MATERIALS: Telephone card file (like Rolodex Petite File) or file box with file cards and alphabet dividers, pen, area Yellow Pages

Enlist your children's help in compiling a telephone directory of all the stores your family has occasion to call. That way your fingers won't have to do quite so much walking when you need a chimney sweep or want to have a pizza delivered.

A card file of some sort makes more sense than a page listing because you can easily pull out old numbers and replace them with new ones: for instance, when your haircutter moves to a new location or you find a cheaper hardware store.

Sit down with your children and make a list of all the commercial places and professional services that come to mind. Include the newspaper delivery service, the bike shop, the library, the Chinese take-out restaurant, the TV repair service, the skating rink, the frame-it-yourself shop, the all-night pharmacy, and so on.

Then have your children do the real legwork—looking up all those telephone numbers in the Yellow Pages and copying them onto separate file cards. They'll have to do some careful categorizing to decide under which headings to look, and they'll have to use their alphabetizing skills both to find the original listing and then to file their cards.

As more places come to mind, jot them down and ask your children to find the numbers and add them to the file. They can be responsible for generating their own numbers—the sports shop, the hobby store, the Homework Hotline, the pizza delivery service, you name it.

Price Problems

AGES: Beginning readers, older readers
MATERIALS: Food labels or cash register tape, paper and pencil

Who says reading and math don't mix? You and your children can write out word problems for one another to solve based on the prices of the food in your pantry.

Remove product labels that have the prices still attached, or keep the cash register tape if your supermarket uses universal product codes. Write out a word problem involving some of the items for your child to solve. For example: "I bought one big box of raisins for 79¢. I also bought a package of snack-size boxes for $1.29. How much money did I spend altogether on raisins?"

A more advanced mathematician may be able to handle problems involving several different operations. For example: "Last week I bought oranges at two pounds for a dollar. This week they are three pounds for a dollar. I paid $2.50 this week. How many pounds of oranges did I buy? How much would the same amount have cost last week?"

After your children solve the problems you pose, ask them to write problems using the labels or tape. Then it's your turn to solve the problems.

Bargain Hunter

AGES: Older readers
MATERIALS: Newspaper ads, paper and pencil

A little comparison shopping is good for the pocketbook and encourages your children to develop critical thinking skills, important for all kinds of reading.

Look through ads in the newspaper with your children and discuss how different stores offer many of the same items at different prices. (Most newspapers run large supermarket ads regularly on a particular day midweek.) Together, make a shopping list of food and household items that you really need to buy. Then turn over the list to your children so they can comparison shop in the newspaper before you do the actual shopping at the food store.

After rereading the ads in the paper, your children write the name of the local store offering an item at the lowest price next to that item on the list. Provide a calculator or scrap paper so they can do the arithmetic required to figure out whether a five-pound bag of potatoes selling for $1.99 represents a savings compared to potatoes selling for 29¢ a pound. Unless you plan to shop at several stores, you might also ask your children to figure out which store offers you the largest overall savings.

On the Road

Does your family do a lot of traveling? Take these ideas for a road test the next time you pull out of the driveway.

You really do need a good stock of ideas to keep your children occupied on long drives. Some of the better activities for a road-weary crew are the ones that come spontaneously, like singing, rhyming, and storytelling. Intersperse these with ongoing activities, like looking for all fifty states' license plates or playing Navigator. Your children can play these awhile, drop them, and then come back to them.

Supplement the activities in this chapter with those in "The Gang's All Here." You'll find a number of word games and memory games equally good for the car and the family room because they require the family to have nothing more than their verbal wits about them.

The surest way to keep the children cheerful is to stay ahead of them. Drop an activity when you sense they are beginning to tire of it and have another ready to go.

Book Bumper Stickers

AGES: **Beginning readers, older readers**
MATERIALS: **Strip of paper (about 3" or 4" wide) or letter-size envelope (#10), wide-tip marker, letter stencils or stick-on letters (optional), clear contact paper, scissors**

Advertise your family's enthusiasm for reading right where everybody can see it—on the bumper of your car.

Before your children print their bumper stickers, they'll need a catchy slogan. Since it's the family car, the whole family may want to be in on the brainstorming session. Keep the message short and direct. For example:

· "We Break for Books"
· "Have You Read Your Book Today?"
· "Honk If You Like to Read!"
· "We (heart symbol for Love) Books!"
· "Backseat Reader"
· "Do You Know Where Your Library Is?"

Have your children print the slogan in bold, dark letters on the strip of paper or on the front of a letter-size envelope. They can use stencils, stick-on letters, or write freehand.

Cut out a piece of clear contact paper to the dimensions of the bumper sticker plus one inch all around. Remove the backing, center the bumper sticker facedown on the adhesive surface, and stick the whole assembly onto the car bumper. Smooth from the center out to remove air bubbles. The contact paper will be easier to peel off than a glued-on bumper sticker. When your family tires of one message, simply replace it with another.

When In Rome . . .

AGES: All ages

When in Rome . . . read about Rome! The same applies for everywhere you travel with your children. Whether you're headed for the beach or a national landmark, let your first stop be your local library, where you and your kids can check out books related to your itinerary.

For a shore vacation, you might recommend *Harry By the Sea* or *The Maggie B.* to a young child. An older reader might enjoy *Island of the Blue Dolphins, Call It Courage,* or *Paddle to the Sea.* Or bring a collection of John Masefield's sea poems and take turns reading aloud to the rhythm of the waves.

Historical novels are fitting for a tour of a landmark city. Are you planning a weekend in Boston or Williamsburg? *Johnny Tremain* or *Toliver's Secret* offer colorful accounts of the Revolutionary War period. A biography of Lincoln can accompany you to Gettysburg.

Stories on the Go

AGES: Prereaders, beginning readers, older readers
MATERIALS: Storytelling cassettes, car tape deck or portable cassette player

Storytelling tapes are an effortless way to amuse your children on a long trip. If your car is not equipped with a cassette deck, bring a portable cassette player along. If you take the player on a train or plane, plug in a set of lightweight headphones so the other passengers won't be disturbed.

Children who don't suffer from motion sickness can bring books and read-along cassettes—the store-bought variety or homemade recordings. Queasier travelers can sit back and listen without reading along. If you plan to travel through the night, a favorite book recording can substitute for your usual bedtime story.

You and your older children might enjoy listening to old radio theater re-releases available on cassette, such as "The Lone Ranger" and "The Green Hornet." Sing-along tapes are also great for travel; they can revive a tired troop or lull a toddler to sleep.

Almost There!

AGES: **Beginning readers, older readers**
MATERIALS: **County or state map (optional), paper, pencil**

When children follow their own homemade maps, they won't need to ask you, "How long before we get there?" The information will be right in front of them.

This idea is useful if you plan to drive forty-five minutes or more. Beforehand, draw a simple map of your trip, with your children, marking each good-sized town or city you'll drive through. Also mark in any landmarks or familiar sights (the Coppertone billboard, a skyscraper, a favorite restaurant) along the way. You don't have to put a lot of time into making the map. Either help your children draw the map freehand, or they can trace a county or state map, marking in towns and landmarks selectively.

To help the children keep track of where they are, number the locations on the map. Then instead of the wearying "How long before we get there?" you'll hear an authoritative "That was number five. Three more towns to go!"

Navigator

AGES: Older readers
MATERIALS: Road maps, a copy of your itinerary, highlighter or light-colored marker, pencil, and pad

If the pilot (driver) is willing, your child can be the navigator on the family's next car trip.

In preparation for the trip, the navigator reads the itinerary, then uses a highlighter to trace your planned route on the map, circling the various destinations. The pencil and pad are for keeping track of mileage. The navigator is also in charge of giving directions to the pilot, watching for signs and markers along the way, and answering the impatient questions of younger brothers and sisters: "Are we there yet?" *"When* are we going to be there?"

If your navigator also marks down the places your family stops for the night and special sites you visit along the way, the annotated map will be a nice souvenir of your trip.

Just Passing Through

AGES: Beginning readers, older readers
MATERIALS: Paper, pencil, notebook, stamped postcards

Whether you drive along the highway or back roads, you'll pass through a number of small towns. With this activity, your children can help them jump off the map from relative obscurity.

Give the children a notebook to record the names of all the unknown places you drive through without stopping on your trip. When you finally do stop for the night, or perhaps when you return home at the end of your trip, have them alphabetize the list. Then suggest they write away to the local Chamber of Commerce in each town for visitor information.

Your children may learn of a tiny Native American Museum or old windmill that will make a stop worthwhile should you find yourselves traveling through those parts again. Or you may learn about a new campground or popular diner where you can stop regularly along a route you travel often, say to Grandpa's house or the beach.

Rhymesters

AGES: Prereaders, beginning readers, older readers

Rhyming is like the flu: Often you don't know it's coming on until it hits you, as when someone says, "Give me the keys, please." Warning: Rhyming can be very contagious, especially among children.

Pass the time as you drive by spontaneously stringing along a list of rhyming words with one child, or with a whole carpool full of rhymesters. Say a word, then let the children call out rhyming words until the possibilities are exhausted. Depending on the children's ages, you might want to accept nonsense words—after all, they do rhyme!

When you have a long period of time to fill, try one of these rhyming games, which are appropriate for older children:

- *Rhyming Ghost.* Play Ghost, but instead of naming letters in sequence until a word is spelled, players take turns saying rhyming words until one player cannot think of another word that rhymes. That player gets a G as a penalty. The game continues with a new word each round. When players accumulate all the letters in the word *ghost,* they drop out of the game. Play until there is one player left in the game—the winner. Or quit while you're really ahead—when the kids begin to show signs of boredom.

• *Hink Pink.* This rhyming game will challenge older children. Players take turns coming up with clever definitions that will relate a pair of rhyming words. The player poses the definition as a question, and the other players try to guess the answer. For example, what is the name of the disease that makes plaid skirts lose their pleats? Kilt wilt! What do you call the god of love when he shoots the wrong person? Stupid Cupid! That's a Hinky Pinky because there are *two* rhyming syllables; you can also make up Hinkety Pinketies for word pairs with *three* rhyming syllables.

• *Limericks.* Kids love to make up these five-line nonsense poems. Using the popular formula, "There once was a . . . from . . ." they can make up silly poems in the car or on the train. Limericks can be about members of the family, passers-by, or imaginary people. For example:

> There once was a sister named Mary
> Who packed more than she could possibly carry.
> From New York to Lancaster,
> We all moved right past her,
> 'Cause that suitcase caused Mary to tarry.

> There once was a boy named Len Brown
> Who drove south with his window rolled down.
> The sun hit the van
> And gave him a tan
> Before Lenny ever left town!

Detour, Exit, Falling Rocks

AGES: Beginning readers, older readers
MATERIALS: Pad, notebook, or clipboard and paper, pencil

In this road activity, the riders on the left side of the car take on the riders on the right side in a race to spot words that begin with all the letters of the alphabet.

The two sides compete to find a word for *every letter, in order.* Team members assign themselves a window or direction, then look hard and fast at road signs, billboards, restaurant and store signs. Players call out the words as soon as they spot them so the other players can corroborate the sighting. The first team to go through the alphabet wins.

Depending on the patience of the players, you may want to eliminate letters like *Q, X,* and *Z.* Although you may pass a motel advertising queen-size beds or a school zone sign, it may be a while before you pass two such signs so each team can get by the hurdle. And if you're driving in the summer, it's unlikely you'll find *X*-mas advertisements. Another alternative might be to allow players to use the letters they find on license plates. Easier yet, require that the words the players call out only have to *include* rather than *begin with* each letter.

Finding words in alphabetical order, or competing to find words, can frustrate beginning readers. If young children are participating, play a cooperative game, where both sides of the car call out words in any order. Have one player write the alphabet on a pad or in a notebook and enter words alongside each letter as the players spot them. The object is still to see if the players can find at least one word for every letter of the alphabet.

Backseat Scavenger Hunt

AGES: Prereaders, beginning readers, older readers
MATERIALS: Paper and pencil

If you prepare a backseat scavenger hunt for a long car ride, your children may be too busy looking out the window to notice how long you've been on the road.

Before you head out, make up a long list of various things your children are likely to see from the car (or bus or train) window. For example: a license plate beginning with the letter *C*, an old tire, a tow truck, an overpass, a city that is named after a woman, a McDonald's restaurant, a silo, and so on.

Give the children the long list to work on together or divide up the list so that each child is looking for different items. Or let them make up lists for each other.

For children who can't yet read, make a picture list by cutting out magazine pictures of signs and other common roadside attractions, like cows and pay telephones. Glue the cutouts on a piece of paper.

The children cross items off their lists or circle the pictured objects as they find them. If they wish, they can call out when they see something so the other players can corroborate. Let the winner of the backseat scavenger hunt be the first one out of the car when you stop to stretch your legs, or the one who gets to ride in the front seat for a while.

License Plate Games

AGES: Beginning readers, older readers
MATERIALS: Map of the United States or list of the fifty states, crayons, notebook

Keeping track of unusual license plates or plates from different states is a favorite pastime on very long car trips. Here are some variations your family may want to try.

- *States Plates.* Photocopy a map of the United States that includes all fifty states or make a list of the fifty states. Family members see how long it takes to find a license plate from each state. The first player to notice a new plate colors in that state on the map or circles the state on the list.
- *License Plate Bingo.* Make copies of the map for everyone. The first player to see plates from three (or four or five) adjoining states, marks them on the map and gets Bingo. Only the first player to notice a plate can make a mark.
- *Out-of-State Graph.* Families that travel near home can keep track of all the out-of-state plates they see as they drive around town. Have your children make a graph to see which states are best represented in your area.
- *Collectors' Plates.* Family members keep a constant lookout for unusual license plates—plates with letters that spell words or names, or that form a rebus message (for example, ICU 2 for "I see you, too" or 10 SNE 1 for "Tennis, anyone?"). Collect your findings in a notebook, or check stationery and toy departments for a novelty pad with empty license plates that your kids can fill in. Older children may want to brainstorm their own vanity plates.

Travelog

AGES: Beginning readers, older readers
MATERIALS: Notebook or blank book (or postcards for variation),
pen, colored pencils

Keep a family journal on your vacation trips, as well as a photo album or souvenir scrapbook. When it comes to reliving your adventures, you'll find that words often say more than pictures.

Have all the members of the family take turns writing an entry in a notebook or blank book at the end of each day's travel or stay. (Children who don't write yet can dictate to a parent or older brother or sister.) Leave the substance of the entry to the writers. They may want to describe something you all saw, recount a mishap with the luggage, or retell an anecdote about a historic place you visited. Take along a box of colored pencils in case your writers want to illustrate their entries.

Back home, help your children intersperse the journal entries with photos and other paper souvenirs, and paste them all in a scrapbook.

Your children may prefer to keep a postcard travelog. From every place you visit, the children mail themselves a picture postcard describing what they have seen or done in that particular place. When they arrive home, a stack of postcards will be waiting for them. Your children can then reorganize the cards, punch one or two holes in the top of each card, and insert binder rings to hold the deck together. From time to time, flip the cards over one by one, read, and remember.

Unpacking Grandmother's Trunk

AGES: Beginning readers, older readers

In this activity, your children recall Items in sequence, from A to Z, as they play a game especially appropriate for going places.

Your family probably knows at least one version of the game Grandmother's Trunk. In the original game, one player starts by saying typically, "In Grandmother's trunk I found an afghan . . ." The next player repeats what the first player has said, then adds a second item beginning with *B:* "In Grandmother's trunk I found an afghan and a bowtie." The third player repeats what the second player has said and adds a third item beginning with *C:* "In Grandmother's trunk I found an afghan, a bowtie, and a coat."

The game continues as the players take turns repeating the sequence of items from memory before adding another item beginning with the next letter of the alphabet. If a player omits an item, he or she drops out of the game. The game continues until there is only one player left or all the remaining players have correctly unpacked Grandmother's trunk (or your family's suitcase) from A to Z. Your family may decide to assist one another so that all players remain in the game till the end.

You can change the lead-in to reflect your family's current activity or destination. For example, if you're going camping, begin "We're going on a camping trip and we're taking along . . ." If you're heading out to the supermarket, begin "We're going to the supermarket and we're going to buy . . ."

You may want to add yet more alphabetical elements, as in this version which challenges vocabulary as well as memory: "I love my love with an A. I went to Alaska and bought her an alabaster apple . . ."

Black & White
& Read All Over

My Name in Print!
Newspaper Solitaire
Fun with the Funnies
Off with Your Headline!
Newspaper Scavenger Hunt
Read It and Weep
Weather vs. Weather
Have Newspaper, Will Travel
Classified Fiction
Negative Advertising
Campaign Coverage
News to Share

Extra! Extra! The newspaper is an ideal supplement to your family's reading. Where else than in the newspaper can they find out at once about the President's trip abroad, a new medical breakthrough, a promising young ballerina, the discovery of sunken treasure, a bike sale, and a new bestselling children's book? Television and radio offer only a fraction of the newspaper's scope.

Newspapers provide the very latest information about every facet of your children's world. The newspaper's best virtue is that it has something for everybody. A sports fan can consume an entire section of the paper; a young musician can check the classifieds for a used instrument; a political activist can jeer or cheer over the results of an election; a preschooler can pick out familiar letters or ask Dad to read aloud the caption under a photo.

Many Sunday editions include a syndicated children's supplement, like *The Mini Page* and *Pennywhistle Press*. These supplements feature articles and puzzles directed at your young readers. You might want to save these pages for a quiet activity time during the week.

Before you recycle your newspapers, keep in mind that they offer a cheap source of letters, words, and pictures to cut out and use in a variety of art and reading-related activities.

My Name in Print!

AGES: Toddlers, prereaders
MATERIALS: Section of newspaper, pen (not black)

Invite a younger child to come sit on your lap and "read" the newspaper with you. Choose a section such as Sports that has a lot of headlines. The larger print will make it easier for your child to find individual letters.

Begin pointing out letters that your child can recognize, circling the letter with a colored pen as you say it: "There's an *s*. There's a *b*. Look, two *o*'s together! Here's *s* again. Do you see another *s* in this word? What letter does Seth start with? *S*, right?"

Turn to a fresh page of the paper. Write your child's name in large letters in the margin at the top of the page. (Use both upper- and lowercase letters with preschoolers, even if they haven't learned to recognize many small letters yet; for toddlers, use all capitals.) Say the letters out loud as you print them.

Now ask your child to scan the headlines and find each letter in his or her name in sequence. You may need to help with letters such as *a* and *g*, which are often configured differently in newspapers from the form most children learn. After your child has found and circled each letter, repeat the full spelling aloud: "We found your whole name. *S-e-t-h, Seth!*"

If you still have your child's attention, turn to another new page and begin again. Maybe this time look for a sister's name or your name (small children love to use Mommy's and Daddy's first names).

Newspaper Solitaire

AGES: Prereaders, beginning readers
MATERIALS: Newspaper, highlighter or colored pencil, pad and pencil for keeping score (optional)

When you're too busy to play with them, show your children how to play one of these self-directed games that reinforce letter or word recognition. Supply each player with a newspaper and a highlighter or colored pencil.

• *Find the Letter.* Prereaders pick a newspaper article, then highlight or circle a designated letter (of their choice) every time it appears. The children can try to beat their own scores, or play against other family members.

   When there is more than one player, players choose different articles, but look for the same letter. There's no time limit; this is not a test for speed. All the players have a chance to finish before they count and compare their scores.

• *Find the Word.* Beginning readers also choose an article, but they go through the text highlighting a new word they have learned. Suggest a frequently used word, like *the, and,* or *said.*

• *Find All the Words You Know.* Beginning readers highlight *all* the words they recognize (they must also know the meanings of the words). Save the articles so the children can repeat the game several months later to check their progress. The second time around, suggest they use a different color pencil or highlighter. Now they can instantly distinguish their new vocabulary and count how many more words they have learned.

Fun with the Funnics

AGES: Prereaders, beginning readers, older readers
MATERIALS: Comic strip, scissors, pen, envelope, sheet of plain white paper, cellophane tape

When you offer them the newspaper, do your children head straight for the comics? Next time, beat them to it and use their favorite cartoon strips to make one of these quick games.

• *Out of Order.* With a few snips of a scissors, you can make a sequencing puzzle for prereaders or beginning readers. For a prereader, choose a cartoon strip like "Peanuts," which doesn't have many words. First read it aloud to your child, asking questions as you go, like "What happens in the *first* picture? What happens *next? Then* what does she say?"

After you finish, cut apart the individual frames, number them on the back in their original sequence, and slide them into an envelope. Give your child the envelope and a piece of paper, and explain how to put together the puzzle: "Take the cartoon pictures out of the envelope. Turn them over on top of the white paper so the numbers are hidden. Now see if you can put the pictures back in order, the way we looked at them before."

Show your child how to peek under the frames to check that the order is correct, then let him or her tape down the pictures. Don't be surprised if taping the pictures is your child's favorite part of the activity.

For a child who can read, cut apart the frames before he or she ever sees the comic strip. Present them in an envelope on which you have written the directions.

• *Punch Line, Please!* Cut out your child's favorite self-contained comic strip (not a serial strip that has a continuing story line). Copy the punch line (the words in the last voice balloon) on a piece of paper. If you have correction fluid, white out the punch line on the strip; otherwise, cut out a new voice balloon and glue it over the original one.

Now you can give your child the comic strip and ask him or her to come up with a punch line. Encourage your child to compare his or her words with the original punch line you copied.

To make the activity more challenging, snip off the last frame of the cartoon strip altogether. Now there is no longer a picture context for the punch line. Tape the rest of the strip on a piece of paper, and draw a box where the last frame would have been. Ask your child to complete the cartoon, illustration and all.

Off with Your Headline!

AGES: Beginning readers, older readers
MATERIALS: Newspaper, scissors, paper, and pencil

Cut the headlines off a few articles you think will interest your children and you have an activity that tests their ability to identify the main idea in a news story or any other story. Brothers and sisters might enjoy setting up this challenge for each other.

Go through the newspaper and cut out a few short articles that your children will find appealing. Fold down the headlines or cut them off so they can't read them. Then ask your children to read the articles and come up with their own headlines. Each child gets a different article. Give them pencils and paper to write down their ideas.

When they have written new headlines, reveal the originals. Compare them and have your kids decide which more clearly tell the reader what the article is about.

Here are a couple of variations that also help develop reading comprehension:

- *Mix and Match.* This is a much simpler version. Cut out several articles, cut off their headlines, and hand all the pieces to your child. Your child reads the articles and matches each one with a headline. If possible, cut out articles on the same or similar subjects.
- *Caption Cutoffs.* Your child can play another mix-and-match game with news photos and captions. Cut out the photos, cut off the captions, and turn the severed pieces over to your child to reconstruct. Your child will have to observe the photos closely and pay attention to details in the copy of the captions.
- *Off at the Neck.* This is a more difficult version, requiring more thinking and writing. Rather than snipping away only the headline of an article, cut the article off after the lead paragraph. Challenge your child to write a new lead paragraph, drawing the most important ideas from the body of the article.

  You might want to introduce the style of writing that journalists refer to as the "inverted pyramid"—working from the most important to the least important details.
- *Context Puzzle.* Cut apart a newspaper story after every three or four lines. Give your child the pieces and challenge him or her to put them back together as a complete article. Your child will have to read carefully, taking clues from the context of the broken sentences.

Newspaper Scavenger Hunt

AGES: Beginning readers, older readers
MATERIALS: Newspaper, paper, pencil

Make a game of familiarizing your children with the different sections of the newspaper. Send them on a scavenger hunt for information to be found from the front page to the classifieds.

As you read through the newspaper one morning or evening, make a list describing various items you run across in each section. Your list might include:

• A photo of a world leader.
• A headline about a business merger.
• A sports statistic.
• The high temperature in a major city.
• The price of a pound of meat.
• An angry word.
• The cheapest 1982 Chevette for sale.
• A movie that begins at 7 P.M.
• A picture of Snoopy.

Give your child the list and ask him or her to find a sample of every item, cut it out of the paper, and paste it on the list. If more than one child wants to play, divide the list between them or make separate lists for different issues of the paper (more time for you, but less frustrating for your children).

All children who complete a list are winners in more than one respect. Not only have they found all the items, but they now know their way around the newspaper and have a better idea of the incredible variety of material that's there for the reading.

Read It and Weep

AGES: **Beginning readers, older readers**
MATERIALS: **Newspaper, stationery, pen, stamped envelope**

Do your children have a natural, if somewhat maudlin, fascination for sad stories in the news? You may find that their compassion produces a passion to read.

Call your children's attention to a human interest story you think will interest them—the plight of a family left homeless after a fire swept their third-story apartment, the attempt to rescue a beached whale, the discovery of an abandoned puppy.

After they've finished reading the article, encourage them to talk about it. Speculate about what special belonging might have perished in the fire, why the whale came ashore in the first place, or who might take in the puppy. Suggest that they turn on the evening news to see if TV reporters cover the same story, and make sure they have an opportunity to read any follow-up stories in the next day's newspaper.

Your children may be anxious to "do something" for the victims. Perhaps they'd like to write a note expressing their concern and support, draw a cheer-up picture, or make a small contribution to a fund that has been set up. They can send mail care of the newspaper. Explain to your children that they probably won't receive a reply, but encourage their good intentions within reason. If you don't limit their involvement, you may find yourselves with a new puppy!

Weather vs. Weather

AGES: Beginning readers, older readers
MATERIALS: Newspaper, television

Your children will soon discover that sometimes the newspaper says one thing and the television newscaster says another. This activity encourages young readers to become more aware of conflicting reports so that they will begin to question their accuracy and become sensitive to an important reading issue—viewpoint.

You might begin with something as seemingly straightforward as the weather report. Have your children watch the TV news forecast for the next day's weather. In the morning, they can compare the television forecast with the forecast printed in the morning newspaper. They can also look up the telephone number for the United States Weather Bureau and call to hear its recorded forecast. And they can see the weather for themselves as the day progresses.

Were the predictions accurate? Did the reports differ in any way? Discuss why this might be. The evening news may offer its own insights; for example, the weather forecaster may report that shifts in wind patterns brought on an unexpected storm.

Older children may now be intrigued enough to compare news stories. How does a newspaper article about an air crash compare with the television coverage? Does one medium report more facts? Does one offer more eyewitness accounts? If there are discrepancies, how do the reporters handle them?

Whenever you and your children discuss a news event, encourage them to question the various sources of information, especially if they detect bias or sensationalism.

Have Newspaper, Will Travel

AGES: Prereaders, beginning readers, older readers
MATERIALS: Newspaper, file cards, glue, highlighter, pencil and paper

An older child may enjoy planning a pretend trip while looking through the travel section of the newspaper, while a younger brother or sister may be excited just to find so many pictures of airplanes and boats.

Most travel sections are published in the Sunday edition of major metropolitan newspapers and feature a different city, region, or country in each issue. There are a variety of ways your children can use this material:

- *Travel Itinerary.* Your children can read the main articles to find out about the people, sights and side trips, various restaurants and accommodations, and shopping for a featured tourist spot. Using this information, they can plan their own itineraries for a pretend trip. They may want to estimate the costs based on newspaper advertisements run by airlines, cruise lines, resort hotels, tour packagers, restaurants, and other companies.
- *Travel Flashcards.* Help prereaders and beginning readers look through the travel section and cut out transportation pictures and words. Give them file cards to make their own flashcards. They paste a picture of a vehicle on each card and print or paste on the name of the vehicle: *airplane, train, boat, car, balloon.* Take along the cards on your next family trip.
- *Stock Locations.* Your young writers may discover the perfect setting for their next stories in the travel section. Suggest that they keep portfolios of interesting places—both pictures and descriptions.
- *Travel Information.* Is your family planning a real trip? Maybe your children can find articles and ads related to your itinerary. Do the

newspaper ads list places one can write for more information? Suggest that your children cut out the articles and save them in a scrapbook along with whatever other souvenirs they bring home from the trip.

Classified Fiction

AGES: Beginning readers, older readers
MATERIALS: Newspaper, paper and pencil

Imagine finding an ad for Chitty Chitty Bang Bang under Cars for Sale, or a description of Mary Poppins's unique qualifications under Positions Wanted (talk about character references!). That's what your children do as they try their hand at writing creative classifieds for favorite story characters.

Together, read aloud some of the ads in the classified section of the newspaper. Point out the different conventions—the short phrases, abbreviations, and jargon.

Ask your children to think of something they might want to buy or sell through the classifieds. Walk through the process of writing an ad: Make a list of all the information you want to give the reader, then substitute conventional wording and abbreviations.

Here are some ideas to get your kids started:

- *Fictional Lost and Found.* Lots of story plots revolve around something missing. A child can write an ad to place in a fictional Lost and Found. For example: "LOST: 6 mittens. Reward—rattail pie. The Three Kittens."
- *Fantasy Real Estate.* Deciphering real estate ads is a challenge in itself. They are riddled with abbreviations and jargon. After figuring out a few real ads, a child can write a fictional one. For example, is your birdhouse empty? Your child can advertise the vacancy: "WANTED: family of wrens for vacant birdhouse w/nest

in lg. yd., birdbath, feeder, nr. berry bush. Nice nghbrs; no pets or jays. If inter'd, fly nth. to 1402 48th Ave."

- *For Sale.* Your child might place an ad to sell the likes of Danny Dunn's homework machine (under office equipment) or Mike Mulligan's steam shovel (under heavy equipment).
- *Position Wanted.* How would Amelia Bedelia advertise her housekeeping skills? Perhaps Encyclopedia Brown wants to do some free-lance sleuthing—after school hours, of course.
- *Personals.* If you answer this ad, you'll meet Chester, a musical cricket: "Lonely violinist new in town seeks friends. Interested? Meet me in the subway at Times Square." Your children might want to write personal ads describing themselves or fictional alter egos.

Negative Advertising

AGES: Older readers
MATERIALS: Newspaper, dictionary or thesaurus (if you have one), pencil and paper

The language of advertising is usually colorful, exciting, and positive. In this activity, your children will enjoy using their vocabulary skills to turn advertisements on their heads.

Have your children choose advertisements from a newspaper or magazine (the more hyped-up the language, the better). Ask them to circle all the adjectives, then to rewrite the ads, replacing each of those words with an antonym.

When they're finished, ask them to read their devastating piece aloud. The advertisement for that lovely new restaurant in town will never know what hit it!

Campaign Coverage

AGES: Older readers
MATERIALS: Newspaper or news magazine, scrapbook, rubber cement

Put your young reporters on the campaign trail of their favorite candidates for office on either the local or national level. They can give updates over dinner on the latest fast-breaking news stories, and develop a scrapbook of news articles and analyses.

If more than one child is participating, they can draw straws to pick which candidate to follow in a race. If it is a presidential election year, there should be enough candidates to go around so that Mom and Dad can participate, too.

The reporters read every article about the contest or issues that they can get their hands on. When everyone else is finished with the newspaper or news magazine, they clip out related articles and paste them into scrapbooks. The scrapbooks might also include quotes from speeches heard on the radio or television, travel itineraries, published interviews, campaign literature, photos, political cartoons, polls, and standings.

Encourage your children to report to the family regularly, assessing their candidates' current chances for election and commenting on other aspects of the campaign, such as the candidates' stands on important issues, the opponents' strategies, and the political climate in general. Children with opposing candidates can hold a debate toward the last days of the campaign.

After the election, your children may want to continue covering the postelection activities of a winning candidate, or they may want to read more about some of the issues raised during the campaign.

News to Share

AGES: Beginning readers, older readers
MATERIALS: Manila envelopes, pens, newspapers and magazines, scissors

When you see an article about your child's favorite musician, do you call attention to the item, read it aloud, or cut it out of the paper and put it on your child's desk? Here are a few more ideas for making a time and place to share news in your home.

- *A Time to Share.* Incorporate news sharing in the family dinner hour once or twice a week. Have family members take turns picking an interesting article to read, then later share with the rest of the family. This activity can spark some thoughtful discussion at the dinner table—sometimes a welcome departure from the usual small talk, school talk, and office talk.

- *Clipping Service.* Many businesses and organizations hire a special service to read through newspapers and magazines and clip out articles that are pertinent to them. Your family can act as its own clipping service if family members are willing to read with one another's special interests in mind.

  Have each family member write his or her name on a manila envelope and underneath list any subjects of special personal interest: animals, astronomy, football, flower gardening, movie classics, vegetarian cooking, sculpture, and so on. Store the envelopes in a convenient place.

  When someone comes across an article that might be of interest to another family member, the finder reads far enough into the article to decide whether it is worth clipping. If it is, that child cuts out the item, dates it, and slips it into the other person's envelope.

- *Well-Placed Articles.* Items that are of interest to everyone in the family can be posted on the refrigerator with a magnet, tacked on a bulletin board, taped to a mirror or the back of the cereal box, or read aloud. In short, place an article of general interest where no one can fail to notice it.

Rainy-Day Ideas

Words in a Mist
Egg-Carton Sorter
Clothesline Games
Put Your Room in A-B-C Order
B Is for Book
A Book About Me
Rainbow Book
Photo Phone Book
Household Word Hunt
Pickup Popsicle Sticks
Concentration Games
Busy Box
Tiny Worlds
Doll Costumes
Book Buttons
Pretend Office
Book Nooks
Bedroom Library

Reading can take place rain or shine, but certain activities lend themselves especially well to those long periods when wet weather, illness, or early nightfalls require your child to be indoors.

Of course, you'll want your children to occupy their indoor time with worthwhile activities, and what can be more worthwhile than reading? As preparation, help your children find a comfortable nook where they can settle down with books or a quiet activity when they feel in the mood. Then fill a "busy box" with activity books and art supplies that they can use to amuse themselves.

To prevent an outbreak of cabin fever, you'll need a full docket of ideas to meet your youngsters' constant need for something to do. This section offers a number of reading-related art projects, activities, and games ranging from bookmaking to word hunts to a game of pickup sticks that teaches letter or word recognition.

Words in a Mist

AGES: All ages
MATERIALS: Frosty or foggy window or mirror

Lead your small children to a window on a bitter-cold night. Together, breathe against the glass so that your warm breath condenses on the pane. Now you have the perfect slate for printing letters and drawing shapes.

Use a finger to draw and write. Three- or four-year-olds can copy or trace your letters, then try to make their own. Let toddlers draw pictures or try to make letters formed by simple strokes, like L and T. When you run out of room, just breathe again to "clean" the slate. Toddlers love this game because it stimulates both their visual and tactile senses at once.

An older child will already have had considerable experience scribbling messages on dusty shelves, dirty cars, and frosty car windows. You may discover telltale traces of fingerwork in smudgy statements like these: "Clean me." "Guess who?" "Hi there!" You can always respond in kind; for example, slip inside the bathroom while your child is showering and leave "Good morning!" on the misted mirror.

It's the simple, yet magical things you do to interest your young children in letters and words that impress them with how spontaneous and fun reading can be. Like you, they'll probably never outgrow the impulse to find something to read in the least likely places.

Egg-Carton Sorter

AGES: Prereaders, beginning readers
MATERIALS: Egg carton, felt pen, construction paper, magazines, scissors, glue or cellophane tape

There must be a dozen sorting games you and your children can invent using the inside of an empty egg carton. Here are a few to get you started: One reinforces letter recognition, another color words, another letter sounds. This is the kind of idea you can turn over to an older child, who may enjoy making these games for a younger brother or sister.

- *Letter Lotto.* Print a different capital letter in the bottom of each section of an egg carton. Cut out twelve paper eggs. Print the matching lowercase letters on the eggs. Have your child put the lowercase eggs in the corresponding uppercase sections.
- *Rainbow Words.* Use color markers to make a different color spot in the bottom of each section of an egg carton. Repeat each primary and secondary color twice. Cut out twelve paper eggs. Print the corresponding color words (*red, orange, yellow, green, blue,* and *violet* or *purple*) twice, one word on each egg. Your child reads the words on the paper eggs and places them in a section with the corresponding color spot.

• *Sorting Sounds.* Print a different lowercase letter in the bottom of each egg-carton section. Leaf through a magazine with your child and cut out several small pictures of objects that begin with each of the letter sounds. Let your child paste or tape the pictures on paper eggs.

Have your child place the pictures in the sections labeled with their beginning letters. For a self-checking game, print the name of the pictured object on the back of each egg. Your child can turn over the egg and see if the first letter in the word matches the letter in the bottom of the carton.

Clothesline Games

AGES: Toddlers, prereaders, beginning readers
MATERIALS: Clothesline, snap clothespins, basket of clothes, large file cards, felt pen

It's another rainy day, so hang it all! On the clothesline, that is. String an indoor line across two chairs (about a child's shoulder height), take the clothes out of the dryer, and play one or two of these learning games. If you have some art projects planned for later in the day, keep the clothesline up after you play and use it as a drying rack or an art gallery.

• *Clothesline Categories.* Invite your children to sort through the basket of laundry for items in a certain clothing category—shirts, pants, socks—then ask them to hang the clothes on the line for your inspection. (You may have to help small hands with the clothespins.)

Then your children can remove the clothes, sort through the basket, and hang clothes in a new category.

To vary the game, ask your children to hang up all the clothes of a certain color.

• *Sizing Things Up.* Your kids sort out clothes in one category, such as

T-shirts or socks, then hang them up in size order—first Daddy's socks, then Mommy's, and so on down the line.

- *Letter Lineup.* Print large upper- or lowercase letters (whichever your children are learning) on large file cards or pieces of construction paper. Give your children the cards and a handful of clothespins. Call out all the letters for which there are cards, giving each child a turn at sorting and hanging. Then admire the long letter lineup.

  If a child is first learning the ABCs, hang up the first letter card, then ask him or her to find a matching card and hang it next to yours. Say the letter together. If a child is learning the alphabet sequence, shuffle twenty-six letter cards and have your youngster hang them in the right order.

- *Word Lineup.* Print different clothing words on cards and present them to your child in a box (call it the "laundry basket"). Ask your child to hang the "clothes" on the line in alphabetical order.

  A variation is to give your child the clothing cards along with a laundry basket containing real clothes. Your youngster finds an article of clothing to go with each word card and hangs the two together—a way to reinforce reading vocabulary.

Put Your Room in A-B-C Order

AGES: Beginning readers, older readers
MATERIALS: Paper and pencil

Have your children take an alphabetical inventory of all objects in a room by listing everything they see in A-B-C order.

A simpler version of the game is to have your children try to find twenty-six objects in a room, each beginning with a different letter of the alphabet. Set a time limit and award a point for each item written next to the letter. To simplify the game further, have the children choose one letter and see who can find the most objects beginning with that letter in a set amount of time.

B Is for Book

AGES: Prereaders, beginning readers
MATERIALS: Loose-leaf binder, standard-size paper, scissors, magazines and catalogs, glue

There are a great many alphabet picture books (collectors call them *abecedaries*) available at libraries and bookstores, but your children will learn most from the books they make themselves.

An ABC book is not put together in one-two-three. Plan to let your child work on one letter page at a sitting, two if he or she is already well versed in the ABCs. You can go in order from A to Z, or have your child choose a letter at random each time.

You or your child prints the letter in upper- and lowercase at the top of a sheet of paper (or cut out the letters from advertisement headlines in magazines). Keep a supply of magazines and color catalogs on hand. When your child sees an appealing picture of an object that begins with that letter, he or she cuts it out and pastes it on the paper.

When finished, you and your child can insert the page in a loose-leaf binder. The page may have two pictures on it or eight, limited only by the size of the pictures and your child's patience for looking. If you have lots of pictures, let your youngster devote more than one page to a letter.

A Book About Me

AGES: Prereaders, beginning readers
MATERIALS: Scrapbook or album with static-cling pages, family photo and photos of your child, drawing paper and crayons

Preschoolers are very egocentric, so they will enjoy creating a book about themselves. This self-important work should have a place on your child's bookshelf where it can be reread as many times as your young author likes.

Collect photos of your child with family, friends, favorite toys and books, and engaged in favorite activities. Let your youngster paste the photos in the scrapbook or insert them on static-cling pages.

Offer to be the secretary as your child dictates captions to you: "This is our whole big family." "I am holding Grover." "I like to cut paper." You can write the captions directly into the scrapbook or onto strips of paper that are positioned in the magnetic sleeves. If an important event is missing from the photos, your child might want to draw a picture and mount that, too.

Rainbow Book

AGES: Prereaders, beginning readers
MATERIALS: Six sheets of paper, color markers or pens, small scissors, old magazines, glue, hole puncher, colored ribbons

In this activity, bluebirds fly on the page labeled Blue and frogs hop on the page labeled Green in a beginning reader's rainbow book. While assembling this homemade book, your child differentiates colors and learns to recognize color words.

To get your child started, label each sheet of paper with a different color word—*red, orange, yellow, green, blue,* and *violet* (you may prefer to write *purple*). If possible, write each word in the corresponding color ink. Have your child say the words as you write them.

Set out some magazines, full-color catalogs, last season's greeting cards, and the like. Your child browses through these materials for pictures of different-colored items, cuts out the pictures, and pastes them on the appropriate pages. When the pages are full (front and back, if your child likes), help punch holes along the side or top of each page and bind them together with colored ribbons—all the colors of the rainbow would be nice.

Photo Phone Book

AGES: Prereaders
MATERIALS: Shirt cardboard or other sturdy paper, photos of family and friends, picture of emergency vehicles, scissors, glue, list of phone numbers, pencil

Have you ever been mystified by a phone bill listing long-distance calls you know you never placed? Maybe it's time to teach your three- or four-year-old how to use, not play with, the telephone.

If your child can read numbers, he or she is ready for a first personal phone book (actually a reference *card*). First collect photos of friends, grandparents and other close relatives, and your immediate family. Cut out all the faces. On the cardboard or piece of sturdy paper, paste the faces in a column, in alphabetical order according to the way your child refers to the person. For example, Grandmother may be filed under *G* for "Granny." Also paste on a small picture of a fire engine, ambulance, or police car.

Next to each picture, print a phone number. If you prefer, you can print the numbers with broken lines so your child can trace them. Near the emergency vehicles, print 0 (for Operator) or 9-1-1, if your community uses this number.

Give your child the phone card along with a play telephone on which to practice making calls. When you think your youngster's ready and responsible enough, let him or her make a call to Grandma or a friend on the real telephone, referring to the phone card for the number.

Make sure your young caller understands how to use the Operator or 9-1-1 number in case of a real emergency. And give careful instructions about when and when not to make calls without your supervision.

A beginning reader might like to make a more sophisticated

phone card, including the names of the people as well as their faces and phone numbers.

Household Word Hunt

AGES: Beginning readers, older readers
MATERIALS: Large paper grocery bag, marker, pencil and paper

Do your children need an active indoor activity? Send them searching the whole house over for words they can recognize.

First you need to come up with lists of words found on familiar household items—words your children recognize or can sound out with your help. A beginning reader might be sent off to find words like *shampoo, flakes, beans,* and *toothpaste.* An advanced reader can hunt for *polyester, riboflavin, detergent,* and *recipe.* If more than one child is playing, make up a different list for each player.

Give your children the word lists and large paper bags on which you've printed these directions: "Read the first word. Find something in our house that has the word on it. Put it in the bag. Find something for every word on the list, then bring the bag back to me."

When the bags are full, your children unpack them with you, pointing out the listed word on each item and saying it aloud. Or trade the original list for a blank piece of paper and pencil. Then as your children remove the items, they write the listed word on the paper and put the item away. Writing the words will help your youngsters commit them to memory. You might also ask to have the lists put in alphabetical order.

This game offers practice in word recognition, but more important, it makes children more aware of the around-the-house reading they do every day.

Pickup Popsicle Sticks

AGES: Prereaders, beginning readers
MATERIALS: Popsicle sticks, permanent marker, empty juice can,
contact paper or wrapping paper

Very young children love collecting things in containers. In this word-recognition game (a little like old-fashioned pickup sticks), children pick up popsicle sticks and keep what they can read.

Rinse and save popsicle sticks or buy a package of sticks at a crafts supply store. Write a word your child is learning to recognize on each stick with a permanent marker. Cover an empty frozen juice can with contact paper or wrapping paper, and label it Marty's Sticks (use your child's name).

Present your child with the game, gift-wrapped if you like, and explain how to play. Your child pours the sticks out of the can, scattering them every which way, and then picks them up one at a time, telling you what is written on each stick. If correct, your child keeps the stick and continues to play. The object is to see if the player can pick up all the sticks. If your child reads a word incorrectly, the round ends. All the sticks are gathered up and the game starts again.

Concentration Games

AGES: Toddlers, prereaders, beginning readers, older readers
MATERIALS: Index cards, felt pens

Your children can be the contestants in a number of different games based on the old TV game show "Concentration." All you need is a homemade deck of cards featuring picture words, letters of the alphabet, early vocabulary words, or word pairs. Matching and memory skills are involved in every version.

To play Concentration, pairs of cards with matching elements (pictures, letters, or words) are shuffled together and placed facedown on the table in rows. Players take turns turning over two cards at a time. If the cards match, the player gets to keep the cards and go again. If the cards don't match, the player turns them facedown in their original positions and passes to an opponent. Players use the information they learn from their own turns and their opponents' turns to remember the locations of the cards. (See Coupon Card Games in "Ashopping We Will Go" for other card games.)

- *Match the Pictures.* Draw or paste matching pictures on pairs of cards. Show the pictures to your toddler before you play. Say the words the pictures represent, and have your child repeat them. Practice matching while the cards are still faceup. When you play real Concentration, play with only a few pairs at a time.
- *Match the Letters.* Print matching uppercase or lowercase letters that your preschooler recognizes on pairs of cards. Review the letters before you play Concentration. Play with six pairs, then eight, increasing the number of cards as your child becomes more skillful at remembering their positions.
- *Match the Words.* Print matching words on pairs of cards. For rein-forcement, choose words from a beginning reader's reading vo-

cabulary; many older readers like the challenge of new words. Give your children some cards so they can help come up with word pairs. Play with as many as twenty pairs, and throw in some odd words if you like.

- *Match the Rhymes.* Print pairs of rhyming words (*pity/city, seen/ queen,* for instance) on cards, one word on a card. Be sure they are all words your children can recognize and pronounce. You might ask them to come up with half the rhymes.

You can play Concentration with other kinds of word pairs, such as antonyms (words and their opposites) and homonyms (words that sound alike but are spelled differently).

Busy Box

AGES: All ages
MATERIALS: Box with lid, wide-tip marker, items to fill box (see suggestions below)

Put together a busy box for your children. What's a busy box? It's what you point to while saying, "I'm busy right now, but I've planned some activities to keep you busy, too."

Choose a sturdy box or container—molded plastic file boxes are great—and paint a label or the child's name in bright letters (e.g., "Lillian's Busy Box"). Then fill the box with a variety of books, games, and art supplies. Here are some ingredients to consider:

- Storybooks
- Activity books (dot-to-dot, word-search puzzles, crosswords, coloring books, water-paint books)
- Art supplies (crayons, watercolor paints, paintbrushes, pencils and sharpener, color markers, colored chalk, glitter)
- Sewing cards and laces
- Beads and cord for stringing
- Paper (ruled construction paper, newsprint)

- Scissors (child-size for younger children)
- Stickers and sticker album
- Collage materials (old magazines, fabric scraps, bits of wrapping paper and ribbon, sequins, old greeting cards)
- School glue or glue stick
- Flannel board and felt for cutouts
- A magnet and a few metal objects (jacks, paper clips, keys)
- Compact games (dominoes, card games, jacks)

(For safety's sake, do not give toddlers any objects that can be swallowed or that can cut them.)

Put together a busy box for the car, too. If you pack items in a shirt box, it will fit more easily under the car seat. Some items are more appropriate for the road than others. For example, save yourself and the children some frustration by excluding small items that can get caught between the seats. Flannel boards and magnetic board games, on the other hand, are excellent because the pieces adhere; likewise, pads are better than loose sheets of paper.

If grandparents don't already have a busy box stored in a closet for the children's visits, you might suggest that it would make a nice gift. Be sure to show the baby-sitter where to find your own box for times when the going gets rough.

Tiny Worlds

AGES: **Beginning readers, older readers**
MATERIALS: **Shoe box or other medium-size box, dollhouse furniture and accessories, modeling clay, magazines, scissors, cardboard, glue, small dolls or figurines, other tiny objects as required**

Children are charmed by whimsical stories about miniature creatures like the Borrowers, Thumbelina, and Stuart Little. What more appropriate project can there be for recreating these characters' tiny worlds than constructing a diorama?

Perhaps your children would like to decorate Stuart Little's bedroom inside a shoe box. The book describes how the mouse's four-poster bed was fashioned out of a matchbox and clothespins. Your children can reconstruct the little piece of furniture as lovingly as Stuart's human parents did using the very same materials.

Your children may also enjoy making a diorama that recreates a scene from a favorite story of more human proportions. For example, they might like to scale down the old house from *The Lion, the Witch, and the Wardrobe* by arranging dollhouse furniture and accessories in a box. They can set the furniture and other objects in bits of modeling clay to keep them stationary. Any missing elements can be cut out of magazines or catalogs and pasted on the walls, or backed with cardboard and fixed in clay inside the miniature scene.

Perhaps your young readers would like to recreate a forest scene from *Hansel and Gretal* using twigs and dried plants, or if they're a good deal older, the landscape of *Dune* using real sand and glue. Supply the basic materials, then let your kids look around the house for things to improvise, such as a cork for a stool or a bottlecap for a round picture frame.

If your prereaders have favorite picture stories, they'd probably enjoy helping you make a miniature replica of an illustration, for example a scene in the bunny's bedroom from *Goodnight Moon*.

Dioramas are also interesting ways to recreate the scene of the crime in a mystery or detective novel. After your children set up the scene according to the book's details, they can use cardboard suspects to retrace the steps of the characters and try to establish whodunit, or reenact the crime after the mystery has been solved.

Doll Costumes

AGES: Beginning readers, older readers
MATERIALS: Fabric scraps, needle and thread; or crepe paper and tape

Do your children like to play with dolls? One day when you have a lot of time on your hands, suggest that all of you dress up the dolls to look like book characters.

Let your children select the fabrics and tell you what kind of clothing and accessories the characters need. They can refer to the book illustrations or look in an encyclopedia under a fashion heading for authentic details. Depending on a child's abilities, you may have to do the sewing yourself or just lend a hand.

For temporary costumes, you can use colored crepe paper bound together with cellophane tape instead of fabric and thread. Smaller children will enjoy helping tear or cut out pieces of paper to wrap around the dolls.

When you're all finished, your children can use the dolls to retell the stories to the rest of the family. For example, a Barbie doll decked out as the shepherdess Heidi can meet her unfriendly grandfather, played by a Ken doll or GI Joe. If you run out of dolls for all the character roles, cut out paper dolls and paper costumes.

Book Buttons

AGES: Beginning readers, older readers
MATERIALS: White cardboard or posterboard, compass or round object, scissors, felt pens, clear contact paper (optional), pin backs and glue (available at hobby shops or crafts stores) or double-stick tape

Make reading your family's cause célèbre by designing your own campaign buttons to wear on T-shirts, lapels, or coat collars.

First have family members brainstorm to come up with a slogan for their buttons. Each person may want to come up with an individual slogan, or you can all agree on one. The more clever the slogan, the more attention your buttons will attract. For example:

• "Snuggle Up with a Book."
• "Reading Is Power "
• "I (heart symbol for Love) Books."
• "Beware: Wordmonger"
• "Book Crazy"
• "A Good Book Is Easy to Find."
• "Have You Read Your Book Today?"

Constructing the buttons is an easy enough task to leave to the children. They can use a compass to make circles on posterboard, or trace a round object, then cut out the buttons. Have them hand-print the slogans on the buttons, or if you want to get a little fancy, they can apply transfer lettering or stick-on letters.

If you keep a supply of clear contact paper, laminating the buttons will offer protection when they're worn outdoors. To make the buttons wearable, your children will have to glue a pin to the back of each button, or attach a piece of double-stick tape.

Your children can put the same slogans on their T-shirts if you supply fabric paints (available at crafts stores and fabric stores).

Pretend Office

AGES: Prereaders, beginning readers
MATERIALS: Storage box or desk-organizer tray, desk supplies (see suggestions below), desk lamp, old briefcase or shopping bag with handles

If your young children see you working with paper, pencils, and the like at home or heading off to an office, they'll want to do likewise. And they'll prefer to borrow your real things rather than substitute play props—to rummage through your desk and try out all your supplies.

Let your children see what you do at your desk or worktable. While you do your work, invite them to sit alongside you and do their "work," whether that entails drawing a picture, pretending to read a report, or practicing to write a newly learned letter of the alphabet.

Suggest to your children that they set up their own "office." If they have desks, fine; if not, set up a work station at a play table or the dinner table. Fill a box with all kinds of real supplies and a few play props. For example:

- Assorted writing tools
- Eraser and correction fluid
- Rubber stamps and a stamp pad
- Paper clips
- Notebook, message pad, and writing paper
- Envelopes
- Pretend postage stamps (e.g., magazine or book stamps from sweepstakes mailings, Easter Seals, National Wildlife Federation stamps, novelty stamps sold in stationery stores)
- File folders

- Pencil holder or desk organizer
- Play telephone

Plug in a desk lamp, and lend them some work clothes. Then let them set up their own office space, leaving you free to go back to your own work.

If your children like to play school or run a pretend business, you can set them up similarly. School supplies might include a blackboard and chalk, a package of stars or assorted stickers, preschool workbooks and puzzle books. A business might require a cash box (a shoe box), play money, price labels, and a receipt pad.

Book Nooks

AGES: All ages
MATERIALS: See suggestions below

A book nook is any inviting place for your children to read, away from the hustle and bustle of the household. Your home may already offer some built-in nooks: a window seat, loft, attic dormer, or hearth. A few pillows and a good reading light are all the furnishings you need.

But if the architecture does not lend itself to cozy corners, you may want to improvise. For example, how about setting up a campground in your children's room? Drape a sheet or blanket over a card table or some chairs for a tent. You can also buy a pop-up tent that is attached to a fitted bedsheet, or put up a real tent that does not require staking. Inside the tent go a few cushions, a sleeping bag, a battery-operated light, and maybe a book or two inspired by the setting, like *Three Days on a River in a Red Canoe* or *The Legend of the Bluebonnet.* When your kids are not camped out with a good book, the tent makes a great place for creative play or time alone.

A large appliance box makes a nifty room-within-a-room. Cut off the top and line the bottom with a carpet scrap and some old pillows. Your children may consider this their cabin, cave, or reading room.

Here's another unusual environment you or your children can set up in a jiffy: Create a jungle or woods with a circle of large houseplants. What better place to read animal and nature stories?

If your home already feels like a campground or jungle, head for the one room with guaranteed privacy—the bathroom. There you can convert a bathtub into a temporary nook. Just load it up with pillows and let a child or two "test the waters" with a magazine or book.

While a comfortable chair will often do, a special place that inspires the imagination may also inspire your children to settle in for a good long read.

Bedroom Library

AGES: Prereaders, beginning readers, older readers
MATERIALS: Bookshelves or cinderblocks and boards, box or crate, oatmeal carton, utility knife, poster paints and paintbrush

When your children place books on a bookshelf or in a bookcase, they are setting them apart as items of value. Shelving books also helps your children keep track of them—to distinguish the library books from the books they own, the picture books from the chapter books.

If your children's room has no bookcase or built-in shelves, building shelves together might be a weekend project you'd all enjoy. If you're not very handy or don't want to spend a lot of money on materials and tools, here are three alternatives that can work as well:

• *Cinderblocks and Boards.* You can buy cinderblocks (or bricks) and particle-board shelves inexpensively at a hardware store. Choose sizes of blocks and boards and a place to set them up that will ensure that the structure is sturdy and childproof. Don't make the shelves higher than your child.

- *Crate Bookcase.* You can buy a plastic milk crate or cube in a department store, or ask the produce manager at your local supermarket to save you a wooden crate. Even a sturdy corrugated cardboard box will do.

   Lay the crate on its side with the open side facing out. Stack books upright or on their sides inside the crate. A child may want to paint the crate before filling it with books.

- *Desktop Bookcase.* Glue the lid onto an empty cylindrical oatmeal carton, then lay the carton on its side. About an inch from each end of the cylinder, make a crosswise cut halfway through the carton (a cut at each end), then cut clear across. You will have cut out a large, curved rectangular section. After decorating this little bookcase, a child can set it on a desk and fill it with books, spines up. The ends of the carton will prevent the books from falling out.

TV Tie-Ins

Before You Watch
Check the Listings
Mad About Movies
Variations on a Theme
Based on Books
Read More About It
What Next?
Typecasting
Scriptwriter
Substitute Commercial
Places in the News

Are you concerned that your family spends too much time in front of the television at the expense of other worthwhile activities—like reading? Maybe you don't want to wean yourselves entirely, but you may want to establish reasonable limits. Or you may decide that the problem is not too much TV, but the kinds of programs you're watching. Changing your viewing habits may be the answer for your family.

The purpose of these activities is not to point out the shortcomings of TV, but to use television to keep your children thinking, learning, and reading. A few activities offer ideas for dealing with issues like too much TV, but most feature creative writing, reading, or critical thinking activities centering on children's show-time interests.

The more you involve yourself in choosing and viewing the television programs and movies your children watch, the more influence you'll have over their selections and impressions. You'll be able to pick up clues to their special interests that will help you redirect some of their pleasure and enthusiasm from the screen to the book. For example, a child who loved *Mary Poppins,* the movie, will probably enjoy reading *Mary Poppins,* the book. Likewise, a television documentary on the recovery of sunken treasure may motivate a child to read a book about pirates or deep-sea diving.

The major networks have long provided classroom teachers with viewers' guides, sample scripts, and other educational materials to use along with their regular and special programs. You can call your local stations to see whether materials are available for programs of special interest to your family.

For more information about programs directed specifically at your child, you can inquire whether your library ties into KIDSNET, a computerized clearinghouse that classifies programs and indicates whether supplementary resources are available. *Parents' Choice* reviews children's materials provided by various media, including books, television, movies, recordings, and home video (see "Further Resources for Parents and Children"). If you want to become actively involved in the movement to improve programming for children, contact Action for Children's Television (see "Further Resources for Parents and Children").

Before You Watch

AGES: All ages

Did you know that 99 percent of American homes have at least one TV set? In fact, there are more homes with TV sets than with indoor plumbing!

It's up to each family to decide what role television plays in their family life, how much to watch, which programs to view, and even where the set is to be located in the home. Here are some ideas to keep in mind before you turn on the set.

- The TV set can be simply another home appliance whose use is monitored by the parents. Many parents set limits on their youngsters' viewing so that the children have time and energy to develop a multitude of interests. Most kids are comfortable with rules—even welcome them, despite occasional gripes—if the rules are fair and the children understand them.
- You might consider placing the TV set on a table with rollers so that it can be unplugged and moved out of the way when not in use. Some parents find that storing the TV in a closet or their own bedroom encourages the whole family to choose only those programs they really want to watch.
- If your set goes on the blink, you may want to use this as a chance to take an extended vacation from TV. Wait awhile before having it repaired, and see what other kinds of activities—like reading, conversation, evening walks, games—your family turns to instead.
- Try not to set up television viewing as a reward for reading. If you say, "You can watch a half hour of TV for every half hour you read," your children may get the message that reading is a chore and that TV is a treat you value highly.
- Try looking at your own TV viewing through the eyes of your children. If they see you thoughtfully choosing a show to watch and turning on the set only when you want to see something special, they may want to do likewise. If they see you spending time with books, magazines, newspapers, board games, hobbies, and other alternatives to TV, they will learn valuable lessons about spending their free time.
- Of course, kids pick up a whole range of habits from parents. If they see you watching hour after hour of television, they may follow suit.
- When you sit down with your kids to watch a show together (an excellent idea in its own right), talk with them about the program. What do they like? Dislike? What's happening in the story? Was it believable? The point here is to use the TV show as a way to talk

with your children, not to turn the conversation into a quiz. Look for ways to use TV shows as conversation starters.

Check the Listings

AGES: Beginning readers, older readers
MATERIALS: Television guide or newspaper listing, paper and pencils

How do your kids know what's on television? Do they flip channels —an annoying habit at best—or do they read the schedule of programs in a television guide?

Encourage previewing what the networks have to offer by reading the listings with your children in the newspaper, a television guide, or the magazine you receive as a member of your local public television station.

Reading the listings gives the whole family a chance to think and to make decisions about their television viewing. You may also want to establish some guidelines ahead of time: for example, no TV until homework is finished, only a set number of shows per week, or only between certain hours. You may wish to sit down and work out a set of rules with your children.

The following activities can give your previewing some direction.

- *Family Guide.* Sit with your children and read through the weekly TV listing in the Sunday paper. Divide a piece of paper into sections for the days of the week. In each section, list the shows you agree to watch. Or you may want to circle programs in the newspaper listing.

  Previewing the week's offerings serves a few purposes: You can make sure your children know about a TV special they wouldn't want to miss; you can resolve conflicts before show time (Jonathan gets to watch his program Tuesday night, and Jeremy gets to watch his on Friday); you can influence what the children watch by discussing their choices; and it gives you a regular opportunity to limit their viewing.

In addition to their regular favorites, help your children find shows that feature their personal interests or parallel what they are learning at school.

- *From Hollywood to the Library.* Clip articles and help your kids find books about topics treated in TV shows and movies. Tape an article on the refrigerator or near the phone where passers-by will notice, or put it inside your child's lunch box. A show's subject or star, or even the place where it was filmed, could lead your children to reading.

- *TV Categories.* Have your child list program categories as headings on a piece of paper: situation comedy, news, dramatic series, documentary, soap opera, sports, cartoons, and so forth. While reading through a day's scheduled programs in a television guide or newspaper listing, your youngster writes the names of as many shows as possible in each category. Which categories are most represented? Which are least represented?

Mad About Movies

AGES: Beginning readers, older readers
MATERIALS: Newspaper

Children love to go to the movies, so they'll gladly take responsibility for planning which one to see next. Take advantage of their enthusiasm by suggesting some reading tie-ins.

First ask your children to read aloud mini-reviews of films they are interested in seeing, perhaps after dinner while everyone is still at the table. These short synopses usually appear somewhere in the weekend newspaper. Agree on one or two films that appeal to everyone in the family. If you come across a full review, ask the children to read that aloud, too.

When the children decide which film to see, give them the task of checking listings for theaters and viewing time. If the movie they choose is based on a book, encourage the family to read the story before seeing the film so you can make comparisons. It might be fun to read the book aloud together, although in this instance you may not want to wait until you finish reading to see the movie.

Variations on a Theme

AGES: Prereaders, beginning readers, older readers

Borrow a good idea from "Reading Rainbow," an educational television program that motivates children to read. Read a book to your children on a topic you know appeals to them, then gather a bunch of other books on the same subject that they can choose from to read on their own.

Use the thematic approach when you help your children select books at the library. Show them how to look through the card catalog or microfiche for titles on specific subjects. Encourage reluctant readers especially to find all the titles they can on a topic that holds their interest. A comprehensive list of books about horses or inventions may be just the thing to keep them reading.

You might want to try a "Theme of the Month" idea to encourage members of your family to share their different interests through reading. Each month let it be another person's turn to have the whole family read a book on his or her favorite subject. That person may want to make some recommendations, but the other readers are responsible for finding and checking out their own books.

For example, if the theme of the month is dinosaurs, your family may borrow these books: *Digging Up Dinosaurs* (for a beginning reader), *Dinosaurs! A Drawing Book* (for an artistic child), *Dinosaur Wrecks* (for the joker in the family), and *Comet* (for a parent or older child who enjoys scientific theory). Read *Danny and the Dinosaur* to a preschooler.

Wait a week or two after the topic has been announced before everybody reconvenes, perhaps over dinner, to talk about the books they are reading on the shared subject. Whether they are enthusiastic about a particular book or not, everyone will have learned a little something about another reader's special interest.

Based on Books

AGES: Prereaders, beginning readers, older readers

How many children would have overlooked *The Little House on the Prairie* and all its sequels if the books had not inspired a long-running television series? How many older readers would have picked up classics like *The Scarlet Letter* or *The Scarlet Pimpernel* without all the hoopla surrounding the made-for-TV movies based on their stories? Had you even heard about Maria Von Trapp's autobiography before the movie *The Sound of Music* was released?

Television is at its best when it brings books to life and to mind. Besides "Reading Rainbow," CBS Storybreak, and ABC Weekend Specials, programs that are designed to interest children in reading books, networks feature many special programs based on books your children may have read or may want to read in conjunction with watching the televised version.

If possible, have your children read a book *before* viewing an adaptation on the silver screen or for television. That way they can compare the treatment of plot and characters as they watch and discuss the scriptwriter's departures from the original story. If you keep an eye out for early reviews and previews, you can have the book in the house in time for your children to read (or for the family to read aloud) before the movie is scheduled to be aired or released in local theaters.

Of course, you can ride on the crest of your children's enthusiasm just after they see a production, and make a special trip to the library or bookstore to find the novel or historical biography on which the movie was based.

Read More About It

AGES: Prereaders, beginning readers, older readers

Good television can be a springboard for reading. Borrow a good idea from CBS, which has created a "spot" following its docudramas called "Read More About It." In this public service message, created in cooperation with the Center for the Book in the Library of Congress, a member of the cast comes out of his or her role to encourage the audience to read one of several related nonfiction books recommended by the Library of Congress. Your children might appreciate the same kind of recommendations coming from Mom or Dad after viewing a program on a subject that captivates them.

Both public and commercial stations offer a rich array of special educational programs, notably those of the National Geographic Society, ABC After School and Weekend Specials, documentaries, and docudramas based on historical figures.

If you know ahead of time about a special program, check out a few related books at the library and have them available for your children immediately after the program, while their enthusiasm and interest are high. For example, if your children are planning to watch a documentary on space travel, they might enjoy follow-up reading about astronauts, space technology, or astronomy.

Your children may express interest in a new subject after listening to the news or turning by chance to a special program. Don't miss this opportunity; take them to the library the very next day to find a book or two that tells more about the subject.

What Next?

AGES: Beginning readers, older readers
MATERIALS: VCR (optional)

If your children have a favorite sitcom or dramatic series, make the most of the minutes you have during commercials. That's really about all the time your children will need to review what they know about the characters and simple plot and predict the outcome of the show.

Turn down the sound as soon as the script breaks. Ask a child, "What do you think is going to happen next?" or "How do you think the story will end?"—depending where you are in the plot sequence. Shows that air for thirty minutes usually have two commercial breaks. Your child may very well be able to predict the entire sequence of events after the first break.

If you have a VCR, you can try one of these variations:

- *Stop the Cameras.* Tape a movie or hour-long show while it is being aired, but plan to view it later. Stop the tape at crucial intervals—when you learn a character's secret, after you witness a significant event, or at a cliff-hanger (probably where the station takes its own break)—and ask your children those same questions. Encourage them to support their predictions with insights into the characters and foreshadowing in the plot.
- *Write Your Own Ending.* Watch a show with your children until just before the end. Then turn off the TV and turn on the VCR.

  While the VCR tapes the end of the show, family members write their own endings. (A couple of paragraphs will do, but a short script is more fun.) Take turns reading your endings aloud, then play back the one you recorded on the tape. Were any of the endings the same or similar? Vote for the one you thought was best.

Typecasting

AGES: Older readers
MATERIALS: Paper and pencil

Have you always wanted to be a director? Here's your opportunity. You and your children take on the tasks of a production company planning to shoot a made-for-TV movie or major motion picture based on a book you've all read. If possible, plan this activity *before* you see a movie or television adaptation.

Everybody plays the director by considering which real actors and actresses to cast in the major characters' roles. Could Molly Ringwald play the part of awkward and tempestuous Meg in *A Wrinkle in Time?* Who would play the young and vulnerable Charles Wallace? In deciding who would best be cast in each role, your children will be voicing their insights into the various characters. The differences in their perceptions can be a springboard for further discussion.

Using a similar approach, the directors also choose the best location for the shoot based on details the author provides for the story's setting. You may want to concentrate on a central scene rather than the whole book. Choose a musical score for the same scene—a hit song or classical theme that would set the appropriate mood.

If possible, compare your imaginary production with a real movie or television production. What did your family think of the director's casting job? Did an actor or actress play a character differently than you would have? Did the setting appear as you had imagined? Did the musical score put you in the appropriate mood for the scene? In what ways did the commercial production depart from the book? Which did you like better, and why?

Scriptwriter

AGES: Older readers
MATERIALS: Paper and pen (or typewriter or computer), stationery and stamps, video camera and VCR (optional)

After predicting a punch line or event on a favorite show, your child may pipe up, "I remember when I wrote that!" With this activity, your youngster will get the chance to come up with some new lines.

Suggest that your child write to the producer of a favorite show requesting a sample script (a librarian can give directions to a reference listing the network's address). The whole family can read the sample script aloud, each person taking one or two parts as needed.

After coming up with a plot, your child may want to review some of the scriptwriting conventions and take a turn at writing a show segment. When finished, your scriptwriter can ask family members to assemble for another reading—this time a reading of his or her own script.

Upon hearing the lines, the scriptwriter may want to make some changes or additions. If your family has a video camera or access to one, it might be fun to tape the script using the family players and a few simple props and costumes.

Substitute Commercial

AGES: Beginning readers, older readers
MATERIALS: Paper and pen, cassette recorder and cassette tape (optional)

Out of every hour of commercial television your family watches, you'll see twelve minutes of commercial messages. You can continue to watch, turn down the volume and talk about something else, or you can substitute your own commercial.

- *Invent a Product.* What new product or service would your children like to advertise in a thirty- or sixty-second commercial break? They should plan their substitute commercial for half as long to compensate for false starts and typical underestimations.

    Perhaps the children can come up with a jingle or catchy slogan. If you have a cassette recorder, encourage them to prerecord the commercial once they have written and rehearsed it; otherwise, they can rehearse and perform live.

    During one of the station breaks, quickly turn down the volume or turn off the TV altogether and let the kids take over. Whenever they feel like repeating their commercial, let them. Don't you have to listen to real commercials again and again?

- *Public Service Message.* In addition to airing commercials, networks donate commercial time to public service organizations to air their messages.

    Your children may enjoy producing a public service message. This may require a little reading and research at the library. Perhaps they can instruct their audience in home fire safety, ask their cooperation in saving water or electricity, or warn them about a local outbreak of mumps or chicken pox.

Places in the News

AGES: Older readers
MATERIALS: Atlas or world almanac (and globe if you have one),
state map, paper and pencil

Few children can visualize a map of the United States, let alone the
location of other countries in the world. Here's a way to use television newscasts to help your children learn about geography here
and abroad.

Keep an atlas or world almanac, a globe if you have one, and a
state map next to the television. When you turn on the evening
news, hand your children pencils and paper and ask them to write
down the names of every place mentioned by the newscasters. They
might also want to jot down the context in which these places were
mentioned.

Following the national news, help your kids look up each place in
the ready references and, if possible, pinpoint it on a globe. (Use a
state map to find places mentioned on the local news.) Does location
have anything to do with the news story? For example, is there a
border dispute or does an unfriendly neighbor nation pose a threat?
Is geography a factor? Has an earthquake shattered a region, or has
drought produced a famine?

If your children enjoy record keeping, they might like one of these
related activities:

• *Color-In Map.* While listening to the national news, your children
  can have handy a box of crayons and a map of the United States.
  They can make the map by tracing a map from a reference book or
  by tracing the pieces of a U.S. map puzzle. When a state is mentioned, they color in that area on the map.

  This activity will help your children define geographic regions and learn the locations of states. They may be surprised to see how long it takes some places to make the news.

• *Record Number of Places.* Your children can keep a running count of the different cities, states, countries, or famous people mentioned in a single news show. They'll listen more closely and become more familiar with these names in the news if they're trying to establish a new record.

The Four Seasons

Most reading activities are fun year-round, but you may want to reserve some ideas for special times and days of the year. For instance, your children would probably enjoy making a Monster Dictionary on any rainy Saturday, but if you can hold off till Halloween, you'll catch them at their most ghoulish. And although ice cream sounds good to them anytime, your kids will get a lot more vicarious pleasure alphabetizing their favorite flavors on a hot summer day.

Calendar activities can involve your children in keeping track of an eventful year, beginning with a New Year Calendar, supplemented by a School Break Calendar, and finishing up with a Countdown Calendar before the end-of-the-year holidays. Why not fill in a calendar now with some reading activities they can look forward to in the coming months?

Words for All Seasons

AGES: Prereaders, beginning readers
MATERIALS: Construction paper, seasonal catalogs, newspapers and magazines, scissors, glue

Your children can usher in each season with a lively collage of words that describe it best. They'll need lots of printed materials to search through for their words.

Give your children construction paper (they can choose a seasonal color) and a collection of newspapers, magazines, junk mail, and colorful seasonal catalogs from stores. First they label their paper with the name of the current or approaching season. Then they look through the printed materials for words to describe it. Words and phrases are cut out and pasted on the page. If they want to use words that they can't find in print, there's no reason why they can't write them in.

What to do with the finished product? Perhaps your kids would like to fold them and send them as seasonal greeting cards (Grandpa would love to receive one), hang them in a window, or use them to fashion wall calendars.

Prereaders can make a picture collage along the same lines. Label a piece of construction paper with the name of the current season or the upcoming season. Then sit with your young ones and look through publications for pictures that remind them of that season. Encourage them to cut out the pictures, then position and paste them.

Book and Character Costumes

AGES: Toddlers, prereaders, beginning readers, older readers
MATERIALS: *For book jacket:* Large box, paints and brushes, utility knife, face paints. *For character costume:* Varies with each costume

Have your children run out of ideas for an original Halloween costume? Suggest that it might be fun to dress up as a favorite storybook character—or the book itself! This idea will appeal to all the book lovers in your family—parents, too, if you have occasion to dress up.

- *Book Jacket.* Your children can wear what every well-dressed book wears—a dust jacket.

   First your children design and paint the front of a large box to look like a book jacket. Each child can design his or her own. The jacket cover should feature the title of the book, the author's name, and an illustration. Cut armholes and a head hole out of the top and side panels.

   When it's time to dress up, help a child into the jacket. As a final touch, make up the child's face as a character in the book, or as a bookworm crawling out of the book.

- *Character Costume.* If you have more time and ambition, help your children think up character costumes. Very young children will probably choose an animal character from a picture book or Mother Goose. Older children can turn to their own favorites.

   Have a young child describe the character to you: What animal features does it have (ears, tail, whiskers)? Does he wear a certain kind of clothing? Does she carry something special? Have an older child research the period of the story or novel for authentic costume details.

   You don't have to spend a lot of time sewing an elaborate

coverup; a leotard and tights or thermal underwear will do for animal skin while you concentrate instead on face makeup, masks, or accessories. Sew felt bear ears on Corduroy's hooded sweatshirt, and let your child rip off a button on one side of his or her old corduroy overalls. Give Katy No-Pocket an apron with a huge pocket for carrying her Kangaroo baby (a sock puppet will do) and her Halloween treats.

People characters can dress up in clothes you scrounge up and accessories you sew. Take little Laura Ingalls to a rummage sale or thrift store to find her a prairie skirt and shawl. Help Amelia Bedelia sew an old-fashioned bonnet, or Ferdinand a red cape.

Planning a character costume encourages children to be inventive and to read for details. More thought and energy are spent on the costumes than money, so your children may learn a simple lesson in thrift as well.

Trick or Treat?

AGES: All ages
MATERIALS: See suggestions

If the trick is to get kids to read, hand out Halloween treats that will encourage them to do just that. You may be remembered as the one who gave out the longest-lasting treats.

You can't very well give a book to every child who knocks on your door, but you can give something fun to read or something that's reading-related. For example:

• *Word Puzzles.* Buy a children's puzzle magazine. Remove the staples and separate the pages. Give each child a two-sided page with word-search puzzles, crossword puzzles, or other word games on it. Roll up the page around a pencil and tie with ribbon.
• *Workbook Pages.* Wrap a pencil in a page from a children's workbook. Activity books for preschool and primary grades are dis-

played at many supermarkets and variety stores. You can also order a collection of sixty double-sided creative task sheets titled *Trick or Treat* from David Lake Publishers. (For a mail-order catalog, write David Lake Publishers, 19 Davis Drive, Belmont, California 94002.)

• *Crayons or Colored Pencils.* Hold out a big bowl full of crayons or colored pencils and let each trick-or-treater choose two or three. You can buy crayons most economically from school supplies catalogs or outlets (check the Yellow Pages under School Supplies or ask your children's teachers); you'll also find that some variety stores sell a bag of Crayola three-packs around this time of year.

• *Stickers.* Children of all ages love to collect stickers. You can give out prepackaged Halloween stickers for a pretty penny, or you can buy sheets of stick-on letters (a package of ten for less than a dollar) wherever you buy office or stationery supplies. That should trick kids into making lots of words!

• *Comic Books.* For trick-or-treaters you know well enough to recognize behind their masks, you might want to save something special. Buy a variety of the children's current favorite superhero comic books and let good friends choose.

Monster Dictionary

AGES: Beginning readers, older readers
MATERIALS: Paper, crayons, felt pens, report binder (the kind with a clear acetate cover) or a hole puncher and yarn

Prepare to be horrified by the ghoulish creatures that spring from your children's imaginations. Suggest this project as a family collaboration on Halloween, when everybody is feeling a little weird.

A monster dictionary is a catalog of monsters that appear in alphabetical order along with a picture and a definition of sorts. Divvy up the letters of the alphabet among family members. For each letter, someone creates a monster, draws the creature's picture

on a page labeled with the appropriate letter, gives it a name beginning with that letter, and describes its habits. Here's an example:

"O for Octoculus, a monster whose eight bloodshot eyes are all very
nearsighted and therefore render him harmless. If you encounter an
Octoculus, stand right under his nose; he'll never see you. If you see
an Octoculus coming out of an optician's office, run for your life!"

When all twenty-six monsters have been duly depicted, have your
children design a cover and assemble the pages in a book. They can
insert the pages in a clear report binder, or they can punch holes
along the left side and tie with yarn or place in a three-ring binder.

If you have time to stop at the library beforehand, check out a
monster book or two to launch this project—anything from *Dracula*
to *How to Care for Your Monster*. When your children have finished
making their monster dictionary, ask them to choose a favorite entry
as a creepy story starter. (See also Ghost Stories in "Read It
Aloud.")

Words Aplenty

AGES: Prereaders, beginning readers
**MATERIALS: Construction paper, child's scissors, stapler, old news-
papers and magazines with food features**

Words spill over in this activity as your children fill a cornucopia
with cutouts from newspapers and magazines.

You may be able to find a small cornucopia (a cone-like basket) at
yard sales or thrift stores. Many families use them as centerpieces on
the Thanksgiving dinner table. If not, your children can construct
paper horns in a couple of minutes. Have them trace a plate on a
piece of construction paper, cut out the circle, then cut out a small
wedge. Form a cone by overlapping the ends of the remaining circle
and staple in place. Make a small cone for one child to fill, or a larger
one for a cooperative effort.

Encourage your children to fill their horns of plenty with plenty of words—food words, that is, cut out of magazines, newspapers, expired coupons, or other printed matter. Help read or pronounce unfamiliar words. If you have the time, give a hand clipping out the words.

A younger child who doesn't read at all can participate, too, by cutting out food pictures instead of food words. Talk about the different items—the colors, tastes, and textures. Have your youngster repeat the names of unfamiliar foods and add a couple to your food shopping list. Older children can busy themselves while increasing their reading vocabulary; younger children can expand their speaking vocabulary.

Winter Picnic

AGES: Prereaders, beginning readers
MATERIALS: Picnic basket or lunch box, picnic blanket, lunch or snack, books

Brighten an otherwise bleak, wintry day for your children with an unseasonably good idea—a picnic!

If you usually bring a basket on your picnics, take it out of storage; otherwise a lunch box or bag will do. Your children, intrigued by now, can help you pack a lunch or snack and a few books to read aloud together. If you get the chance, make an earlier trip to the library to check out *Winter Picnic*, an appropriate story about a boy who persuades his mother to join him for a picnic in the snow.

Spread a blanket on the floor, preferably in front of a window looking out onto the yard or street. Invite your children to join you there for your winter picnic. Although the scenery is different, the mood can be the same—leisurely and companionable. With your minds on eating and reading, the walls around you will disappear.

Book Ornaments

AGES: Older readers
MATERIALS: Empty matchboxes or paper clip boxes (the kind with tiny sliding drawers), plain paper to cover the boxes, scissors, fine-line markers, hole puncher, ribbon

Get your family in the holiday spirit *and* the reading spirit. Decorate your tree with homemade ornaments that look like miniature books —your children's favorites, of course!

Collect small matchboxes or paper clip boxes. Remove the drawers and save them for another project. Cover the outsides of the boxes with plain paper. Then invite your children to decorate the fronts of the boxes with fine-line markers so that they look like miniatures of their favorite books. Have them include titles, authors' names, and tiny cover illustrations.

Punch a hole in the top of the book's spine and insert a piece of colored ribbon. Tie a bow at the end of a good-size loop and hang the book ornament on the tip of a tree branch.

A word of caution: Paper decorations are not safe to use on trees with electric lights. If you plan to light your tree, you might want to string the book ornaments along the mantel instead, or tie them onto a ribbon streamer.

Countdown Calendars

AGES: Beginning readers, older readers
MATERIALS: Calendar, notebook, pen or pencil

Does your family keep a traditional Advent calendar or count down the days to Christmas? Here are some variations your children might enjoy that will help put them in the holiday spirit. Families who celebrate Hanukkah can instead count *up* the nights during the festival, and all families can adapt these ideas for a countdown to the New Year.

• *How Many Words Till Christmas?* This kind of Christmas list gets very long, but it's self-fulfilling. Each day beginning a month before and continuing until the holiday arrives, your children write down words they associate with Christmas—a nice variation on the traditional Advent calendar.

 If your calendar has large squares for each day, your children can write their words directly on the calendar. Otherwise, they can keep a notebook. They can write the date, the number of days before Christmas, and at least one word or phrase that comes to mind when they think about the holiday season.

 Your children may prefer to look for their words in print, then cut them out and paste them onto calendars so that the final product, with all the interesting graphics, will look very festive.

• *Activity Countdown.* Have you already purchased one of those pretty countdown calendars in which you would ordinarily put candies or prizes behind the numbered doors?

 Instead, put a written message describing a family activity. For example: bake cookies, read a Christmas story or poem, write a letter to Santa Claus, make greeting cards, help at a Christmas bazaar or other fund-raiser, shop for a toy to donate to the hospital's pediatrics wing, decorate the tree, and so on.

The idea is to make each day a special day that draws the family together.

- *New Words Countdown.* Make your own countdown calendar and write a new word for a child to recognize behind each flap.

For Christmas, you might want to cut out a paper tree. Before mounting the tree on a contrasting piece of paper, cut out a window for each day till Christmas. Mount the tree and print a new word in each window. Then cover the windows with tree ornaments cut out of scraps of holiday wrapping paper (use cellophane tape or a small piece of masking tape rolled sticky side out to attach the ornaments). Each day, your child removes one ornament and reads the new word behind it.

For Hanukkah, you can draw a large paper menorah on a piece of construction paper. Each night of the holiday, add a paper candle on which you have printed a new word for your child. Perform this little ritual just after you light the real candles on your family menorah. Perhaps the words can be holiday related: *menorah, dreidl, miracle,* and so on.

Ring Out the Old . . .

AGES: All ages

MATERIALS: *For time capsule:* Storage box or container, paper and pens, family souvenirs (see suggestions). *For yearbook:* Scrapbook or photo album, family photos taken over the year, paper and pens, rubber cement. *For message:* Pencil and paper

If your family could look back on themselves a year from now or many years from now, what would they think? As part of your New Year celebration this year, compile a family yearbook, deliver a State of the Family Message, or pack a time capsule to be opened the same time next year—or the year 2000, if you can stand to wait that long!

• *Family Time Capsule.* A time capsule is a container holding artifacts and documents of present civilization that is buried or otherwise preserved for future examination. Your family can bury a time capsule to preserve memories of the past year.

Find a container in which you can place family souvenirs and papers. A locking plastic file box or an under-the-bed storage box would be good. Invite your children to decorate the container with paint, stickers, or a decoupage of the day's newspaper articles. Write the date on top and the future date on which the capsule will be opened and reexamined.

Here are ideas for what you might place inside your capsule before you "bury" it somewhere in a closet:

• Recent photos of family members, including extended family.
• Stubs of theater tickets. (Write the name of the movie or show you saw on the back of each stub.)
• Clippings from the local newspaper or school newspaper that mention family members.
• The family's favorite cartoon or comic strip.
• Samples of artwork by each family member.
• Letters the children wrote home from camp.
• Itinerary and picture postcards from a family trip.
• Dried flowers from the summer garden.
• A copy of the menu from your favorite restaurant.
• A worn-out article of clothing from each person's wardrobe. (T-shirts won't take up too much room.)
• Current events clippings or an end-of-the-year issue of a news magazine.
• A list of the five favorite books read by each family member that year.
• Personal statistics for each family member (age, height, weight, hair color, school grade level).

Same time next year, won't your family be astonished at how much the world and they themselves have changed in so short a time! After examining the contents of your time capsule, you may decide to repack and exhume it again in future years. Meanwhile, have ready a new capsule to bury away in the closet alongside the old one.

- *Family Yearbook.* Do your children enjoy looking at your old school yearbooks? Suggest that it might be fun to borrow the same format to make an annual family keepsake.

Fill a scrapbook or photo album with family photos taken over the year. Somewhere in the middle of the book, label a blank page for each family member. On this page place a closeup snapshot of the person, and include a montage of personal information, views, and self-reflections.

The family decides as a group the categories under which they'll each write about themselves. Possibilities include: close friends, favorite book and author, favorite food, five words that describe you, your happiest day, your worst fear, what is most important to you, what you want to be or achieve.

Have everybody first write out their ideas on paper, then copy them neatly into the yearbook alongside their photos.

- *State of the Family Address.* Taking its cue from the President's yearly address to Congress, your family might want to collaborate in preparing a similar kind of self-assessment.

Have one person act as secretary while everybody comments on the family's present circumstances and relationships. Perhaps Mom's going back to school changed the daily routine, or Grandma's moving in forced two brothers to figure out how to share a room and still get along. A parent's job promotion or job loss would certainly have affected the household budget.

When everybody has finished, the secretary organizes and writes up the notes, then delivers the State of the Family Message aloud. Everybody present signs the paper, which can be buried in a time capsule, inserted in a family yearbook, or otherwise filed away for the future.

. . . Bring in the New!

AGES: Prereaders, beginning readers, older readers
MATERIALS: Calendar (for New Year Calendar), paper and pencils

Begin the New Year with a look ahead. Can family members accurately predict what will happen in the coming months? Can they carry out their best intentions? Make a few predictions and resolutions and see what happens. Meanwhile, mark your calendar so no one forgets important dates and events.

- *New Year's Resolutions.* This year, have family members put their personal New Year's resolutions in writing. Suggest that the lists be short and reasonable; it's unlikely that messy rooms will be kept neat *all* year long.

    The family might also make some resolutions as a group; for example, you may resolve to double the production of your vegetable garden or devote a certain amount of time to volunteer work.

- *Predictions.* Family members make some predictions for the new year together. The predictions can be about the family, politics, science, world events, sports—anything. Who will win the World Series? What will be the bestselling book? Will it rain for the third year in a row on Toby's birthday? Will Slipper have kittens?

    Have someone write out the predictions, attributing them to the family members who made them. Save the list in a secure place till the following year, when you can reread the predictions and determine if they were indeed accurate.

- *New Year Calendar.* Some people observe an old New Year tradition by tossing the pages of last year's calendar out the window (literally) and opening the new calendar to January 1. Your family can start to look forward to the New Year with its own calendar event.

    Shop together before the holidays for a new calendar, or ask your children to make one themselves. On New Year's Eve, take down the old calendar, but before you hang your new one, take some time to fill in some important dates and scheduled events.

Refer to the old calendar for family and friends' birthdays and anniversaries. Write in important school dates—the school play, field trips, holidays, spring break, summer closing, and so forth. Fill in the date when your cousins from Omaha are coming to visit, the week you plan to take your vacation, the Saturday the library is holding its annual book sale, the evenings that *Anne of Green Gables* will be aired on television.

When everybody has contributed all the calendar information they have at the time, turn back to January 1 and hang the new calendar where the old one used to be. Now that you all have an idea of what you can look forward to, celebrate!

Frog and Toad Are Valentines

AGES: Prereaders, beginning readers, older readers
MATERIALS: Red construction paper, felt pen, assorted materials for decorating (e.g., bits of lace, paper doilies, tissue paper, glitter, sequins, glue)

While your children are making valentines for their favorite friends, let them also make them for their favorite book characters. Here are a few novel approaches to suggest.

- *Literary Lovers.* What kind of valentine would Romeo send to Juliet? Florid, no doubt! And what charming hearts would Pat and Martha exchange? Or Wilbur and Fern? Your children imagine themselves as literary characters and make appropriate valentines for their literary loves. The sentiment should be true to character.
- *To Curious George, with Love.* Young readers often feel about books and book characters the way they feel about their friends, so they won't think it at all unseemly to design a valentine for Curious

George or some other literary favorite. Perhaps George's valentine says, "You drive me bananas, Valentine!" or "I'm curious to know if you'll be my Valentine."
- *Spot Sends His Love.* Younger children will be thrilled to receive valentines from their favorite characters. If you don't have time to make them, have the characters sign store-bought cards. If you do have the time, draw or trace pictures of the characters and write an appropriate message: "I'd spot you anywhere, Valentine!"

School-Break Calendar

AGES: Prereaders, beginning readers, older readers
MATERIALS: Calendar, pen, list of reading activities (see suggestions)

Here are some ways to keep books open even though the school doors are closed. The long summer break leaves more time than ever to read or participate in reading-related activities.

You can set up a whole calendar of events to make sure your kids experience a little reading fun each day throughout the summer vacation. Start small, if you like, with an activity calendar for the week-long winter or spring break. Meanwhile, keep a running list of ideas that involve reading books or other materials, practicing pre-reading or reading skills, improving vocabulary, or motivating the family to read and learn.

Here is a month's worth of ideas to fill in a school-break calendar. Choose the ones your children will enjoy, repeat some, and add your own ideas to the list:

- Make up a recipe for a refreshing summer drink. Write out a recipe card.
- Go to the library and sign up for the summer reading club.
- Write an alphabetized list of the furniture in your bedroom.

- Search for something tiny enough to fit in your pocket and make up a story about it.
- Look out your window and write down the names of everything you see.
- This is the longest day of the year. Find five of the longest words you can in the dictionary, then after dinner tell the rest of the family what they mean.
- Today (July 28) is Henry Ford's birthday. Look in the newspaper for the names of ten different cars and five different trucks.
- Read a book to your younger sister.
- Press some flowers between the pages of your book for somebody else to find.
- Trade books with your best friend.
- Write a letter to your grandmother about what you did this week.
- Today is Arbor Day. Find a book about trees. See how many trees you can identify in your neighborhood.
- Make a crayon rubbing of an object you find outside.
- Make a map of your yard. Label the patio, trees, swing set, and so on.
- Tonight there is a full moon. Sit outside and tell a scary story.
- Cut out words from the newspaper. Send someone a mysterious message.
- Make a scrapbook of our houseboat trip. Write captions under all the photos and picture postcards.
- Trace an illustration in one of your brother's favorite books. Give him the picture to color.
- Find an unusual fact in today's newspaper and share it with us at dinner.
- Make up a new fruit. Describe its flavor, texture, and appearance.
- Start a reading marathon. See if you can read all the books written by your favorite author, by the end of the summer.
- How many out-of-state license plates did you see today?
- Read the most exciting paragraph in your book to the rest of the family. Try to persuade someone else to read it.
- Write the four food groups at the top of a piece of paper. Look in the refrigerator. List all the foods you find under the correct heading.
- Write the number words from one to twenty.
- Find a long word on the cereal box. Can you find smaller words inside the big word?

- What is the tiniest sound you can think of? Write a poem about it.
- Write all the words you can think of that sound like the noise they describe: *crash, squeak, gurgle,* etc. Look up the word *onomatopoeia* in the dictionary.
- School begins soon. Make a list of the supplies you need, then let's go shopping.
- Today is Choosing Day. Choose your favorite activity from this month's calendar and do it again.

Almond, Butter Pecan, Chocolate

AGES: Beginning readers, older readers
MATERIALS: Paper and pencil

On a blistering hot summer day, think ice cream. With your children, fantasize about the long list of flavors on the board at your local ice cream parlor. How do they keep track of so many flavors? Alphabetical order!

Pretend you're the proprietors of an ice cream store. Get out your pad of paper and encourage your children to think of all the flavors of ice cream they can. List the flavors in the order they come up with them. Then turn over the list to your children to alphabetize. You might have to show a younger child how to alphabetize by the second or third letters if your list includes *peach, peppermint,* and *pistachio.*

When all the flavors are in the right order, choose your favorites, head out to the ice cream store, and splurge!

Local Treasures

Check Out the Library
Zoo Stories
Museum Scavenger Hunt
Museum Tie-Ins
History That Rubs Off
Graveyard History
Local History
This Old House
Old Stores in Town
New Kid on the Block
Bookstore Events
Community Players
Reading on the College Level

You don't have to go far to find resources that will stimulate your children's interests and, in turn, their desire to read. Begin at the local library, where books abound on every possible subject, and where ongoing services and programs are designed to lure young readers. Then knock at your own front door; your home or hometown may have a colorful history that a few extra visits to the library will help unfold.

Encourage your children to look for people resources—local

craftsmen with skills to share, old-timers with stories to tell, local history buffs who know something about the arrowhead your children stumbled upon in the woods behind your house.

You're fortunate if your community houses an art or history museum, or a nature center or zoo. Familiarize your children with these local treasures; visit regularly and follow up with trips to the library so your children can read more about the exhibits that excite them.

Even the most ordinary places have hidden treasures—old stores, bookstores, parks, even a graveyard with historic headstones.

Have your children contact the local arts council to find out about community cultural events, such as photography exhibits or after-school dance classes. Is there a summer-stock theater or a year-round theater company that performs in the high school auditorium? How about a children's drama group, or a puppeteer who performs at the annual Fourth of July picnic?

You and your children can play tourist in your own community by reading materials available from your local Chamber of Commerce. You might discover local treasures where you least expect—in downtown architecture, in an old postcard collection you find in an antiques store, on a landmark sign along the highway. The most valuable treasures are those that intrigue your youngsters enough to pursue the subject.

Check Out the Library

AGES: Toddlers, prereaders, beginning readers, older readers

Have you and your children taken a guided tour of the library? It may be worth your time to check out the library before you check out books. A librarian will be happy to show you around if it's not a busy time.

Depending on its size and the number of people it serves, your local library or library branch may have more to offer than just books. You might take a few minutes to inquire about some of the services and programs listed below.

• *Library Card.* Most libraries will issue personal library cards to your children if you agree to be responsible for the materials they check out. Make a big deal about your children's first "charge cards." Take them to the library to break the cards in the very day they arrive; buy children's wallets in which they can carry them, or have your kids laminate the cards in one of those coin-operated machines you find in malls or supermarkets.

• *Story Time.* Ask if your library has a regularly scheduled story-time program for your toddler, prereader, or beginning reader. During this time, a children's librarian will read to the children, perhaps sing or play games, and sometimes show a short filmstrip. Make story time a part of your family's weekly routine.

• *Audio Tapes.* Your library may have special facilities where you can listen to recordings of readings or music. Even if there are no facilities, the library may have a collection of records and tapes that you can borrow. The young children's section may have books that come with read-along cassettes.

• *Filmstrips.* Some libraries have small video machines on which young children can watch filmstrips. The librarian may set up a filmstrip at a scheduled time, or your children may be able to request a filmstrip at any time.

• *Reading List.* Your librarian can recommend books appropriate for your children's reading levels and interests. You might ask a librarian to make each child an individualized reading list (if the library is not busy), or ask to see an annotated list. Sometimes the library will offer brochures the librarians have prepared that recommend books in certain categories ("Out of This World Science Fiction") or for certain age or reading levels ("What's New for Preteens" or "Best Bets for Beginners"). For reading suggestions from national organizations, see also the "Further Resources for Parents and Children" section of this book.

• *Summer Reading Club.* Do your children equate the closing of school with the closing of books? Many libraries, sensitive to this syndrome, sponsor summer reading programs designed to motivate children to continue to read—in fact, read more—during the school break.

• *Display Cases.* Do your children have special collections of baseball cards, arrowheads, or costume dolls? They may be able to reserve a time to set up one of their collections in the library's display cases. They'll also enjoy investigating the changing exhibits displayed by other young readers.

• *Local History.* Your library (or a branch of your library system) may house a collection of local historical documents, artifacts, and other memorabilia. Your children may use these materials for school reports, or they may just enjoy looking at old photos and news clips that are on display.

• *Entertainment.* Your library may occasionally present performances by local musicians, storytellers, pantomimists, and the like. The library may also offer weekend movie matinees for children and classical films for teenagers and adults on weeknights.

• *Art Gallery.* Libraries often display the work of local artists and photographers, and sometimes sponsor contests in which children can participate. If the walls in your children's room look a bit bare, they might want to borrow a framed poster available from the library's take-out collection.

Zoo Stories

AGES: Toddlers, prereaders, beginning readers, older readers
MATERIALS: Books about animals and the zoo, zoo guide, paper and pens

Are you planning a trip to the zoo? If possible, plan a trip to the library first to check out a bunch of books related to your excursion. Then suggest one or two of the following activities that your children might enjoy in preparation for their trip or to extend their experiences afterward:

• *Follow the Tracks.* Save the zoo guide you picked up at the information booth. Back home, your children can use the guide map and an animal reference book to draw their own picture map with each animal's footprints or paw prints leading to its location in the zoo. Next time you visit the zoo, use this map to guide you to your favorite animals.

- *Animal Safari.* Before a trip to the zoo, your older readers can set up their own zoological scavenger hunt. Using library books or encyclopedias, they make up a list of animal riddles for each other to solve. For example, one riddle might read, "What has three toes on each foot, one or two horns on its snout, weighs about four hundred pounds, and eats plants?" The answer lies in the rhinoceros yard.

  At the zoo, the children exchange their lists, then set out to hunt down the animals' identities by matching the riddle clues with the zoological information provided on the cage signs.

- *True-to-the-Zoo Stories.* When your children understand such ideas as the predatory relationships between various animals and the importance of natural environment, they can tell or write their own realistic animal stories. Preface this suggestion by reading aloud a story that offers some zoological insights, such as *Bringing the Rain to Kapiti Plain.*

- *Zoo Fantasies.* Books like *Just So Stories for Children* (how the camel got its hump, etc.), *If I Ran the Zoo* (about acquiring some zany species), and *McBroom's Zoo* (these zany creatures spin out of a tornado) may inspire your children to tell or write their own zoo fantasies. Or they might like to create an *A-B-C Fantazoo,* a picture encyclopedia that includes a drawing and a short description for twenty-six imaginary species.

- *Behind the Scenes at the Zoo.* When you arrive at the zoo, check the feeding times for various animals so you can be there to see. Books like *Behind the Scenes at the Zoo, Zoos in the Making,* and *Doctor in the Zoo* can help older children appreciate the zoo operations that they don't get to see. A young child will enjoy *Sam Who Never Forgets.*

- *What's New at the Zoo?* The purpose of modern zoos is as much to educate the public and protect and preserve animal species as it is to put the animals on display. When the story of a successful breeding experiment hits the news, clip out the article and save it for your child to read. When you visit the zoo, head for the cage with the pregnant Mom or the new zoo baby.

  Also look for newspaper and magazine articles about endangered species, and make sure you pay a respectful visit to those animals, too. The announcement of the removal of a species from the endangered list calls for a celebration—perhaps another trip to the zoo.

Your children can write to the National Wildlife Federation (1412 Sixteenth Street, N.W., Washington, D.C. 20036) for more information about wildlife preserves in your area or a copy of the endangered species list. Your family may also be able to become members of your local zoo (usually for a membership fee) and receive periodic newsletters that might interest the children.

Museum Scavenger Hunt

AGES: Older readers
MATERIALS: Museum brochures, scissors, glue, paper, pencils

If you have a museum in your community, a scavenger hunt is a fun way to acquaint your children with the variety of exhibits on display.

Drop by the museum to pick up brochures and other illustrated literature. Cut out pictures of some of the objects and artifacts on display and paste these on a piece of paper. Read through the literature and write some questions about other exhibits that can be answered by observing the exhibits carefully or reading the documentation. These pictures and questions make up the scavenger list.

Present copies of the list to your children in the museum lobby. Explain how the game works: "You're going on a museum scavenger hunt. You have to find all the objects shown in the pictures. When you find the object, write down what it is. You also have to answer all the questions. Take your time; it's not a race. Just see if you can finish the list before we leave the museum." With that, your children are off.

If you want to reward the children for getting through the list, let them select a postcard or other inexpensive souvenir from the museum gift shop before you head back home.

Museum Tie-Ins

AGES: Prereaders, beginning readers, older readers
MATERIALS: Books related to museum exhibits

If your children are excited after seeing a museum exhibit, take advantage of their interest and enthusiasm. Stop at the library on the way home so they can check out books on subjects related to what they have just seen.

For example, if you viewed an exhibit of Kachina dolls at the local doll museum, your children might want to read a book about the Hopi Indians or read aloud from a collection of Native American myths. After seeing a pioneer exhibit at an American history museum, you might want to introduce them to historical novels like *Caddie Woodlawn* or *The Little House on the Prairie* books.

You can also encourage your children to do some related reading before you view an exhibit. In anticipation of a trip to a railroad museum, younger children would undoubtedly enjoy train stories and picture books, such as *Freight Train* and *The Little Engine That Could.* Older children would benefit from reading an artist's biography or a book that teaches beginners how to look at and appreciate art before they confront the paintings on a museum wall. Ask your librarian for suggestions.

Museum-going, like many other activities, may present yet another opportunity to home in on your children's interests, and whenever possible, tie in those interests to books and reading.

History That Rubs Off

AGES: Beginning readers, older readers
MATERIALS: Large pad of newsprint (or ask at a local newspaper office for a "roll end" of newsprint), jumbo-size crayons with the paper labels removed or rubbing sticks (available at stores that sell art supplies), camera and film, scrapbook, glue, pen

Here's a way to extend Giving Words the Rub, which appears in the "Out and About" section. Collect souvenirs of local history with your youngsters by rubbing building plaques and cornerstones, landmark signs, and the plaques on statues and monuments in your city or town.

"Rubbing" refers to the technique of placing paper over a raised inscription or engraving, then rubbing over the surface with the broadside of a crayon or rubbing stick. An impression of the lettering or design will appear on the paper.

Help your children supplement the text of a rubbing with a little library research. For example, the date on the cornerstone of an important building—perhaps your children's school or the county courthouse—can lead you to an old issue of a local newspaper, where you may find a photo of the architect and mayor placing the cornerstone. The local history room in the library may have papers documenting the commission of a statue to commemorate the city's centennial or the return of a war hero.

Keep a scrapbook in which the children paste photographs of the objects they rubbed and small rubbings. Encourage them to write captions or include notes on any related findings. Display larger rubbings on the wall.

Along with picture postcards, rubbings make inexpensive souvenirs of your family's travels. On trips to historic places, bring along your supplies for rubbing. Before touring an old church, inquire whether your children may rub the surfaces of monumental brasses (sheets of brass set into the walls or floors which have been engraved with figures, coats of arms, or inscriptions). There is usually a nominal charge. Always check first with a guide or other official before you rub the surface of a stone or brass plaque; if rubbing contributes to the erosion of an old engraving, you will be asked not to do it.

Graveyard History

AGES: **Older readers**
MATERIALS: **Large pad of newsprint, jumbo-size crayons, with their paper labels removed, or rubbing sticks**

If your children are mature enough, consider a visit to a cemetery that has historical headstones from the Revolutionary or Civil War period, stones with especially interesting epitaphs, or stones bearing the names of past notables, such as the town founders. Bring along supplies for making crayon rubbings.

Take turns reading aloud the epitaphs carved into the headstones. Choose a few of the more interesting or oldest stones to rub. (See History That Rubs Off in this section.) After your outing, suggest one or more of these activities to your children as a follow-up:

- *Rubbings Scrapbook.* Help your children assemble their rubbings in a large scrapbook. Then go to the historical room at the library, a local museum, or the local newspaper office to look for more information about the people whose stones you rubbed. For example, the date on a soldier's stone may help establish the battle in which he was killed. If you have rubbed the stone of a local college's founder, you may find a photo of him or her greeting the first students.
- *Graveyard Art History.* Like painters, tombstone cutters had (and still have) personal styles that distinguish their stones from each

other's. By careful examination of the lettering and design, you may be able to collect the rubbed work of one artisan. Using a graphic arts book, your children can try to identify the typefaces and symbols the cutter used.

- *Sad But True.* Read aloud headstones bearing pithy epitaphs composed by people before they died, or afterward by their families. Your children may be particularly touched to read the tender message carved on an infant's stone, or the words of love a widower chose to inscribe to his wife. In fact, they'll probably speculate for days about these far-off events.

Local History

AGES: Older readers
MATERIALS: Camera, access to old photos and published materials, scrapbook

Your children can consider themselves local historians after visiting and researching some original landmarks in your city or town. Wondering how the city got its name or seeing a photo of your town when it was a cluster of small farms may spark their interest.

- *Place Names.* Is your street named after a famous writer or statesman? Does the regional park have the same name as the group of Indians that first lived in the area? Do you know how your town got its name—where the spring or the field had been in Springfield?

    As you and your children investigate some of the place names in your area, you may uncover a wealth of local history. A librarian can get you started by showing you the library's collection of local historical documents and artifacts. If your children are really interested, they may find themselves searching through old records at the county courthouse or looking through collections of old newspapers at a local newspaper office for the sources of some lesser-known names.

• *Before and After Pictures.* If you live in an older town or district, your children may be fascinated when they compare the way the town looked fifty or a hundred years ago with the way it looks now.

Walk around the older parts of town. Bring along a camera so the children can photograph the present-day scene: a new housing development, a row of shops, kids on ten-speed bikes riding down Main Street or another commercial block, traffic on the four-lane highway.

Follow up your excursion with a trip to the library or a local museum. Can you find old photographs or drawings of these same sites taken or drawn decades or even centuries ago? Perhaps you'll come across an old picture postcard showing county fairgrounds where the mall now stands, or a small plaque in the park noting that here an important general once dispatched a message to his troops. Where ten-speeds and dirt bikes now ride, horse-drawn carriages may once have had the right of way!

If your town has held an anniversary celebration to mark its founding, your children may be able to clip out old photos from a commemorative publication. They may want to mount these, along with recent photos, in a scrapbook. Other "Before and After" items for the scrapbook might include department store advertisements (see Old Stores in Town in this section), photos of the original and present-day grammar schools (published in a school newspaper or yearbook), maps the children have copied from the ones on display at the municipal building, picture postcards from the local museum, and so on. Beside each item, ask your children to write a caption relating it to your area's local history.

• *Oral History.* If your children have a tape recorder, they can record their own interviews with old-timers in the neighborhood, the archeologist sent to oversee a building excavation, or a neighbor who moved to your town years ago and remembers his or her first impressions.

Recordings are special because they capture a person's exact words and preserve an authentic voice. If you don't have a recorder, the children can take notes and write up an account afterward. Before they go on an interview, help your children prepare a list of questions based on some reading they have done about the area's history.

This Old House

AGES: Older readers
MATERIALS: Copy of house title (optional), access to old local newspapers or historical papers and photos (optional), camera, paper and pen, glue

Do you live in an old house or building, maybe one of the original ones in your neighborhood? If your home has a heritage, your children may enjoy learning more about it. Afterward, they can produce a visitor's guide for guests who want to take a tour.

A copy of the title on your house will provide the names of the original and subsequent owners. Depending on how far back they have to go, your children may be able to find old newspaper articles that mention the family that first lived in your house, or they may have to look through the papers (letters and other documents) and publications of the local historical society.

The children may be interested in learning a little about the architecture and workmanship of the house, especially if the house has remained relatively unchanged over the years. Books on period architecture can help them identify all the features of the house, from the general style to the design of the mouldings around the doors and windows.

A nice way you and your children can share what you learn is to produce a guidebook: a *Visitor's Guide to the Mitchell House*. In a photo album or scrapbook, assemble all your findings. Older children can write about colorful occupants in the past and describe the house's outstanding architectural features in captions alongside photos. Help them draw a detailed floor plan that points out new features as well as old ones.

Children who live in newer homes can produce a similar book, concentrating on the more unique features of their house (a frog-shaped door knocker, the secret play space under the stairs), and various items of interest (Grandpa's watercolor paintings, the rocking chair that has rocked three generations of babies to sleep).

A guide to your house is also a considerate gift to leave the new owners if you happen to be moving.

Old Stores in Town

AGES: Older readers
MATERIALS: Library materials, current and old department-store catalogs, old newspapers, paper and pencil

Does your town have an older downtown? Your children might enjoy comparison shopping in the present and past in some of the original stores, such as Woolworth, Sears, a local independent department store or food market, or a family-owned restaurant.

This activity may involve a little library research. Your children pick a store and a year, say twenty years ago, and look through back issues of the local newspaper for ads run by the establishment. Upon finding an ad, they jot down various items and prices.

Next the children visit the same store and do a little comparison shopping. How much does the same loaf of bread cost today? How much more must they pay for their sneakers? How much more expensive is their favorite dish on the menu than it was twenty years ago?

If you live in a newer community, your children can still comparison shop in the past and present. They can use the library's newspaper microfilm to check past prices for brand names in any local supermarket, maybe the same chain if not the same store they plan to check prices in today.

They might also enjoy comparing a current Sears Roebuck catalog with the 1897 facsimile published by Chelsea House (check your library for a copy). They'll undoubtedly get caught up in this compendium of turn-of-the-century merchandise, complete with testimonial letters, descriptions, and engraved illustrations.

New Kid on the Block

AGES: Beginning readers, older readers
MATERIALS: See suggestions

Is a new family with children moving into your neighborhood? Your own kids can play welcome wagon by producing a packet of homemade maps, guides, and other materials to help the new kids learn their way around.

Here are some of the items the children might want to put together:

- A homemade map of the immediate neighborhood with the names of the neighborhood children written on the drawings of their respective houses.
- Published tour guides collected from nearby museums, historic landmarks, or the zoo.
- A notice printed by the public library listing its hours.
- A list of important phone numbers: the best pizza parlor that delivers, the skating rink, the Homework Hotline, the local movie house, your children's own home phone.
- A list of shops the children can recommend from experience: the bike repair shop, the Women's Auxiliary bookstore, the corner candy shop, the ice cream parlor that serves the thickest shakes, a haircutting salon, a department or variety store that sells school supplies cheap.
- A map that shows how to get to the park.
- A list of do's and don'ts: Don't walk on Mr. Cummings's lawn. Do keep a lock on your bike.
- The secret password to the children's clubhouse.

- A photo of the neighborhood children with a caption telling who's who.

When they've collected all the materials, give your children a large manila envelope in which to put them. They might want to first decorate the outside of the envelope with drawings and stickers and write a personal greeting. Have them deliver their package in person so they can introduce themselves—the first simple gesture of friendship.

Bookstore Events

AGES: Older readers

Besides an opportunity to browse or buy, your local bookstore may offer a calendar of literary events, some of which may interest your family. When you visit a local bookstore, ask to put your name and address on a mailing list for upcoming events.

Here are the kinds of events your family might enjoy:

- *Readings.* Some bookstores set aside an evening every week for a poetry or short story reading by local or visiting authors. You might want to do a little prescreening of the writer's work to make sure it's appropriate for your child.
- *Book Signings.* Large publishing companies send their celebrity writers, including children's authors, on tour to sign books at bookstores. Local newspapers will publish an announcement in the book review section and cover the event, and the store may publicize the event on local radio stations.

  Small bookstores often sponsor informal book signings by local writers whose books have been published by small publishing houses or private presses. At an event like this, you may have an opportunity to talk to the writer, whether or not you buy a book and have it signed.
- *Remainders and Other Sales.* Some bookstore chains are strictly dis-

count. Others occasionally purchase remainders, books that are sold at considerable discount after the regular trade sales have dropped off. Some bookstores have a bargain table or an entire basement filled with books at sale prices. It pays to ask.

• *Nonprofit Bookstores.* Some auxiliary groups run nonprofit used bookstores. People donate their old books and the sponsoring organization sells them at bargain prices from a small storefront. Proceeds go to a charitable cause. You and your children might pick up some real treasures if you're willing to rummage through dusty bins and shelves.

Community Players

AGES: All ages

Many communities boast a number of different kinds of theater groups, perhaps ranging from a troupe that performs only Gilbert and Sullivan to a pantomimist who entertains people standing in long lines outside a community playhouse. Your community may even have its own children's theater, where young players directed by older volunteers perform short plays and storybook adaptations.

Your children can contact the local community arts organization to find out exactly what your town has to offer. Encourage them to ask the organization to send a seasonal schedule of classes and events that may interest them. Besides theater activities, they can find out about local art shows, special exhibits, dance performances, concerts, and the like.

Younger children will enjoy puppet theaters, school pageants, children's theaters, and other juvenile performances. Older children will enjoy plays put on by high school and adult groups as well as performances by their talented peers.

Reading on the College Level

AGES: Older readers
MATERIALS: Campus catalog, course list, campus newspaper, picnic lunch

If there is a university or college in your community, encourage your children to be frequent visitors. Besides experiencing the aura of books and learning just by being on campus, they can take early advantage of its rich resources.

On a warm spring or fall day, pack a picnic lunch and go with your children to the campus. Stop at the admissions office for a campus catalog, a list of the semester's courses, and a copy of the campus newspaper before you look for a spot to settle down and eat.

Let the children read through the materials. They might like to pretend they're students by choosing their courses from the course list and expressing interest in a few of the extra-curricular activities described in the catalog. Read aloud the calendar of events to see if there are activities, productions, or sports events scheduled that might appeal to your children. Before you leave, be sure to visit the campus bookstore and browse among all those scholars and tomes.

Subscribe to the campus newspaper, if you can, or go onto campus regularly to pick up the issue that features the calendar of events. Here are some of the cultural events your children may enjoy:

- Theater groups and dance troupes (dramatic, improvisational, operatic, ballet, modern dance)
- Concerts, symphonies, and recitals (jazz, rock, orchestra, individual artists, folk music)
- Art shows (student and professional artists' works)
- Poetry and short fiction readings (by student writers and guest writers)

- Lectures (campus and guest speakers on virtually every subject, including literature your older child may be reading)
- Political rallies (speeches by local figures and national leaders)
- College sports

Out and About

Reading Out
Seeing Things
Position-Words Walk
Nature Exhibit
Giving Words the Rub
Safety Walk
Alphabet Hike
On the Ball
Jump-Rope Jingles and Other Game Songs
Backyard Theater
Ring Around the Ground

Fresh air lends a fresh perspective to your children's reading-related activities, and often leads them right back to their books.

For example, a walk in the woods or the park is an invigorating way for children to practice using observation skills, or to learn position words, safety rules, or the alphabet. Meanwhile, your children's encounters with wildlife may sufficiently arouse their curiosity so that they willingly follow the outing with some informative reading.

Even everyday playground activities can orient your children to reading. A game of catch can become a contest of word opposites, and jump rope can be accompanied by rhyming songs and chants.

Actual reading can precede or follow any number of outdoor games and activities.

Children are as apt to use their imaginations outdoors as indoors. Take time with them to look for castles in the sky or get down and build them in the sand. Help the children improvise the stage, props, and costumes for summertime theater productions based on books and published plays, or their own literary inventions. And get out there and read with them, making activities that appear unrelated to reading, like a picnic or beach outing, an excuse for bringing books.

Reading Out

AGES: All ages

Share the pleasure of reading outdoors with your children, and show them that books aren't just for indoors.

Make your next family picnic a "book-nic." Before setting out for the park or beach, pack some books along with the blanket, picnic lunch, and play equipment. For outings like this, your children may prefer lighter reading fare, such as detective novels, short stories, magazines, or comic books. Although you might make a few recommendations, let your readers choose their own material to bring along.

If you are taking a young child to a nearby park, bring a book to read aloud before the two of you enjoy a picnic lunch or snack. If your child is old enough to read, bring books for both of you so you can sit quietly and read together after your lunch.

Of course, you don't have to plan an excursion to encourage your children to do a little outside reading. Just lay out a towel on the lawn or place a comfortable piece of lawn furniture in a strategic spot in the yard—beneath a shade tree, for example, or behind some bushes that block the street sounds. Don't forget to bring a book for yourself.

Seeing Things

AGES: All ages

The next time you go on a picnic, lie on the beach, or just take it easy in the backyard, spend a few minutes looking up at the clouds with your children. What you see there—a princess' slipper or soldiers on the march—may be the start of a new fairy tale or adventure story.

Seeing pictures in the clouds, finding rocks that resemble other objects or animals, noticing branches that form a *Y*, building a volcano or castle in the sand, nibbling a slice of cheese into the shape of a boat—these whimsical pastimes encourage your children to use their imaginations, to see possibilities.

Using imagination is an important skill for reading. The more freely your children can immerse themselves in the imaginary worlds conjured up by words, the more pleasure they'll get out of their reading. Likewise, the more practice they have imagining aloud, the fewer inhibitions they'll have for creative storytelling and story writing, both natural offshoots of reading.

Position-Words Walk

AGES: Toddlers, prereaders
MATERIALS: Paper, crayons, stapler or hole puncher, yarn

Someday when you plan to take your child to the playground, first pay a visit to the library and look for the book *Rosie's Walk* by Pat Hutchins. Read the story aloud with your child to initiate this activity. Rosie is a carefree red hen who goes on a walk that takes her *under, over,* and *through* various obstacles in her path, all the time unaware of the fox who is stalking her. The fox, of course, runs into disaster with every obstacle he encounters.

After reading, you can make up your own "walk" using the playground equipment. Make a point of remembering the exact sequence of the obstacles you and your child must negotiate along the way. As you duck *under* the slide, and ride *up* and *down* on the seesaw, repeat these concept words several times with your child.

Once back home, you can play a game that provides a visible reminder of the fun you had, while helping your child retain the concepts. First, take out some blank paper. At the top of each page, number and describe an obstacle in the sequence. Use simple phrases or sentences ("Around on the merry-go-round" or "I went down the slide"). Encourage your child to illustrate these various points on your walk, then assemble the pages in a book which you can title "Davie's Walk" or "Alison's Walk." Ask your child to retell the story using position words as the two of you look through the book together.

You can set up a similar obstacle course indoors on a rainy day. Just use furniture and household objects. Your kids may want to set up a course for you.

An obstacle course is also fun for acting out *The Three Billy Goats Gruff.* You can be the troll who lurks *under* the bridge (a few dining room chairs) waiting to pounce on your billy goats who come trip-trapping *over* the bridge.

Nature Exhibit

AGES: Beginning readers, older readers
MATERIALS: Collection of leaves, field guide for trees, wax paper, self-stick labels, pen, shirt box or other shallow box, clear contact paper (optional)

Take a nature walk in mid-autumn to admire the colorful foliage, or in early spring to collect wildflowers. Help your children gather as many different leaves or flowers as they can, then have them bring home their collections to identify and display in a family "museum."

As soon as possible, sandwich the plant material between sheets of wax paper, then place the sandwich under a few volumes of the encyclopedia or other heavy books. Your children might also like to slip a few flowers in the pages of their favorite books for the next reader to discover.

In a few days, the leaves or flowers will be pressed flat and ready to mount. Meanwhile, make a trip to the library to borrow a field guide to the trees or wildflowers in your region. Help the children search through the book for the trees or plants represented in their collection. Suggest the kinds of information they might print, on self-stick labels; for example, generic name, Latin name, date found, place found.

Give each child the top or bottom of a large shirt box for a display case. After they arrange their pressed leaves or flowers to their liking inside the box, they glue down the items and stick on the labels.

To make a display permanent, laminate the bottom of the box with clear contact paper. As you lay the tacky side of the contact paper over the specimens, press out from the center to remove air bubbles.

Now the collection is ready to exhibit wherever you have set up your family museum—on a folding table in the basement or garage, on top of the bookshelf in the children's bedroom, along the wall in a hallway. You can set a shirt-box display case on a table or countertop, or put an adhesive hook or double-stick tape on the back of the box to hang it.

Giving Words the Rub

AGES: Toddlers, prereaders, beginning readers
MATERIALS: Large pad of newsprint or other paper, jumbo-size crayons with paper labels removed

Children are delighted as numerals and letters appear like magic when they rub the surface of a license plate. Making a crayon rubbing involves placing a piece of paper over an engraved or raised surface, then rubbing over the surface with the broad side of a crayon. An impression of the surface emerges on the paper.

Take your children on a walk around your neighborhood to make crayon rubbings that reinforce letter, number, and simple word recognition. Begin with your house number, then proceed to your car, where your kids can rub the numbers and letters on your license plates. At the street corner, lift up a child to rub an old street sign or stop sign. (Note: Some license plates and most *new* road signs are printed flat rather than embossed.)

Encourage your children to look for other interesting textures to rub: the sidewalk, tree bark, leaves sandwiched between two sheets of paper, or a brick wall. Can they identify each rubbing when you look at them later at home?

Look for rubs indoors, too. Household rubs might include names on appliances, keys, and coins in a piggy bank. If you have one of those gadgets that embosses labels on strips of plastic, make some labels of the names of family members and give the labels a rub. For small objects, like coins, a pencil rub sometimes produces clearer results than a crayon rub.

Safety Walk

AGES: Prereaders, beginning readers
MATERIALS: Pad or sketchbook, box of crayons, backpack

You can turn any walk into a safety walk. Heading to the bus stop or a friend's house is as good a time as any to begin pointing out road signs and discussing rules for crossing the street. Or you can plan a special walk just for the purpose of acquainting your children with pedestrian safety.

Small legs tire quickly, so choose a short, familiar route for your safety walk, ideally a sidewalk route with plenty of signs and one or two intersections. Bring along a sketch pad and a box of crayons in a backpack, if you have one; that way your hands will be free for holding when you cross the street.

As you and your children walk, take turns pointing out various safety features. You might also want to tie in other learning concepts: What colors are the lights in the traffic signal? What shape is the stop sign at the corner? What shape is the yield sign where the roads merge? What number is on the speed limit sign? Can your children recognize the word *school* on the school crossing sign? Watch a few drivers as they obey the sign or signal, and talk about how they do it.

Pause after each new sign to draw its picture. Outline the shape for your children, and print any words, numbers, or symbols that appear, but let the children color in the signs themselves.

If a child is about to start school, take at least one safety walk along the exact route the neighborhood children take. When you get home, draw a map of your walk, including all the signs and road marks you both can remember.

Alphabet Hike

AGES: Prereaders, beginning readers
MATERIALS: Paper bag, felt pen, pad or small notebook

You can turn an ordinary walk through the neighborhood or park into an alphabet hike. As you cross the lawn, pick a clover for *C* and a dandelion for *D;* on the sidewalk, find a penny for *P* (or call it money for *M*).

On a pad, list all the letters of the alphabet. As you walk, your children look for items that begin with as many different letters as possible. Write the name of the item next to the appropriate letter on the list. Remind them occasionally about the letters they still need.

You might want to take a paper bag along to collect items. Later on, when you return home or stop to rest or have a picnic, your children can try to arrange the objects in alphabetical order.

If you don't have the time for a hike, your children can blaze their own trails. Perhaps instead of an alphabet hike, they'd like to go on a color hike, picking up items that match the color words or color swatches on their lists.

On the Ball

AGES: Beginning readers, older readers
MATERIALS: Ball

Players have to stay on the ball as they toss words as well as a ball back and forth in this fast-paced game for the yard or playground.

Line up your children a short distance across from you (or you can play with just one child facing you). As the leader, you think of a secret word (say *sight*) and call out a word that rhymes with it (say *kite*) as you bounce or throw the ball to one of the players on the line. The player who catches the ball calls out a word that rhymes with yours, perhaps *right* or *white*, while throwing the ball back to you. You catch the ball and immediately send it off to the next player in line along with another word to rhyme.

The object is to see how long you and your players can keep the ball moving without pause. When the rhythm is disturbed by a player who falters or drops the ball, reveal the secret word and begin again. After a few good rounds, let the children take turns being the leader.

For variation, players can call out words that begin with the same letters (coat, clap, count) or words that mean the opposite (summer/winter, black/white) rather than words that rhyme. Slow down the game for beginning readers; speed it up for older children.

Jump-Rope Jingles and Other Game Songs

AGES: Beginning readers, older readers
MATERIALS: Jump rope (or about six feet of clothesline), pocket-size notebook or spiral-bound deck of index cards, pen or pencil

You may be startled one day to hear your daughter clapping hands with a friend and singing, "I Am a Pretty Little Dutch Girl," just as all the little girls did twenty years ago. Like nursery rhymes and songs, jump-rope jingles, hand-clapping songs and chants for choosing sides are bits of oral literature passed on through every generation. Their meanings are left to the folklorists; their rhymes and rhythms are what make them memorable to children.

Give each child a small notebook (something that will fit in a jacket pocket) in which to collect rhymes for jumping rope and clapping hands, chants for choosing sides, and ditties for various other games. The notebook is not so much for learning the lyrics as for keeping track of them. When your children's friends catch on, you may see lots of children with little notebooks on the driveway, sidewalk, or school-yard sharing songs and adding to their collections.

Besides the ones learned by listening, your children might like to invent a few personal rhymes. These, too, go into the little notebook. A copy of the collection of old and new jump-rope jingles or hand-clapping songs would make an original gift for a friend or younger sibling.

If your library has a book of jump-rope jingles, your children can check it out and quickly add a few more to their repertoire. Your library or bookstore may also carry *Wee Sing and Play*, a cassette and read-along booklet that features a collection of songs for jumping rope, choosing sides, and playing games.

Backyard Theater

AGES: Prereaders, beginning readers, older readers
MATERIALS: Garage or other improvised stage (see suggestions), large appliance box, utility knife, book of short plays or original script, simple props, costume collection or old clothes

Plays become part of your children's reading repertoire when they organize a summer-stock company to perform in a garage or backyard theater.

As soon as your children begin to tell their own stories, they're old enough to participate in improvisational skits based on their favorite storybooks. These shows may involve little more than having the children dress up as their favorite characters and say lines of dialogue from the story or act out a part of the story while making up their own lines. Older children can choose short plays from a children's anthology or adapt short stories or historical accounts for their stage productions. Ask your librarian for suggestions.

If you have a box of costumes (old clothes are just fine), let the players dig in. They can also fashion masks and other no-sew costumes out of paper bags, boxes, crepe paper, and tape. Props can probably be found around the house, although it will require some imagination to see a kitchen chair as a throne or two chairs as the front seat of an automobile.

You can help your children set up a simple outdoor stage using the garage or a part of the backyard, or you can make portable sets. Here are some possibilities:

• *Garage Playhouse.* A garage or carport makes an unusual site for a summer-stock theater. The players perform in the garage, storing sets and costumes at one side, out of sight. A theater sign can be tacked on the front of the garage. The children can set up lawn chairs, stools, or sit-upons (the kind scouts weave out of newspaper) for seating, or the audience can share blankets.

• *Clothesline Theater.* A couple of old sheets, snap clothespins, and a sturdy clothesline suspended between posts or two trees make another instant theater.

Pin the sheets side by side on the line so they hang smoothly. Weigh down the far ends if necessary. When it's curtain time, one of the players or a stagehand gathers up each side of the curtain from the inner corner and pins it up on the clothesline.

• *Folding Theater.* One or two large appliance boxes make interesting portable sets or stage walls for a "traveling company," in this case a group of players that set up stage wherever there's room.

Use a utility knife to remove the ends of the cartons, then cut along one fold to open the side panels, making the cardboard into a single, continuous piece. The panels can be propped like a decorative screen or room divider, either directly behind the players (one box) or curving from behind and to the sides of the players (two boxes). The children can paint sets directly on the panels, or clip on removable paper sets. Fold in the panels to store the sets.

Ring Around the Ground

AGES: Prereaders, beginning readers, older readers
MATERIALS: String (a yard or more), sketch pad or notebook, pencil, books on plants and insects

Let your children discover nature in their own backyard or another nearby "green" spot. As they focus their attention on a tiny plot of ground, they practice using their observation skills, first to see all the natural details, then to classify them. Later, they may enjoy researching their findings and writing up a field guide to the backyard or neighborhood park.

Give the children notebooks and pencils and a yard of string or rope to arrange in a circle on the ground. Have them get down on their bellies or squat if the ground is damp and look carefully in the area enclosed by the ring. What do they see?

At first they will notice the larger and more stationary objects— grass, stones, a clump of clover, and the soil. But as they concentrate, they will begin to notice smaller details. They may spy a few busy ants toting food, or a ladybug climbing a blade of grass. Perhaps a spider will lumber through the territory, or a worm may poke through the soil if it's damp. In spring there may be tiny weeds with delicate flowers; in fall, a selection of fallen leaves that can be traced to various trees in the yard.

Everything the children observe goes into their notebooks. They may want to categorize things generally at first, as Live or Not Alive, or Plant or Animal. They can write the names of what they see and include small sketches. Later, older children may want to consult a field guide or nature book to try to identify their findings and learn their true botanical or animal names and classifications.

A ring around the ground can lead to a more ambitious study of backyard nature. Your children can thoroughly investigate the yard or a park over one or more seasons—lifting rocks, climbing trees, poking in the garden, and so on—then write up their notes in *Mike and Abby's Field Guide to the Backyard* or *Shary's Field Guide to Chestnut Park.*

The Gift of Reading

Reading Coupons
Homemade Books
How to Make Gifts
Ex Libris
Bookmarks
Note Clip
Read Generously
Finding the Right Words
Birthday News
Book Pets
Go-Together Gifts
Treasure Hunt
Reading Countdown

Children can produce many thoughtful gifts *by* reading and *for* reading. For holidays and the birthdays of family and good friends, encourage your children to use their own talents and resources—especially reading resources—to craft homemade items rather than buying gifts from stores.

An older child can create picture books to read aloud to younger brothers and sisters, or compile a family history album to present to a grandparent. Young ones can make any reader a bookmark.

When they are on the receiving end, your children will enjoy gifts of reading that come from you. Wrap up a stuffed animal with a book about an animal, or choose a nonfiction book about a child's new interest. When you have to be away for an extended period, leave a book or something else to read for each day of your absence.

Reading Coupons

AGES: Beginning readers, older readers
MATERIALS: Construction paper, scissors, marking pens, stapler or hole puncher and ribbon (optional)

Reading aloud is a gift children can give as well as receive. A coupon for Grandpa (designed and decorated by your child) might say, "I will be happy to read to you for fifteen minutes so that you can close your eyes and relax." Or the giver may wish to be more specific: "This coupon entitles you to a poetry reading from the works of your favorite poet, Robert Frost, by your favorite (and only) grandson, Peter."

Supply your child with paper, scissors, and an assortment of felt pens for printing the wording of the coupon and drawing a decorative border. A standard-size sheet of construction paper will produce six 3" × 6" coupons (just fold and cut). To make a coupon book, line up and staple the coupons along one short end, or punch a hole in each coupon and tie the bunch together with a colorful ribbon.

Reading coupons make thoughtful gifts from older brothers and sisters to younger children. Parents can make them, too: Stuff a book of coupons in a Christmas stocking or enclose one coupon inside the cover of a new book for a child's birthday.

But why wait for a special occasion? If you hide a coupon in a different place each week (the middle of a cereal box, a coat pocket, or lunch box), your child can look forward both to discovering and redeeming it on a regular basis.

Homemade Books

AGES: Prereaders, beginning readers, older readers
MATERIALS: See suggestions

Your children will put a lot of reading and writing skills to use when they make their own books. The difference between the bookmaking projects in this section and those included in other sections is that the children make these books to give as gifts rather than keep for themselves.

- *Illustration Coloring Book.* Do you have a young reader in your family with a birthday coming up? Perhaps a brother or sister would like to make a book of color-in illustrations from the birthday child's favorite picture book.

  Give the book artist sheets of white paper (not too opaque) to position over various picture-book illustrations. The child traces the outlines in the illustration (some books are more appropriate for this kind of activity than others), then removes the sheet and writes a caption: "Curious George does tricks on his bike."

  The book artists can choose one illustration to trace and color for a book cover. The tracings are stapled together along the top or the left side to make a book.

- *Family History Books.* Grandparents, especially, will enjoy receiving books about the family's history that are written and illustrated by their grandchildren.

  Your children can approach the family's history in different ways. One child may want to write a short story based on a true anecdote: "The Little Heroine: How Great Grandma Ethel Saved Her Brother from a Fire." Another child might want to research a historical family figure. Or perhaps together the children can write a biography about Grandpa for his sixtieth birthday.

  For a finished look, the kids can assemble the pages of their books in a report binder, staple the pages together and tape over the stapled spine with cloth tape, or punch holes and tie through with ribbons or yarn.

• *Puzzle Books.* Your children can collaborate and produce puzzle books for each other and friends for holiday and birthday presents.

Save samples of puzzles from store-bought books or the newspaper that the children can use as models for creating their own puzzles. Include word searches, crossword puzzles (based on themes or books), acrostics, scrambled words, word tricks (see "The Gang's All Here" section), and other favorites.

Provide graph paper for crosswords, if possible; lined notebook paper will do for everything else. The children can assemble the puzzles pages in a narrow loose-leaf binder or insert binder rings. Remind them to include the answers at the back of the book.

• *Children's Books.* Older brothers and sisters may enjoy writing and illustrating books for a younger child in the family. They can make up their own simple stories, retell old favorites, illustrate ABC books, or make up silly poems to read aloud to a younger sibling. Anything goes in the way of binding the books.

• *Accordion Books.* Parents or grandparents would treasure a small collection of poems written by your children and bound in a lovely folding booklet. The collection can be an individual or collective effort.

Your children will need a sheet of paper at least 18 inches long to accordion-fold into panels 3" to 4" wide. An art-supply store will sell individual "parent sheets" that are at least that long. Another possibility is to tape individual sheets of paper together and accordion-fold along the taped sides. The children will also need two pieces of cardboard for front and back covers, and material to cover the cardboards, such as gift wrap or thin fabric.

The poems are printed on all but the first and last panels of the paper. The end panels are glued to the insides of the covers. Explain to the children how to fold up the book accordion-style. They can keep the book from folding open by tying a ribbon around the construction.

How to Make Gifts

AGES: Beginning readers, older readers
MATERIALS: How-to book, materials for making a handicraft item

Your children can make their own gifts for family and friends by
following the directions in a how-to book. Besides the thoughtful-
ness involved in taking the time to make rather than buy a gift, your
children will learn a new craft by reading.

Well before holiday time or a birthday, let your children browse in
the crafts section at the library. Help them select projects that are
appropriate for the person for whom they're intended, and ones
they can manage without too much assistance. For example, an
older child might find a playdough recipe and cook up a batch for a
younger brother or sister. Perhaps you might agree to help the
children build a birdhouse for Grandpa's favorite shade tree.

Have your children list all the materials they need and accompany
you shopping. Be available to clarify directions or hold a gluey part
in place while your eager but awkward young craftsmen study the
next step.

Encourage your children to learn other crafts from how-to books
—how to tie-dye a T-shirt, how to marble paper, how to build a
small bookcase, how to bake brownies. When they're not making
gifts for someone else, they can make something for themselves.

Ex Libris

AGES: Prereaders, beginning readers, older readers
MATERIALS: Paper (stationery that has some rag content is nicest),
scissors, ruler, fine-line markers, rubber cement

By designing labels that identify books as their own, your children are acknowledging that books are among their most precious possessions. They might like to share that value by making bookplates for the books they give as well as the ones they receive.

To make a bookplate, your child first cuts down a piece of paper to about file-card size, or a little squarer. Next your child decides on some wording: "This book belongs to Sarah Elizabeth Franklin," "From the Bradford Family Library," "For Pearl Wong: Friends and books are forever," or some other appropriate line that identifies the owner of the book and perhaps expresses some sentiment. An older child might enjoy making up a book riddle, a popular convention on medieval bookplates.

After printing the words carefully, your child illustrates the plate with a fanciful border, geometric design, a favorite book character, or even a tracing of an illustration from the book itself. Go to the trouble of purchasing rubber cement for gluing the plate to the inside front cover of the book; other glues and pastes don't apply as evenly and some crack over time. Rubber cement will also allow your child to reposition a plate, and to peel off smears.

If you have access to a photocopier or offset printer, make copies of your children's personal bookplates. Whenever someone gives them a new book, they can glue on their very own labels.

Bookmarks

AGES: Prereaders, beginning readers, older readers
MATERIALS: Sturdy paper or thin cardboard, materials for decorating (see suggestions), clear contact paper

Suggest that your children make pretty bookmarks to enclose in a gift book or to mark the place in your own book where you left off during read-aloud time.

To decorate a set of bookmarks, your kids can choose their favorite medium from among these:

* Tiny pressed flowers
* Marbling (floating oil paint on water)
* Crayons or marking pens
* Picture cutouts from book clubs or book reviews
* A handwritten poem
* Rubber stamps or stickers

If you have clear contact paper, let the children laminate their bookmarks between sheets of the contact paper after they finish decorating. Smooth out the contact on both sides, then cut out around each bookmark. If they like, the children can insert a tassel or piece of ribbon between the contact to hang down from the bookmark.

Note Clip

AGES: **Beginning readers, older readers**
MATERIALS: **Wood scrap for a base (no more than a few inches square), snap clothespin, glue, paint and paintbrush or color markers**

A note clip keeps a clamp on phone messages, lists, and other scraps of information that otherwise get misplaced. Here's a simple and useful gift your children can make for just about anybody, even themselves.

Constructing the note clip is easy: Your child simply glues down one flat side of a snap clothespin on a small wooden base. After the construction dries (best overnight), the clip can be painted or decorated with color markers or paints.

Suggest that your children present their gift with a ribbon tied around the clothespin and a homemade gift tag or card clipped onto the base.

Maybe your children's own desks or dresser tops need a little organization? Suggest that they make themselves clips to hold on to some of the notes you leave in their lunch boxes, a favorite cartoon, a picture postcard from Grandma, or an invitation to a party.

Read Generously

AGES: Beginning readers, older readers

During the gift-giving holidays, many people give their time collecting for charities. Your children may want to hold their own family fund-raiser—a read-a-thon.

Suggest that your children (they may want to involve cousins and friends, too) hold their read-a-thon to raise money for, appropriately enough, new children's books. The books can be earmarked for a local toy drive, a children's hospital, a refugee program, or some other charity the children want to support.

Here's how a read-a-thon works: The children agree to read as many books as they can during a set period of time, say the month before Christmas or the eight days of Hanukkah. They solicit money pledges—an amount for each book or for every certain number of pages—from grandparents, parents, aunts and uncles, and other adults they know well.

The honor system goes into effect as the children keep track of their own reading. At the end of the set period, they report back to their list of pledgers to request payment and say thank you for their participation.

Take the children to a bookstore and let them make the book selections themselves. Tell the manager what they're up to, just in case the store gives a discount on charitable purchases. If possible, have your children deliver the books to the person in charge of distributing them.

Finding the Right Words

AGES: Beginning readers, older readers
MATERIALS: Paper and pencil, dictionary or thesaurus, construction paper, newspaper and magazines, advertising mail, scissors, glue

How would you describe your best friend? With that question in mind, your children go on a search through newspapers and magazines for descriptive words to use in a collage—so much more thoughtful than a store-bought birthday or Valentine's Day card.

It's better to have some words in mind before charging off with a scissors, so provide your children with paper and pencil for a list. Offer a dictionary also, and a thesaurus if you have one. Point out that these references have served many a writer well in the quest for *le mot juste.* Who knows? Your children may even pick up a few new words along the way.

Offer help when it comes time to look for the words on the list. While you scan headlines and copy in the newspaper, your children can search through magazines. Advertising mail, with all its hype, may provide a rich source of flattering words.

When you have accumulated a small pile of words, and maybe a few appropriate pictures, your children can arrange and glue the cutouts on construction paper.

Birthday News

AGES: Older readers
MATERIALS: The Reader's Guide to Periodicals (in your library's reference section) and newspaper microfilm, family scrapbook, baby book, paper and pen or typewriter, access to photocopier (optional)

If someone in your family has an important birthday this year, (thirteenth, sixteenth, fortieth, or fiftieth) commemorate it with a newsletter supposedly published on the day that person was born. The whole family can get involved in this project, using some of the same techniques historians use to find out about important dates in history.

Give yourselves plenty of lead time—at least two weeks—and plan at least two trips to the library. Here are the kinds of things to look for:

• *Headlines.* At the library, one person uses the newspaper microfilm to locate headlines that appeared on the day the birthday person was born.

• *Old Magazines.* Another person can scan news and popular culture magazines published during the week or month of the birth date. What were fashions like? Were there any scientific break-throughs? Who were the top entertainers? What movies were released? Who were the major sports figures and what were their records? What was happening on the national front? Around the world?

• *Birth-Date Trivia.* Ask if your library has the *Day By Day* series published by Facts on File for each decade. (At this writing, they're only up to the sixties, so this reference will only come in handy for researching adult birthdays.) Look up the birth date and pick up some newsworthy tidbits. You might also ask for

Chase's Calendar of Events or some other publication that lists celebrity birthdays and other noteworthy events that occurred on the same day, though not necessarily in the same year.

* *Family Scrapbook.* A family scrapbook or a baby book should have plenty of information and artifacts. What were the birthday person's birth statistics (weight, length, etc.)? Who delivered the baby? Do you have a copy of the birth certificate and announcement? Baby photos?
* *Interviews.* Different family members can be asked to recount the big event. Where were they? Can they remember what songs were on the radio? What the weather was like? Do they have any funny stories connected with the birth?

Family members take notes as they collect stories and materials, then everybody agrees to write up a different article or feature. The lead story, of course, is the celebrated birth. An "Ask Amanda" column may advise what is considered an appropriate length for a mini-skirt; a weather forecast may predict what someone has researched to have been the actual conditions. Names in the news may include Eisenhower, Gandhi, Twiggy, Stalin, or Nadia Comaneci.

Design a Birthday News banner and print the dateline underneath. Make it someone's responsibility to neatly copy or type the finished features on sheets of standard-size paper. If possible, photocopy the newsletter so all the participants can have one. The original goes to the birthday person.

Book Pets

AGES: Prereaders, beginning readers
MATERIALS: Animal story, corresponding stuffed animal

Children will love cuddling up with a good storybook when they can also cuddle up with a beloved character in the story.

In recent years, several popular animal characters have stepped out of the pages and onto the toy shelf: Corduroy, Curious George, Paddington, and Babar, to name a few, are now available as stuffed animals. You can even buy books that are packaged with toy pets—*Spot's First Walk*, for instance, comes complete with pup. If your child's particular favorite has not been reproduced exactly, you are sure to find a generic look-alike.

Giving a book pet along with a book is a nice touch for both usual and not-so-usual gift-giving occasions. Perhaps this year a stuffed Velveteen Rabbit can deliver an Easter basket full of bunny books (*The Runaway Bunny, Goodnight Moon, The Tale of Peter Rabbit* and, of course, *The Velveteen Rabbit*). Or if you have to be away from your child for an extended period, leave a book and a stuffed animal as a reading companion in your absence. (See also Reading Countdown in this section.)

Go-Together Gifts

AGES: Prereaders, beginning readers, older readers
MATERIALS: Gift and related book, gift wrap

Nothing motivates reading like a gift that arrives with a companion —a book.

Your children will enjoy creating go-together gifts for their friends and family as well as receiving them from you. Sometimes the gift will inspire the book, but if you're stuck for ideas, try looking the other way around. Settle on a good how-to book and find a gift to go with it.

Here are some gifts and books that go together well:

· A book on juggling and several bright balls.
· A book about fossils and a bag of plaster of paris.
· A book about hats and a straw hat with materials for decorating.
· A cookbook and an apron or utensils.
· A book about baseball and a bat or ball.

- A book about stamp collecting and a stamp album.
- A book about rubber stamps, a few special stamps, and an ink pad.
- A gardening book and a basket of assorted seeds.
- A house repair book and a new hammer.
- A nature book and a magnifying glass.
- An astronomy book and a star chart.
- A jump-rope jingle book and a jump rope.
- A book about cars and trucks and a few miniature vehicles.
- A story about camping and a small canteen.

Of course the list can go on forever, but that's because there are books about anything and everything. You and your children are the best judges of what kinds of books and activities will appeal most to the people on your list. (See also Book Pets in this section.)

Treasure Hunt

AGES: Prereaders, beginning readers, older readers
MATERIALS: File cards, pencil, small prizes (optional), book or other treasure item

For a special occasion, such as a birthday party, Valentine's Day, or Easter, set up a treasure hunt for your children. The "treasure" itself is insignificant; kids just love the adventure of discovering and following lots of clues.

Set up the hunt so that each clue card leads the hunter to another clue card, and then another, until the hunter finds the last clue card and along with it, the treasure. Or you might want to hide several small treasures to be discovered along the way, say a tiny box of raisins, a whistle, and a novelty eraser. A card that says Treasure or The End accompanies the last gift—perhaps a new book, a story cassette, or you!

How the clues are presented depends on the children's ages and reading ability. Make picture-word cards for prereaders and beginning readers. For example, draw a table or a bush and an arrow pointing to precisely where the next clue can be found. For beginning readers, also print a simple phrase, like "under the table" or "in the sandbox."

For older children, write a riddle: "On top of me you put your plate. Now under me go find clue 8!" Under the table, they would find the last clue: "A whale has beached in the yard. See what it has dragged in from the sea." In the sandbox, they find the treasure—a pair of bookends made out of conch shells.

Plant all but the first clue card (and small prizes, if you choose) in the order they are to be found. You might want to walk through the hunt once yourself to double-check that the clues are in the right places. When it's time for the hunt to begin, hand the first clue card to your child.

Consider these special occasions for a treasure hunt:

- *Valentine's Day.* Hide homemade valentines or valentine candies. Perhaps the children would like to set up valentine treasure hunts for each other.
- *Easter.* Hide colored eggs the children have dyed earlier. A basketful of goodies or a stuffed bunny can be the big treasure.
- *Birthday Party.* Give each party guest a few cards that lead to several small party prizes or treats, rather than one big prize.
- *Mother's or Father's Day.* The children send Mom or Dad on a hunt for treasure. Along with the clue cards, they might hide single flowers, new tools, photos of the children, or homemade coupons for things like breakfast in bed, a dozen kisses, or watering the garden. At the end of the hunt, Mom might discover a ceramic vase or Dad might unlock a new toolbox.

Reading Countdown

AGES: Prereaders, beginning readers, older readers
MATERIALS: Calendar page for the month, something different to read for each day that will be counted, wrapping paper, cellophane tape, file cards, marker

Here's the perfect gift idea for a child who's convalescing or who's left behind when parents are away on business or vacation. For every day your child must be in bed or endure your absence, leave a reading gift to be opened.

Say you will be away from home a week. Before you leave, take a calendar page and circle the date you depart and the date you return. Beginning with your departure date, number the dates in reverse sequence, beginning with the number 7. Next collect seven gifts, preferably things that involve some reading. For example, you might collect a paperback novel, comic book, craft book, sports magazine, model with written directions, cookie recipe and the necessary ingredients, and a T-shirt with a silly slogan.

Wrap each gift separately and label with a different number from 1 to 7. Place the gifts in a large bag. When you present the calendar and the gifts to your child, explain that he or she can open a gift a day, the number gift corresponding to the number of days left before you return.

Reading gifts will help your youngsters pass the time more valuably as they count down the days till you return. (See also Book Pets in this section.)

The Gang's All Here

Oh, D-E-A-R!
Little Sillies
Little Ditties
Family Songbook
Is That a Fact?
That's Nonsense!
Question Games
Initial Response
Word Tricks
Mr. Green Likes Coffee, but Not Tea
Family Trivia
Book Trivia
Luckily, Unluckily
Frame Stories
Book Charades
The Trial of Goldilocks
You're Invited: B.Y.O.B.
Reading Olympics

Reading means fun and games when the family gets together. Whether you take a few minutes at the dinner table to share a startling fact, or play word games on Saturday nights, you are impressing on your children that learning goes on all the time, even at mealtime and playtime—and that it can be fun.

In addition to your read-aloud schedule, you might want to set a regular time when everybody in the family puts down what he or she is doing and picks up something to read. Your enthusiastic participation shows your children that you, too, enjoy reading.

Most of the family activities featured in this section take the form of games—parlor games, question games, word games, singing games, storytelling games. You might also want to invest in a few of the good word games available in stores, like Scrabble, which reinforces vocabulary and spelling, and Boggle, which helps players recognize spelling patterns. Include board games that usually require a fair amount of reading—first the directions, then the spaces and game cards. A game like Clue, for example, reads and progresses like a mystery book, requiring the same mental organization and deduction.

Keep pads and sharpened pencils in the room where your family spends most of their recreation time. When you have ten minutes before a favorite TV show, work in a round of your favorite pencil-and-paper game. If your entire evening is unscheduled, play a parlor game like Charades, or hold a mock trial for a book character accused of a crime.

Oh, D-E-A-R!

AGES: All ages

The next time you hear a young voice say, "Oh, D-E-A-R!" you'll know that's the cue to Drop Everything and Read. The TV and stereo are off, no phone calls are taken, and there are no unnecessary interruptions for the next twenty minutes or half hour.

Make silent, sustained reading an institution in your home. Set aside a time each week, or twice a week, for family reading. (You can adjust the time as your children's reading advances.) When that time rolls around, everybody—parents included—takes time out from what he or she is doing to read *something*. A book, a magazine, a newspaper—even a letter qualifies.

The family can settle in the same room with their various reading materials, respecting each other's quiet but enjoying the companionship. Or readers can go off to their own favorite nooks. If you have a prereader, suggest that the child either look through a picture book or play quietly with a puzzle or toy.

Following the reading, life may resume as usual, or you can persuade family members to stay and talk to each other about what they're reading. You might ask questions about your children's books or share an interesting passage from the book or article you have been reading.

Little Sillies

AGES: Prereaders, beginning readers

> Two little sillies sitting on a seat;
> They got hungry, what did they eat?

"Toasted turtles!" cries one of your little sillies. "Mustard-flavored ice cream with hot fudge sauerkraut!" cries the other. If three children are playing, sing about three sillies. (You can be one of the sillies, too.) Repeat the jingle to whatever tune you like while your sillies think of two more preposterous dishes that might tempt their word-silly appetites.

A Sesame Street variation might have your children dreaming up a menu for Oscar the Grouch, who has a taste for trash. For lunch:

"A melted tire sandwich and french-fried shoelaces," your child suggests. You pick the dessert: "Sardine sundae with a light bulb on top." Yuck!

Where does all this silliness get you? Your children are exploring word combinations, being inventive, and having a giggly good time. Play this kind of game anytime—when you're on the road, waiting in line at the supermarket, or pushing swings at the playground.

Little Ditties

AGES: All ages

Can you hear yourself singing something like "She'll be chopping up the carrots when she cooks, chop, chop!" to the tune of "She'll Be Comin' Round the Mountain"? Your children, familiar with the original song and quick to catch on, can start the next verse: "She'll be slicing the tomatoes when she cooks, slice, slice!" Before you know it, you'll have finished making the salad and you'll have thoroughly amused yourselves.

Children love it when parents make up simple songs about them and their activities or personalize the lyrics to songs they already know. To your infant on the changing table, you might sing about fingers and toes; to your toddler at play, you might sing about toys. Preschoolers especially enjoy songs that call for name substitutions, for example, "Johnny Plays with One Hammer" or "Mary Wore Her Red Dress." About this age, they will also enjoy helping you fill in the patterned rhymes to made-up songs or adding verses to songs they already know.

Spontaneous singing can give you a nice uplift, and your children's own moods will be lightened and brightened as they hear you and join in. Besides amusing everybody, little ditties help pass time. If an errand is taking a parent a long time, a quick verse to the tune of "Where Is Thumbkin?" might relieve the boredom or concern:

Where is Daddy? Where is Daddy?
Where is he? Where is he?
I would like to hug him,
I would like to kiss him.
Hurry please! Hurry please!

Family Songbook

AGES: **Beginning readers, older readers**
MATERIALS: **Loose-leaf binder, notebook paper, pen, songbooks from library (optional)**

Your children can prepare song sheets for the holidays, evenings in front of the fireplace or campfire, long drives, or any other occasions on which the family holds a sing-along.

Label a loose-leaf binder Family Songbook. Inside go the lyrics to your family's favorite songs neatly copied on sheets of notebook paper.

Song sheets are a help when the family is learning a new song or when they are trying to remember all the verses to an old favorite. Guests can refer to the sheets if they are invited to a sing-along; they may also be coaxed to contribute a song before they leave, just as they might leave a favorite recipe.

If your extended family gets together and sings traditional songs during the holidays, or you and your children go caroling, you may want to make a special songbook collection for the occasion. Rather than assembling single song sheets in a binder, you can make copies of the song sheets and staple together booklets to give as holiday keepsakes. If the size of your family makes this impractical, hand out enough copies of the song sheets for every two or three people to share.

Your library will probably have a number of songbooks from which your children can supplement their own song collection. For younger children, ask about picture books that are based on the lyrics of an old song. You and your children can read and sing aloud as you turn the pages to such picture books as *Mary Wore Her Red Dress, The Farmer in the Dell, Roll Over! A Counting Song, Silent Night,* and *London Bridge Is Falling Down.* Usually the illustrator recounts the song's folk origins and includes the music at the very beginning or end of the book.

If you have a cassette player, you can buy song cassettes with read-along songbooks. The *Wee Sing* series is excellent for youngsters and, as you would expect, Walt Disney records and books also make good family fare. For international recordings by and for children, look in your UNICEF mail-order catalog at holiday time.

Is That a Fact?

AGES: Beginning readers, older readers

Over breakfast or dinner, share an interesting fact with your child that you read somewhere—on the cereal box in front of you, in the morning newspaper, in the book you're reading. "Almost half your bones are located in two places in your body. Can you guess where?" you might ask your child. "Wrong—in the hands and feet! That medical reprint I got in the mail is full of facts like that."

Do this every morning or evening, and after about three days' worth of facts, your child may beat you to the punch. "Hey, listen to this! You know what the temperature was for the coldest football game in history? Minus 59 degrees wind chill! Cincinnati beat San Diego—in Cincinnati, of course. January 10, 1984. Now that's cold!"

Agree to take turns contributing interesting or surprising facts at the breakfast or dinner table. Not only will this "side dish" spark conversation, but your children will be impressed with the great variety of reading materials available and the diversity of information they offer.

That's Nonsense!

AGES: Prereaders, beginning readers

Perk up your youngsters with a little nonsense during a long drive or a long wait. Here are a couple of quick and lively ideas that involve nothing more than wordplay, but manage to give your children a little practice learning letter sounds.

- *First Letter Lingo.* "Set's so soo sa sore soo sy some sooz." After interpreting that tongue twister, the *s* sound becomes unforgettable! Maybe your child wants to tell you something that begins with *p*: "Pie pink peas pupcakes par perry pelicious!" Of course, nonsense words like *sooz* and *pupcake*, and the not-so-nonsensical words that are occasionally produced, may give your kids such fits of laughter, they won't be able to finish the sentence.

- *Pig Latin.* Remember the first "ecret-say anguage-lay" you spoke with your brothers and sisters, hoping your parents wouldn't understand? Well, you may as well try it on your own children. Mom might ask Dad casually in the car, "Ould-shay e-way op-stay or-fay ice eam-cray?" Chances are the "es-yay" will come from the backseat.

  The key to this seemingly nonsense language is taking the consonant (or consonant blend) that begins a word and placing it before *ay* on the end of the word, so that *boy* becomes *oy-bay* and *girl, irl-gay.*

Question Games

AGES: Beginning readers, older readers

You can recognize a question game by the standard opener, "I'm thinking of . . ." Here are three games varying in difficulty and focus.

- *"Something That Starts with . . ."* or *"Something That Sounds Like . . ."* The next time you want to occupy your children while you wait in a doctor's office, or while you're painting shelves, play a simple game that reinforces letter sounds or rhymes.

  You might start out something like this: "I'm the sound detective. I'm looking around this room for something that begins with *p*. Aha! I found it! What am I thinking of?" For a rhyming game, you could begin: "I'm putting up my antennae [make devil ears]. I hear lots of words. One is coming in clearly now. I hear something that rhymes with *me*. What word am I thinking of?"

  Let your kids take a turn being the sound detective or putting up their antennae while you try and guess the object or word they have in mind.

- *Teakettle.* Teakettle is a silly variation of Twenty Questions. One player thinks of an activity, say snoring or sweeping. The other players take turns asking yes/no questions, substituting the word *teakettle* for the mystery activity.

  The fun is in asking questions that will put the thinker on the spot, if possible, and the results are often hilarious. For example: "Do you teakettle the floor?" "Can you teakettle with another person?" "Can you teakettle and scratch your head at the same time?"

  No one seems to know why this game is called Teakettle, and your children may want to substitute their own name. For example, can you hamburger?

• *Boticelli.* Play a version of this parlor game where players challenge one another to guess the fictional book characters they have in mind rather than real people. Agree beforehand to limit the characters to ones with whom all the players are familiar.

The first challenger thinks of a fictional character and tells the others what letter the character's name starts with (the last name for characters with full names). The rest of the players try to stump the challenger with questions about other characters whose names begin with the same letter. For instance:

CHALLENGER: I'm thinking of a character whose name starts with *B*.

PLAYER 1: Is this character a hobbit hero?

CHALLENGER: No, it is not Bilbo Baggins.

PLAYER 2: Did this character dress a chicken in fine clothes?

CHALLENGER: No, it is not Amelia Bedelia.

PLAYER 3: Does this character help his father solve crimes?

CHALLENGER: Hmm. I'm stumped.

PLAYER 3: Encyclopedia Brown!

The player who manages to stump the challenger may either guess the identity or ask one yes/no question leading to the character's identity. For example, the player might ask, "Is the character human?" or "Is the character a grown-up?" A round is over when one player uses a turn to guess correctly the character the challenger has in mind. Then someone else volunteers to challenge the group.

Initial Response

AGES: Beginning readers, older readers
MATERIALS: Paper and pencils

Ask Martha Gleason to name her favorite gourmet snack, and she might answer, "Marinated gourds." What advice might her brother

Nicky give a parrot? "Never gossip!" In this game, family players have to keep their verbal wits about them as they respond to questions using words beginning with their own initials.

For each round, a different family member thinks of a question to put to each other player in turn. The player who has been asked must respond speedily in two words that begin with his or her own initials. The object is to come up with an imaginative or clever reply. Unconventional questions help.

This game provides practice in formulating questions and phrasing answers, and lets players show off the unusual words in their vocabulary. It also gives children confidence in their ability to think quickly and creatively.

Players may prefer to write out the questions and as many responses as they can generate in a given amount of time, say three minutes. Although pencil and paper will slow the pace of the game, it will give players with difficult initials more time to come up with good answers.

Here are a few more variations:

• *Monograms.* To make the game more challenging for everybody, have players formulate three-word responses using their middle initials as well as the initials of their first and last names.

• *Anagram Sentences.* Players use all the letters in one person's first name in order to generate words in a sentence. For Martha, they might come up with something like "Mother and Ruth took home artichokes" or "Many abstained rather than hunt alligators." Everybody makes an anagram sentence for every player's name.

• *Attributes.* Your children might like to create this kind of message as a gift for a family member, or a valentine for a friend. First they write the person's name vertically on a sheet of paper. Then they think of a word beginning with each letter in the person's name to describe that person. They write these words across, like this:

M   merry
A   adventurous
R   rowdy
T   trusting
H   honest
A   acrobatic

Word Tricks

AGES: Older readers
MATERIALS: Paper and pencils

If your family has a long evening ahead and no plans, you may need a few tricks up your sleeve to keep everyone entertained. Here are a couple you can pull out when you need them. Only pencils and paper are required.

- *When Push Comes to Shove.* Players pay close attention to spellings and meanings as they set up these little word problems for the rest of the family to solve.

  A player chooses a pair of related words, either opposite or complementary in meaning. Then the player figures out how to change one word to the other by substituting, omitting, and reordering letters a step at a time. The player presents the problem to the others using definitions. For example, to make *push* become its complement, *shove,* four steps are required:

1. Change one letter to make a word that means *fancy*—POSH.
2. Rearrange letters to make a word that means what you do at a store —SHOP.
3. Change the last letter to make footwear—SHOE.
4. Put a victory sign between the *O* and the *E*—SHOVE.

The player can either tell the others the starting word or just provide a definition, depending on how difficult a game you want to play.

   A variation is to give a word pair and see who can make the transformation of one to the other in the fewest number of steps. The pair of words must have the same number of letters and each step involves changing one letter. As an example, if you are turning LEAD into GOLD, you might do it in four steps (LEAD, HEAD,

HELD, HOLD, GOLD), only to be beat out by someone who can make the change in three steps (LEAD, LOAD, GOAD, GOLD).

• *Mind Over Matter.* Family members will need ingenuity to create visual riddles for well-known phrases and expressions using letters and other graphic symbols. After everybody has written a riddle or two, exchange papers and try to solve the riddles.

Sometimes the position of the words reveals the meaning, as in these examples:

• timetime: "Time after time."

• bridge
water: "Water under the bridge."

Size can also be a factor, as with poFISHnd: "Big fish in a small pond." Some word riddles require other graphic effects; for example, "trickle-down theory" might be represented by having the letters in the word *theory* look like they are trickling down the page.

Mr. Green Likes Coffee, but Not Tea

AGES: Older readers
MATERIALS: Paper and pencils

This problem-solving exercise only works once on your family, but then they can challenge other friends and families to figure out what makes Mr. Green so finicky.

Start the game by telling your family a little about Mr. Green. "Mr. Green likes carrots, but not peas," you observe. "Mr. Green likes books, but he definitely does not like reading. He likes tepees, but not tents; food but not eating." By now, you have everyone intrigued.

Pass out pencils and paper. Have the players divide their papers into two columns—one for the things Mr. Green likes, the other for the things he does not like. As you continue to give examples, the players fill in their charts. The object, you tell them, is to discover a pattern in the things Mr. Green is partial to and in those he disdains.

When a player catches on to the fact that Mr. Green only likes things that have double letters in their spelling (he likes letters and spelling, but not words), that player joins you in giving the other players more examples. Play until everyone solves the problem, stopping after twenty or thirty minutes and picking up the game another time, if necessary. Mr. Green likes *all* players to *succeed,* not just a few.

Family Trivia

AGES: Beginning readers, older readers
MATERIALS: File cards, pencils or pens

Can you remember the name of Timmy's third-grade teacher, or the breed of the first family dog? These are the kinds of trivia questions that members of the family read aloud to each other as they take a quick jog down Memory Lane. Play as individuals or teams.

When individuals play, each person takes a small stack of file cards and thinks of a family trivia question to write on the front of each card. The answers go on the back. Here are some ideas to get you started:

• Where did Mom and Dad go on their first date?
• On what vacation did Melanie learn to swim?
• What car was Zack driving when he passed his driver's test?
• What was Katie's first word?
• What is the title of the book four-year-old Kip made Dad read every night for a whole year?

One player collects all the cards, shuffles them together, and lays them in a pile faceup (question side up). The youngest player draws a card from the pile, reads aloud the question, and tries to answer it correctly. If the player gives the right answer, that player keeps the card and draws again. If the answer is wrong, the player places the card at the bottom of the pile and passes to the next player. If a player draws his or her own card, it goes to the bottom of the pile and that player draws again. Play until there are no more cards to pick. The player with the most cards at the end of the game wins.

If you want to play in teams, have team members brainstorm together to come up with trivia questions. The teams take turns drawing a card from the other's pile, and team members may consult each other to try to come up with the correct answer. A team scores a point each time they guess correctly.

Book Trivia

AGES: Prereaders, beginning readers, older readers

What was the name of Mike Mulligan's steam shovel? Whoever answers "Marianne" gets to ask the next question.

Testing each other's memory with book trivia is the kind of activity you can start up and leave off whenever and wherever you please. Play in the evening during a time you set aside for such trivial pursuits. Play on the drive to Grandma's house, while you wait to have the family car inspected, between batches of cookies, or in a ticket line.

There are only two rules in the game: The trivia questions must be based on books with which most of the players are familiar, and the first person to guess correctly asks the next question. Forget about keeping score; it just holds up the game.

Anyone can start off the game with a question. Questions can involve characters ("How big was Stuart Little?") or plots ("How long does Mary Poppins say she'll stay?") or settings ("What was the name of Heidi's mountain village?").

Not only is the game fun and challenging while it lasts, but your readers will get in the good habit of reading for details, however trivial, in preparation for the next time you play.

Luckily, Unluckily

AGES: Beginning readers, older readers

Here's a group storytelling activity that makes great camping and traveling fare. Adverbs and imagination make the fortunes of the characters in these stories swing back and forth.

Everybody sits in a circle (or play in the car). One person volunteers to tell the beginning of a story, for example: "I was walking through the park the other day when I saw an old woman dressed in the most garments I've ever seen on one person. Nothing matched and nothing fit her properly. As she headed over the grass toward me, she stumbled over the hem of one of her skirts, fell forward, and landed at my feet! Fortunately . . . ."

Suddenly the narrator breaks off and turns to the person to the left, who repeats the adverb and continues the story. At the next contrived turn of the story, the second storyteller says *"Un*fortunately . . ." and breaks off, leaving a third narrator to resume. Continue developing the story around the circle two or three times, having the storytellers alternate between the two adverbs.

Frame Stories

AGES: Prereaders, beginning readers, older readers

"Where were you when the lights went out?" may be the theme that ties together an evening of family storytelling by candlelight. Or perhaps the family must spend the weekend snowbound at home. Imagining yourselves as shipwrecked inhabitants of a tropical island, you can pass an hour or more telling tales of your incredible adventures.

Frame stories are a group of tales told by characters who have been brought together by a fictitious event. This kind of storytelling has a long literary tradition your family may enjoy sampling. Perhaps the most popular frame stories are told by an Arabian queen trying to save her own life in *A Thousand and One Nights*.

The next time there is a blackout or your weekend at the beach is rained out, use the occasion as a frame for storytelling. You can ask each family member to assume a fictitious personality and concoct a story for being there, or you can just be yourselves and spin some tales to help pass the time. Frame stories might also serve as a continuing entertainment in front of the campfire on a camping trip or during a cross-country trip.

If your family has a penchant for writing, the storytellers can refine their stories on paper or at the computer and compile an anthology to add to your read-aloud bookshelf.

Book Charades

AGES: Beginning readers, older readers
MATERIALS: Slips of paper, pencils, bowl or hat

When it's just the family, no one is too shy to play Charades. Here are two versions that have players perform pantomimes about the books they're reading.

- *Character Charades.* Divide the players into two teams. Each team goes into a huddle and confers quietly to come up with the names of several familiar story characters (at least one name for each player on the other team). One team member writes the names on slips of paper, then drops the slips into a bowl or hat.

   The teams take turns sending one of their own players to draw a slip from the other team's pile. The player silently reads the name of the character written on the slip, then performs a pantomime to help that player's own team guess the name of the character on the slip.

   The pantomime may involve acting out a scene (Old Mother Hubbard looking for a bone), moving in a characteristic way (the Tin Man walking stiffly), or acting out part of the character's name (putting on a long stocking for Pippi Longstocking). Set a time limit for correctly guessing the character.

   Play for fun instead of points, and don't stop until everyone has had a turn performing a charade.

   Literary Charades. Play Charades using only literary titles—books, poems, plays, and stories. As before, the family plays on two teams, and each team writes a title on a slip of paper for every player on the opposite team.

   The players act out the words, parts of words, or word meanings in the title for their own team using the conventions of regular Charades to show syllables (number of fingers placed on the opposite wrist), number of words (hold up fingers), sounds like (cup hand over ear), and so on. Set a time limit for correctly guessing the title.

Like regular Charades, this game encourages players to pay particular attention to words and word parts.

The Trial of Goldilocks

AGES: Older readers

"This court will hear the case against Goldilocks, who is accused of breaking and entering the home of The Three Bears." And so begins the mock trial of the fairy-tale character who ate a little bear's porridge, broke his favorite chair, and fell asleep in his bed.

Family members assume the roles of lawyers, judge, defendant, witnesses, and jury (everybody plays a juror as well as another role) in an improvisational skit. The lawyers present their cases based on plot details and ask for character witnesses (perhaps Goldilocks's mother, who neglected to give her child breakfast, and who claims that the little girl is only naturally curious).

The court may also schedule the trial of the Big Bad Wolf, accused of two counts of attempted murder and harassment of Little Red Riding-Hood, and a less clear-cut case, that of Jack from Jack and the Beanstalk, accused of murder, grand larceny, and lying.

Does Goldilocks plead guilty on the lesser charge of trespassing? Does the wolf get the book thrown at him? Is Jack acquitted on all counts? Whatever the outcome of the trials, participants will all reach the same verdict about this group storytelling activity—it's imaginative and fun!

You're Invited: B.Y.O.B.

AGES: Beginning readers, older readers
MATERIALS: Construction paper, marking pens

B.Y.O.B. stands for Bring Your Own Book, the theme for a slumber party. Have your children invite their friends to read over as well as sleep over, and help them plan a few book-related party games.

Your children can make their own party invitations out of construction paper and marking pens. Perhaps they can make them look like book jackets, with *"Sleep-Over Party* by Donna Chang" on the front and "the story" (the necessary party information) inside: "Once upon a time, on the fourth of September, as the sun began to set and the old clock in the dining room struck six . . ."

When the guests arrive, you might volunteer to help them warm up by first reading aloud a book or short story. (A young crowd might enjoy *Ira Sleeps Over.*) Follow up with games like Book Charades, Initial Response, or Teakettle (all in this section). The children can make their own bookmarks or bookplates as party favors (see "Rainy Day Ideas") and make up a group story or poem (see The Story Unfolds in "Writing Worth Reading").

Toward the end of the evening, provide snacks while the children read their own books. If they're too giddy to read, move on to other activities.

At lights-out, give the children a flashlight to shine on their faces as they take turns telling spooky stories (see Ghost Stories in "Read It Aloud"). You may want to serve alphabet pancakes for breakfast the next morning (see Edible Alphabet in "Recipes for Reading").

Reading Olympics

AGES: Prereaders, beginning readers, older readers
MATERIALS: Posterboard (or sturdy paper), crayons or paints, scissors, hole puncher, spool of ribbon

In this activity, family members go for the gold (or whatever other color they choose) by entering books they have read in a frivolous series of Olympic reading events.

Together, brainstorm a list of book games and competitions. Keep contests of skill to a minimum, and make them fun. For most events, the books themselves should be the contenders. Here are some examples of records your readers can hope to hold:

- Most number of pages read in seven minutes
- Longest list of characters in a single story
- Fastest oral reading that the family can still understand
- Longest word on a page
- Longest sentence on a page
- Thickest book (not necessarily the one with the most pages)
- Book with the most pictures
- Book with the longest title (number of words)
- Oldest book (earliest copyright)

The family decides when to hold the events (plan an hour or two over several consecutive evenings) and sets some ground rules. For example: Books have to have been read within the last six weeks to qualify (or the next six weeks if you're planning ahead); readers can enter the same book in no more than two events (this encourages more reading); and two readers who enter the same book can tie for a medal.

The children can fashion their own medallions out of posterboard and color or paint them any three colors to correspond to the gold, silver, and bronze medals awarded to the top three contenders in the real Olympics. Help punch holes and string them on lengths of ribbon.

Make sure everybody in the family wins plenty of medals!

Writing Worth Reading

Reading and writing are like the proverbial chicken and egg: It's hard to say which one your children learn first. Most parents assume their children read before they write, but many times that is not the case. Before they learn to recognize and read words, your children may very well use letters as sound symbols to "write" words, putting *HS* under a drawing of a *house,* for instance.

Once children finally do read, writing is a natural spin-off activity that contributes significantly to their language development, and consequently their reading abilities. Having visited the realms of fairy tales, children are sometimes inspired to make up their own tales. Unwilling to give up a beloved character at the end of a book, they imagine and write their own sequels.

Encourage your children's writing by making writing as well as reading a family affair. Collaborate on stories, poems, diaries, and newsletters. Take the time to record and transcribe a young child's dictated stories. Write signs to hang around the house and notes to leave inside the children's pockets or lunch bags. Contribute your say to a wall full of family graffiti.

Taking Dictation

AGES: **Prereaders, beginning readers**
MATERIALS: **Paper, crayons, pen**

Children make up delightful stories long before they can write them. By playing stenographer, you can record those first stories and help your children make the association between spoken words and written words.

Give a small child paper and crayons. You may find that your child is more easily inspired if he or she first draws a picture, then proceeds to tell you about it. As you listen, write down your child's exact words on the bottom of the page. Read back the "story" immediately, pointing to the words as you say them. After rereading the phrases or sentences several times, point to key words one at a time and see if your child can tell you what each word is.

If the drawing technique works well, next ask your child to make successive drawings about a favorite subject, perhaps the park or playgroup. As your child discusses the pictures one by one, write a couple of his or her sentences at the bottom of each page. Staple the pages together to make a book.

Encourage your children to dictate longer and longer stories, with or without accompanying drawings. As they narrate, write out their sentences in full. Read back their stories just as they have told them.

Together, you can assemble the stories in homemade books illustrated by your young authors and "printed" by you. Include a cover with the title and name of the author/illustrator.

A real stenographer transcribes dictation on a typewriter. Your children might be thrilled to see their stories in this kind of print—almost like a real book. After taking down a child's dictation by hand (or you can use a cassette recorder), go to the typewriter or computer keyboard and type up the story. Let your child help you hunt and peck a few letters or key words. Afterward, the story can be illustrated directly on the typed or printed sheets or on separate sheets of paper before you staple the pages together.

Signs of Affection

AGES: **Prereaders, beginning readers, older readers**
MATERIALS: **Posterboard or paper, wide-line markers, masking tape**

When your children return home from sleepaway camp, a hospital stay, or their first overnight at Grandma's house, put up a big "Welcome Home!" sign to greet them as they walk through the door. This small but thoughtful gesture will let them know that they were missed.

Words of welcome and other words on display take on special meaning so that your children quickly learn to recognize and read them. You might hang a banner wishing your child a colossal Happy Birthday, or a big sheet on the front of the garage proclaiming to passers-by that "It's a Girl!"

You don't have to wait for a special occasion. The next time your children are "working" with their play tools, write out a quick sign for the bedroom door: Dan and Jacob's Fix-It Shop. Open Monday and Wednesday mornings (or whenever the workers say). Or after you finish touching up the moldings, print Wet Paint on a cardboard panel and prop it against the door.

Your children will probably follow suit. When you walk past the bedroom, a sign may warn Disaster Area: Enter at Your Own Risk, or say simply, Welcome to Kelly's Room. You can commission your sign makers to design a polite No Smoking sign, Garage Sale signs, or a sign marking the location of The Miller Family Reunion.

Graffiti Wall

AGES: Prereaders, beginning readers, older readers
MATERIALS: Butcher paper or brown wrapping paper, tape, pencils and markers, pencil holder

Can you spare some wall space in your home for hanging a large piece of butcher paper or wrapping paper? If so, you'll have a place where family members can express freely in words and drawings what's on their minds.

Place some pencils and markers in a holder near your graffiti wall. Encourage family members to write whenever they feel the urge in whatever form their ideas take—jokes, aphorisms, verse, exclamations, slogans, quotations, questions, a brief story. Prereaders can draw pictures.

A graffiti board makes writing spontaneous and fun, especially for children who are uncomfortable with the formal essays and compositions required of them at school.

Family Diary

AGES: Beginning readers, older readers
MATERIALS: Journal (a diary, blank book, notebook, or desk calendar)

Like your photo album, a family diary is a keepsake to which you and your children can turn time and time again to reminisce about your experiences together. Unlike a photo album, a family diary rekindles memories through words rather than pictures.

Keep a diary for the year, recording the events and activities in which your family participates. A different family member can write the actual entry each time, but everyone should agree on its substance.

Your family might want to make plans to stay up *next* New Year's Eve and take turns reading from the diary they begin *this* New Year's Eve.

Time Machine

AGES: Older readers
MATERIALS: Journal notebook, pen, brochures from historical site

A trip to a historical landmark, especially a landmark house, is the inspiration for a journal kept by your child in the present but set in the fictitious past.

Before suggesting this activity, you might want to introduce your child to journals like *The Diary of Anne Frank* and *Golden Days,* perhaps by taking turns reading aloud some of the entries.

When you visit a historical site, say a station on the Underground Railway or a pioneer house, have your child pretend to travel back in time in a time machine. Your child assumes the part of someone in the past, perhaps a child living in the house who witnesses the event or events relating to that historic period. Encourage your young historian to record several journal entries dating back to the historic period.

When your child has traveled forward again in time, ask to read the journal or have your time traveler read to you. If your child has enjoyed this activity, you might present him or her with a new journal (a blank book, small notebook, or diary) in which to write personal entries that are not necessarily for sharing.

Sequels

AGES: Beginning readers, older readers
MATERIALS: Paper and pens, stapler, fabric tape

Your children may find it difficult to put down a favorite book, having become quite attached to the characters. You can suggest sequels the author may have written, but if there are none, encourage your children to write one of their own. They may each want to write their own sequels, or collaborate on one sequel.

Besides giving your children a little more time with the characters, writing a sequel will reveal their insights into the characters and challenge them to imagine the plot's most logical extensions. Perhaps the children will want to skip a generation, imagining an aging character or the character's offspring. For example, although Charlotte dies at the end of *Charlotte's Web,* she leaves a sac of eggs. What becomes of them? Can the children imagine Fern as a grown woman?

Have the authors of the sequel read it aloud. Perhaps they would like to make a finished copy. Staple the pages together and cover the spine with cloth tape, then place the sequel alongside the original book on the shelf.

Book of Lists

AGES: Beginning readers, older readers
MATERIALS: Loose-leaf binder, notebook paper, pencils

Wallace family, move over! Now it's your family's turn to compile lists in whatever categories strike their fancy.

Brainstorm a list of lists. Subjects can range from the most mundane (Flavors of Soup) to the most extraordinary (Space Flights). You might want to encourage a few literary categories, like Names of Characters or Children's Authors, and some that reflect your children's special interests, like Kinds of Dinosaurs or Names of Cartoon Characters. If your library has *The Big Book of Kids' Lists*, this eclectic collection (which includes a list of ways to repel Dracula and Kermit's seven good things about being a frog) may inspire other ideas.

Have the children write the title of your book on the front of the binder: *Parsons Family Book of Lists*. Then label a separate page of notebook paper for each category. Now you can all start listing.

Keep your book of lists in a convenient place where everyone can get at it, including visitors. Encourage family members to add items to the lists and come up with new lists. Never remove a list; just when you think you have exhausted a category, another item will pop into your mind.

Younger children may prefer a simpler format using a scrapbook containing words and picture cutouts. You can help your youngsters cut out words and pictures from the newspaper and magazines, then paste them by categories—cars, foods, animals, toys—in the scrapbook. Preschoolers might like to practice writing some lists themselves. Help them spell words in such categories as Names of People I Know, Colors, Numbers, and Body Parts.

Stories in the Round

AGES: Beginning readers, older readers
MATERIALS: Lined paper, pencils

Writing, like reading, can seem like a sedentary activity to your children. A lively session of group writing around the family circle may very well change their mind.

Here are two group-writing formats; the first is strictly a story-building activity in which everybody is continually writing. The second lends itself to writing verse as well as short stories, but family members have to wait between turns. For this one, you might want to plan a concurrent activity—perhaps have a few word puzzles available.

• *Round-Robin Stories.* Everybody contributes to each other's stories as pages of writing are passed from one family member to the next in round-robin fashion.

Have family members arrange themselves comfortably around the room, then hand out sheets of lined paper and pencils. Set a timer for five to ten minutes. Everybody starts his or her own story, writing a paragraph or two in which the scene is set and one or more characters are introduced.

When the timer goes off, pencils go down and the writers pass their stories clockwise to the next family member. The timer is reset. This time, the writers first read the story in front of them, then begin writing where the last writer left off. You might want to establish a rule limiting the introduction of new characters to one or two each round.

Continue until the stories have gone completely around the circle once or twice. Stories can end before they reach the writers who started them, or you can make a final round in which the person who started each story writes the ending. Take turns reading the finished stories aloud.

• *The Story Unfolds.* The whole family can be co-authors of a story that literally unfolds, line by line. You'll need a pencil and a sheet of notebook paper.

To start, everybody agrees on a good first line for a story. This line should be suspenseful or emotive: "One day, I was walking down the street and I saw . . ." won't inspire the same kind of story as will "It was midnight on a moonless night, and I was alone in the cabin . . ."

When the group has settled on a first line, one person writes the line at the very top of the page, folds it over, then writes another line below the first. (A line can contain more or less than a complete sentence, but cannot take up more space than the single line on the page.) The paper is passed to the next person. That person reads the second line *silently,* folds it over, writes a third line, and passes the story on. The story passes around the circle of writers until you have reached the bottom of the page. Hand the paper to the youngest contributor, who unfolds it line by line and reads the story aloud.

More seasoned readers and writers may find it frustrating to have to limit themselves to single-line contributions. If that's the case, provide a wad of notebook paper and limit contributions in terms of time rather than space—two or three minutes at most to develop ideas and write. As before, each person reads the previous writing entry silently, folds it over, adds to the story, and passes on the paper. When you reach the end of the page, begin another and continue for a preset number of rounds. Take turns reading the finished product aloud.

Use a similar approach for writing a group poem in free verse. Participants decide on a theme and first line together. Then they take turns contributing a line of poetry, but they may read only the previous line for context.

Mythmaking

AGES: Beginning readers, older readers
MATERIALS: Paper, pencils

You'd probably be amazed to find out what your children once imagined caused things to happen or to work before they had the real answers. You may have propagated some of the myths yourself —the tooth fairy, Santa Claus, the man in the moon.

Now that you all "know better," you may find it fun to suspend disbelief once again and create your own modern myths. The whole family can participate in this writing activity, or you might suggest it to a young writer who needs some ideas.

To begin, everyone throws out questions that a naturally inquisitive person without answers would ask. It's best if you really don't know the answers. Why are snowflakes perfectly formed? Why don't people have purple eyes? How do spiders know how to spin webs? Who invented the pillow?

Decide on a question and have everybody write a paragraph or two furnishing an imaginatively plausible answer. When everybody's finished, read the answers aloud. If the participants are still game, try another question.

If your myths are worth saving, put them in a binder and set them alongside Bullfinch's or Edith Hamilton's on your bookshelf.

Family Newsletter

AGES: **Beginning readers, older readers**
MATERIALS: **Paper, pens, access to a photocopier, staples, postage stamps**

Do you wonder what Aunt Jill is up to in northern California, or how retirement is suiting your folks down in Florida? Today, *extended family* has as much to do with the distance between family members as the number of relatives you have. One way your children can reach out and touch everyone at the same time is to publish a family newsletter.

The job of editor can rotate among "staff" members. The editor organizes the upcoming issue, making sure that the reporters have contacted the family members assigned to them (by postcard or phone), that stories are written on time, that photos have captions, and so forth. The editor also decides which story will be the lead story, appearing directly below the newsletter's banner, which can be designed by one of the children.

Besides updating the extended family on each other's lives, the newsletter might include some of these regular features:

- A gossip column (who made the honor roll, who has a new boyfriend, who bought a new car)
- An article on family history or genealogy
- Family trivia quiz
- A guest writer's column (a different relative is asked to write a column each issue)
- A calendar of family events

If your own kids can't handle it all, they may want to involve their cousins, or you can give a hand.

When all the features have been written, typed up, or copied neatly, and pasted in position, photocopy the finished pages on letter-size paper. Your children can collate and staple the pages, letter-fold each newsletter, address and stamp it, and put it in the mail.

Relatives will look forward to receiving the family newsletter regularly, so decide with your children what will be a practical schedule for publishing—maybe two or four times a year. A more frequent schedule would require a strong commitment and lots of assistance.

If a newsletter is more than you and your children want to undertake, you might consider writing a periodic letter instead. The letter, addressed to everybody, describes your immediate family's activities, shares what news you have heard from the extended family, and sends your affections. Copies can be sent to the many extended family members who might not hear from you (or at least not in such depth) if you had to write individual letters to everybody.

Excuses, Excuses!

AGES: Beginning readers, older readers
MATERIALS: Paper and pencil

Although you will still have to sign their notes, your children may enjoy writing their own excuses for their occasional absences from school. They'll probably also enjoy making up incredible excuses to help pass the time during an illness that keeps them home from school.

Review the necessary letter-writing conventions with your child: date, greeting, indented paragraphs, closing. Discuss what the note should say before he or she begins writing to the teacher. You don't want the note to be overly graphic; for example: "I was throwing up and having diarrhea all day." Something more like "I had a stomach flu" is sufficient and leaves the rest to the teacher's imagination.

Writing pretend excuses can also be a creative pastime. Your children would probably love coming up with a dire disease or situation that would prevent them from attending school one day, or maybe ever again. "I was bitten by an alligator that crawled out of the drain in the bathtub while I was taking a bath" might be sufficient excuse for staying home a week while the victim receives anti-alligator shots.

Ask a child who stays home for a legitimate reason to draw a picture of the "bug" that he or she is suffering from. Expect some wild-looking germs to jump forth from your child's imagination. Perhaps one of these creatures can become the villain of an original science fiction story, like "The Streptococcus That Silenced Washington."

Picture Postcard File

AGES: Beginning readers, older readers
MATERIALS: Shoe box, oaktag or lightweight cardboard, scissors, pen

Picture postcards are fun to send and receive, and there's a lot of reading and writing involved in the process. You might suggest that your children take up postcard collecting as a hobby. They can sort and save their cards in a homemade file box.

Find a sturdy shoe box. Have your kids cut out subject dividers from oaktag or lightweight cardboard. The dividers should have tabs that rise above the postcards (a standard size card is 3½" × 5") and should be cut just a tad narrower than the width of the shoe box so that they slide easily forward and backward.

The children write subject labels on the dividers, then file the postcards behind them. Cards within a subject category can be filed alphabetically according to the name of the picture that appears on it or the name of the place from where it has been mailed.

Subject categories might include Personal Travels, People, Animals, Historical, Art, Humorous, Scenic, States, and Foreign Countries.

The description that appears on the back of the postcard (the side that bears the message) is informative reading and may inspire your children to do further research. Perhaps they can turn to their postcard file box when they want to find an interesting place or time for the setting of an original story.

Mailbag

In-House Mailbox
Love Notes
Thanks Sincerely
Personal Letterhead
Pen Pals
Pass It On
Free for the Writing
Dear Author
Get Well Soon!
Read and Sign Here, Please
Secret Codes
Join the Club
Welcome to Welcome

Everybody loves to receive mail, and there's plenty of reading and writing involved in the process. When your children discover that a quick postcard produces a science catalog, a replacement part for a damaged toy, or a picture postcard in return for the one sent to a friend, they may make letter writing a habit.

For some youngsters, mail is a hobby as well as a habit. Your children might enjoy collecting postmarks, stamps, even autographs through the mail. Having a pen pal in a far-off place is another incentive for your child to take out stationery and write a letter regularly.

Not all mail arrives in the mail carrier's bag. From time to time, drop notes in your children's lunch boxes or hide them under their pillows. Help them construct their own in-house mailboxes where they can regularly receive family messages or notes written in secret code.

In-House Mailbox

AGES: Prereaders, beginning readers
MATERIALS: Shoe box or other box with lid, utility knife or scissors, stickers or small picture cutouts, glue, file cards, play stamps (magazine stamps from sweepstakes mailings, Christmas or Easter Seals)

Remember the shoe-box mailbox you decorated every year for Valentine's Day in grade school? The same box, minus the doilies and hearts, can serve as a year-round mailbox for your children's "in-house" mail and messages.

Give each child a shoe box—maybe the one that contained their new shoes—and some decorating materials. Cut a slit in the lid and print your child's name and street address somewhere on the box if your child can't, but leave the decorating to him or her.

Break in the new mailbox by delivering some mail, and encourage others in the household to do the same. You might send a note commenting on the pretty mailbox, or forward a birthday invitation that came in the real mail. To send a pretend postcard, write a message on one side of a file card (a letter or picture will do for a nonreader), print your child's name and street address on the other side, and affix a make-believe stamp.

Keep the mail coming. Neither sleet nor hail nor busy day should prevent you or somebody else from writing a quick hello, mailing a reminder about library books, or delivering a favorite comic strip.

Your children will look forward to checking their own mailboxes every day, just as you do!

Love Notes

AGES: All ages
MATERIALS: Notepaper, adhesive-backed notes (optional), pencil

Brighten your children's day by letting them hear from you when they least expect it. Here are a few ideas for sending surreptitious notes your children will enjoy finding.

- *Lunch Mail.* Slip an occasional note inside your children's lunch bags or lunch boxes. Share your plans for the weekend, wish them luck on a test, or just let them know you're thinking about them. If you come across newspaper or magazine articles you think might interest them, slip those into the lunch boxes, too.
- *Pocket Surprise.* Tuck a note in your children's pants or coat pocket. When they put a hand inside, they'll discover your surprise— maybe a message in secret code, a joke or riddle, or a poem you wrote.
- *Post-It Notes.* Post affectionate reminders on the mirror, cereal box, refrigerator, door—anywhere your children are sure to come across them. Remind children about appointments, meeting places, your whereabouts, and other pieces of information. If you wish, you can buy small pads of adhesive-backed slips of paper that stick to most surfaces.

Thanks Sincerely

AGES: Prereaders, beginning readers
MATERIALS: Thank-you notes, construction paper and crayons (optional), stamped envelopes

Is your child old enough to have a birthday party? If so, your child is probably old enough to help you with an otherwise thankless task— composing thank-you notes. The person who gave the gift will probably be more touched by your child's personal note than your own thank-you.

You can involve young children in composing thank-you notes before they can do much, if any, of the actual writing. If you chat with a two- or three-year-old about a gift the child has received, you can usually manage to elicit some original remark to quote in a note to the giver: "You like the big noise the firetruck makes? Okay, I'll tell that to Grandma. I'll put your words right here, see?" Have your very young children sign these first notes with an X or their names, whichever they can manage. You might persuade them to enclose a drawing of themselves with their notes.

Gradually, your children can contribute more and more to your notes, at first dictating a sentence or two and eventually dictating the entire note, including conventions such as "Dear Grandma" and "Hugs and kisses, Larry." When they can write fairly legibly, hand them pencils and big pieces of paper and let them do the whole thing on their own.

Personal Letterhead

AGES: Beginning readers, older readers
MATERIALS: Stationery and envelopes, materials for decorating (see suggestions)

Encourage your children to get in the good habit of writing letters by having them design their very own stationery. Show them a few samples of personal and business letterheads, then give them materials to create their own.

Your children might like to choose from the following art techniques to decorate their writing paper and envelopes:

- Draw a fancy border on both the paper and envelope.
- Use rubber stamps to stamp a design or decorative border around a sheet and the envelope to match. (Children who have a collection of rubber stamps would enjoy *The Rubber Stamp Album*, featuring a wide variety of rubber stamp artists and their techniques.)
- Draw, paste, or rub fancy initials on the top of the paper.
- Draw a small frame and paste in a pressed flower.
- Use picture stickers to make a design, or letter stickers to make a monogram.
- Write names in calligraphy on the paper, and the address and return address in a matching hand on the envelope.

Your children can make lots of one-of-a-kind sheets of stationery whenever the occasion arises to write a letter. Or they can design a master sheet for you to photocopy or have printed at a quick-print shop. Matching envelopes can also be printed.

Pen Pals

AGES: **Beginning readers, older readers**
MATERIALS: **Stationery and envelopes, stamps**

Your children can nurture special friendships through the mail with a far-off relative, a friend who has moved, or a pen pal.

Ask relatives or family friends who live far away to be your children's pen pals. You want someone who will be a speedy and loyal correspondent: Grandparents and aunts and uncles are usually good about this; young cousins may have trouble sustaining their commitment.

If your children have friends who are moving from the area, they can agree to become pen pals. Your children may want to initiate their writing relationship by packing gift boxes with stationery, preaddressed envelopes (with your children's address), a pen, and a booklet of stamps, then giving the boxes to the friends as going-away presents.

Older children might enjoy having foreign friends they can write. Using age, sex, and interests as criteria, various organizations will match your children with youngsters overseas who also seek pen friends. Inquire at the post office or the library for current addresses and names of international pen-pal organizations.

Pass It On

AGES: Beginning readers, older readers
MATERIALS: Stationery or notebook paper, envelope, pen, stamp

A round-robin letter can keep extended family members or a group of old friends in touch with each other. Your children begin a letter, then pass it on. Eventually the letter comes back full circle so the children can catch up on the activities of those to whom they're close in affection rather than distance.

First your children establish a route, listing the names of the participants and their addresses on a route slip that will always accompany the round-robin letter. It may be helpful to include suggested dates for responding, such as "within two weeks."

The children compose a letter that begins "Dear Everybody," then mail the letter to the second person (or family) on the list. The second person reads the letter, adds a message, then sends the letter to the third person, and so on. The chain ends when the letter with all its appended messages arrives back at your home.

A fun variation is to write a round-robin story through the mail. Your children begin the tale, then leave off and send the story to the next person, who adds a few paragraphs and sends on the story. When the story reaches your children, they read it and reroute it so the other contributors can read the finished product, too.

Free for the Writing

AGES: Beginning readers, older readers
MATERIALS: Postcards, stationery and envelopes, pen, stamps

If your children are willing to pay for the postage and take the time to write out their requests, many businesses and agencies are happy to send them (at little or no charge) booklets, catalogs, educational kits, maps, product samples, money-off coupons, and the like.

If you are planning a trip or your children have to write social studies reports, the local Chambers of Commerce and state Tourist Bureaus will send guidebooks, maps, and other information about tourism and events. Find the correct zip code in the Post Office directory.

Call your children's attention to mail-order ads in the back of consumer, news, and trade magazines. Perhaps one of your children would like to write for information about a basketball camp, and another for a catalog of dollhouse miniatures. Sometimes writing a postcard is sufficient; other times, the reader is asked to enclose a SASE (self-addressed stamped envelope).

Your library probably has at least one or two "catalogs of catalogs" in its reference collection. Your children can scan these publications for the names and addresses of mail-order companies whose products meet the children's hobby needs or interests. Many catalogs are free; others cost a dollar or more, but the amount is usually deducted from your first purchase.

The library may also have books, such as *The Whole Kids' Catalog*, that list free materials children can send for. Cereal boxes and food packages are also good sources of send-away materials.

Dear Author

AGES: Prereaders, beginning readers, older readers
MATERIALS: Letter-writing paper and envelope, pen, postage stamp

Do your children have a favorite author or illustrator? Perhaps they'd like to write letters to express their admiration. Children's authors and illustrators enjoy hearing from their fans and often send a reply, which might be incentive enough for your youngsters to give it a try.

To get your child thinking about authors and illustrators in the first place, make it a point to read the biographical sketch on the inside back flap of the dust jacket before you close a book. Discuss where the person lives, whether he or she has children, and how the author's background may have contributed to the book. Compare the different books the writer has written or illustrated. Help your children understand that authors and illustrators are people, like themselves.

You might want to read aloud Beverly Cleary's *Dear Mr. Henshaw*. This story of a child who repeatedly writes to his favorite author may inspire your children to write letters without your prompting.

Before your children begin to write, review some letter-writing conventions with them. If they can't yet write, let them dictate letters to you. Perhaps they can also enclose their own drawings of favorite characters.

In their letters, your children might say that the author or illustrator is a favorite, comment on a book or illustration they particularly enjoyed, and tell how many of the person's books they have read. They might also want to inquire whether the author plans to visit a bookstore in your area for a book-signing event.

A librarian at your local library can direct your children to reference books that list mailing addresses for established writers and illustrators, which are usually care of the book publisher. They might also be interested in reading biographical sketches of their other favorite writers in reference volumes such as *The Junior Book of Authors* or *Teller of Tales: Children's Books and Their Authors*.

Get Well Soon!

AGES: Beginning readers, older readers
MATERIALS: Stationery, envelope, pen, postage stamp

Are there young sports fans in your house? If so, comb the sports page and direct your children's attention to an article about a player injured in a game. Suggest that they write a letter or make a get-well card expressing regret about the injury and hope that the player will recover quickly and return to the game.

Send the message directly to the hospital or care of the player's team. A librarian can lead you and your kids to a reference book for the address you are seeking. Encourage your children to keep up on the player's progress by reading subsequent articles in the sports section of the newspaper or in sports magazines.

Read and Sign Here, Please

AGES: Beginning readers, older readers
MATERIALS: Stationery, envelopes, postcards, pen, stamps

Do you and your kids stake out the back doors at stadiums and theaters to get the autographs of your favorite superstars? Do you elbow your way through crowded bookstores to get an author on promotional tour to sign his or her book?

There's another way your family can beef up an autograph collection. Serious *philographers,* or signature collectors, write letters to the people they admire. More often than not, they receive a reply bearing the person's much-prized signature.

You'll need to supply the stationery, stamps, and some initial guidance if your children express an interest in this hobby. First, suggest that they choose a category of famous people whose signatures they want to collect—baseball players, authors, child performers, astronauts, inventors. List all the people they can think of in that category. Then go to the local library and try to track down their addresses in the latest editions of *Who's Who in America* or *Current Biography.*

Your children's letter to a celebrity should be very personal. A compliment about his performance in a recent TV episode or a question about her preparation for a space flight may generate a letter in reply. Some movie and television performers may simply send an autographed studio photo. If your children enclose a comic strip, article, or photo clipped from the newspaper, a cartoonist or newsworthy individual may be willing to return the item signed.

Serious enthusiasts can pick up many other autograph leads—addresses, tips for collecting, free ads for those interested in trading—by joining the Universal Autograph Collectors Club (P.O. Box 467, Rockville Center, N.Y. 11571).

Aside from the pleasure they get out of their hobby, your children can consider themselves in worthy company. Cicero, Queen Victoria, and Presidents Franklin D. Roosevelt and John F. Kennedy—whose own signatures are greatly valued—were in their own time serious philographers.

Secret Codes

AGES: Beginning readers, older readers

If your children don't enjoy letter writing, suggest espionage. Your young James Bonds might prefer to send and receive their messages in secret code.

Some families have secret languages, like Pig Latin, and secret writing codes they use to communicate with each other, just for fun. There are numerous books on codes and ciphers, written for children. Your children can check one or two out of the library and read to find a suitable code for your family.

Besides showing how to encode and decode messages, most code books include historical anecdotes about the codes, which make for fascinating reading. From code books, your youngsters may go on to spy novels and mysteries for more cryptographic adventures. For example, in the story "The Adventure of the Dancing Men," Sherlock Holmes deciphers a code in which little figures of dancing men represent letters in the secret communications of the underworld.

Join the Club

AGES: Beginning readers, older readers
MATERIALS: Postcards, pencils

Do your children collect teddy bears, fossils, famous signatures, or old postcards? There are clubs and organizations to which your children can write for membership or information about these and scores of other hobbies and interests.

Library books on hobbies and crafts often provide the names and addresses of related clubs and organizations in a resource section or appendix. Your library may also have books like *Clubs for Kids* or *The Whole Kids Catalog*, which have lots of club information for children.

If your children are interested in joining a club, suggest that the best way to go about it is to send a postcard to the club headquarters inquiring about the cost of membership and what you get if you join. Many clubs issue membership cards, periodic newsletters your children can look forward to reading, and, occasionally, free items to add to a collection.

Your children can pursue their more general interests as well by joining clubs like the Boy or Girl Scouts or the 4-H Club. These organizations also provide club reading materials, such as handbooks and newsletters.

Book clubs for children vary in cost and benefits offered. You may wish to write to several (see "Further Resources for Parents and Children"). Most clubs offer young readers a chance to choose from a variety of books, and many children are delighted to receive books through the mail.

Welcome to Welcome

AGES: Beginning readers, older readers
MATERIALS: Paper, envelopes, stamps, map of the United States, scissors, glue

A tour of Maryland might bring you through towns with names like Accident, Boring, Savage, Welcome, and Detour. In New Mexico, you'll find—believe it or not—the town of Truth or Consequences! But you don't have to leave home to collect souvenirs from places with interesting names. Local postmasters throughout the country (especially the one in Happy, Kentucky) will be happy to return your children's self-addressed stamped envelope (SASE) with their post-marks.

You'll have to show your children how to read the Zip Code directory at the Post Office to find interesting or appealing names. You might want to limit your list to a category, such as flower names, animal names, or people names.

Send a SASE along with a brief written request to the postmaster in each town on your list. Slip an index card or piece of thin cardboard inside the envelope so that the cancellation and postmark will be stamped clearly. The postmaster will mail your envelope to you.

Collecting postmarks can also be a fun way to learn a little geography. Tack up a large map of the United States on which your children can pinpoint the cities and larger towns for which you have saved postmarks from the letters and promotional mail sent to your home. Help paste the postmarks along the outside margins of the map and draw lines to the corresponding place names.

Books to Grow On

Visit your local library or bookstore and you will find shelves full of books for you and your children to browse through and enjoy. The range of titles, authors, and subjects is enormous. In fact, more than three thousand new children's books are published every year in the United States.

Of the thousands of books available, which ones do children really like? And which ones do parents, teachers, and librarians recommend?

Reading Is Fundamental posed those questions in a survey sent to a representative committee of eighty-six parents, teachers, librarians, and educators who direct RIF programs in their communities. We asked committee members to draw upon their experience with children and their knowledge of children's books to help us identify books that have won the interest and affection of children and that have inspired children to read. A list of committee members appears in the Acknowledgments section.

We compiled the final list of books from those most often recommended by the committee, with the help of Margaret Coughlan, Children's Literature Center, Library of Congress, and Maria Salvadore, coordinator of children's service at the Washington, D.C., Public Library.

Each of the books listed is followed by a brief annotation to whet your appetite—and your children's. The annotations have been specially developed for the guide by E. A. Hass, children's author and creator of BOOKBRAIN, the computer database of children's books published by The Oryx Press. She is also Dr. Rita Book on American Public Radio's "Paging Dr. Book" program.

Please note that in the listings "H" designates hardcover editions of books; "P" paperback editions.

USING THE BOOK LIST

The books recommended by the book selection committee are grouped into four overlapping age ranges, which we suggest that you use as guidelines. Propelled by their interests and curiosity, children often enjoy reading books that are considered too "hard" or too "easy." When in doubt about a book, take your cue from your children. Most children freely express their likes and dislikes, and you will soon discover whether a certain book is a good choice.

The following list is by no means an all-inclusive one, but merely a guide to the hundreds, even thousands, more that await your children. Your local children's librarian, bookseller, and your children's teachers can help point you toward other books that your youngsters will take to heart. For a list of national organizations that make book lists available, see "Further Resources for Parents and Children."

INFANCY TO THREE

Ahlberg, Janet and Allan. *The Baby's Catalogue.* [H] Atlantic Monthly, 1983.

Did you know that everything begins and ends with babies? At least everything in this book does. It presents all of the new and exciting things in a baby's world through soft, easy-to-look-at watercolor drawings.

Also recommended: *Peek-a-Boo.*

Asch, Frank. *Just Like Daddy.* [H] Prentice-Hall, 1981. [P] Prentice-Hall/Treehouse, 1984.

Little Bear wants to do everything just like Daddy. He tries very hard to walk like him, dress like him, be like him in every way. That is, until they go fishing . . .

Bang, Molly. *Ten, Nine, Eight.* [H] Greenwillow, 1983. [P] Penguin, 1985.

The "four sleepy eyes which open and close" belong to a little girl and her father, as he puts her to sleep. Bright, unusually colored, full-page pictures illustrate every other page of this charmingly tender bedtime counting story.

Brown, Margaret Wise, pictures by Clement Hurd. *Goodnight, Moon.* [H] Harper Junior, 1947. [P] Harper/Trophy, 1977.

Little rabbit is coaxed into sleep as Mother sits quietly, the room grows darker, and the shadows fade away. Alternate full-color and black-and-white illustrations fill this classic bedtime story, ending with "goodnight noises everywhere."

Burningham, John. *The Baby*. [H] Crowell Junior, 1975.

The typical love-jealousy relationship between a little boy and "the baby" is realistically portrayed in gentle, childlike drawings and a simple, understated text.

Also recommended: *The Blanket; John Burningham's ABC.*

Chorao, Kay. *The Baby's Lap Book*. [H] E. P. Dutton, 1977.

Delightfully intricate, soft-pencil illustrations of engaging nursery rhyme characters rollick, roll, and cuddle through the pastel-bordered pages of this read-aloud book.

Also recommended: *The Baby's Bedtime Book.*

Crews, Donald. *Freight Train*. [H] Greenwillow, 1983. [P] Penguin/Puffin, 1985.

Choo! Choo! Chug-a-lug! Chug-a-lug! Whoo! Whoo! You can almost hear the freight train barreling down the track in this primary-colored, geometrically designed book ideal for young children. City, country, tunnels, and bridges are all represented in simple, but exciting shapes.

Dunn, Judy, photographs by Phoebe Dunn. *The Little Duck*. [P] Random House/Books for Young Readers, 1976.

So adorable and fluffy is the duck in this story, you almost feel that you can touch him. Children get the chance to follow Henry the Duck from egg to adulthood through a series of clear, full-color photographs and simple text.

Also recommended: *The Little Kitten; The Little Lamb; The Little Rabbit.*

Eastman, P. D., translated by Carlos Rivera and P. D. Eastman. *Are You My Mother?* [H] Random House/Beginner, 1967.

What a silly story! Parents and children will laugh out loud at the antics of a funny-looking baby bird in search of his mother who was out looking for his first meal when he hatched ahead of schedule. Tirelessly, he asks all of the animals, a tractor, and an airplane the big question: "Are you my mother?"

Flack, Marjorie. *Ask Mister Bear*. [H] Macmillan, 1932. [P] Macmillan, 1932.

What should he get his mother for her birthday? It has to be just right. So the little boy asks each animal—including Mister Bear—

for advice and gets some unusual, not to mention amusing, suggestions.

Also recommended: *Angus and the Ducks*.

Galdone, Paul. *The Gingerbread Boy*. [H] Houghton Mifflin/Clarion, 1975. [P] Houghton Mifflin/Clarion, 1983.

And you were just beginning to get the story of "how babies are born" across to your preschooler. Forget it! This book explains how a little old man and woman were lonely and so decided to bake a gingerbread son. Unfortunately, he's naughty and runs away so fast that no one—including the farmers and the horse and the cow and the fox—seems to be able to catch him.

Gillham, Bill, photographs by Sam Grainger. *The First Words Picture Book*. [H] Coward, 1982. [P] Putnam, 1982.

Vivid photographs of preschoolers doing what preschoolers do will delight young children. Fifteen of the words most commonly used at that age are pictured on the left-hand page and included in an action scene on the right side.

Ginsburg, Mirra, pictures by Byron Barton. *Good Morning, Chick*. [H] Greenwillow, 1980.

"Tap-tap and crack!" What an exciting world this colorful farm is to a newly hatched chick! Everything he does, everyone he meets is an adventure for both the chick and the preschool reader.

Hart, Jane (editor), pictures by Anita Lobel. *Singing Bee! A Collection of Favorite Children's Songs*. [H] Lothrop, 1982.

Piano accompaniment, guitar chords, and words are given for 125 singing games, Mother Goose rhymes, folk and camp songs, holiday songs, and lullabies in this sumptuous collection. Many old friends and some new tunes are brought alive by the exuberant illustrations in full color and black and white.

Hill, Eric. *Where's Spot?* [H] Putnam, 1980.

His mother Sally doesn't know! She looks behind every colorful, lift-up, peekaboo flap, finding every kind of animal except the mischievous Spot. Children will love participating in the search, finding lots of animals they know, plenty of surprises, and maybe even Spot!

Hoban, Tana. *Push, Pull, Empty, Full*. [H] Macmillan, 1972.

The way you look at these unusual photographs is limited only by your imagination. Everyday objects—a jar or a wagon—are seen in a new perspective through the camera lens, becoming larger than life.

Also recommended: *Round & Round & Round.*

Hughes, Shirley. *Alfie's Feet.* [H] Lothrop, 1983.

His brand-new, shiny yellow boots are the best! Alfie is so proud! But wait! Something is wrong. Why do his feet feel so . . . funny?

Also recommended: others in the *Alfie* series.

Hutchins, Pat. *Good-Night Owl.* [H] Macmillan, 1972.

Owl just can't get to sleep. He can't help it if he sleeps during the day when the woodpecker and the bee and the cuckoo are wide awake. Finally it gets dark. Everyone goes to sleep. Everyone except Owl, that is!

Isadora, Rachel. *I See.* [H] Greenwillow, 1985.

For the youngest child, this book offers full-color, easily identifiable pictures of everyday objects and simple words. All elements are carefully selected to relate to a toddler's environment.

Also recommended: *I Hear.*

Jonas, Ann. *When You Were a Baby.* [H] Greenwillow, 1982. [P] Penguin, 1986.

There were so many things you couldn't do when you were a baby —eat by yourself, roll a ball, play with your toys. Aren't you glad you're grown up? This book gets the message across effectively, and may be particularly helpful in dealing with jealousy of a new baby.

Also recommended: *Holes and Peeks.*

Kalan, Robert, pictures by Byron Barton. *Jump, Frog, Jump.* [H] Greenwillow, 1981.

Quick frog! That lily pad is sinking! You'll get stuck in the mud! Caught in the net! "Jump, frog, jump!" repeats the chorus that preschoolers will love to shout out and giggle over.

Kunhardt, Dorothy. *Pat the Bunny.* [H] Western/Golden, 1942.

There is plenty to do in this soothing, old-fashioned classic. You can pat the bunny, play peekaboo, look in the mirror, feel Daddy's beard, and oh, do lots of other things along with Judy and Paul and this book.

Lowrey, Janette Sebring, illustrated by Gustaf Tenggren. *The Poky Little Puppy.* [H] Western/Golden, 1986.

There never was a nosier, pokier little puppy. He just has to check out everything in the garden and on the hill. But one night he comes home late and finds no dessert waiting for him.

Mack, Stanley. *Ten Bears in My Bed.* [H] Pantheon, 1974.

At first, there are ten bears in my bed. Then there are nine, then eight, then seven . . . until finally . . . there's just me. So goes the story of this charming backward counting book.

Martin, Bill, Jr., pictures by Eric Carle. *Brown Bear, Brown Bear, What Do You See?* [H] Holt, Rinehart & Winston, 1983.

Wonderfully bold collage illustration and simple sing-song verses make this book fly by so fast that toddlers will ask for it again and again. Redbird, Purple Cat, Black Sheep, and Gold Fish are only a few of the colorful characters that fill its frolicsome pages.

Miller, Jane. *Farm Counting Book.* [H] Prentice-Hall, 1983.

First we count the number of pigs, ducks, horses, and cows. Then there are delightful quizzes—"Can you count . . . ? How many . . . ?"—all illustrated with authentic, full-color photographs.

Mother Goose (Classic Voland Edition), edited by Eulalie O. Grover, illustrated by Frederick Richardson. [H] Random House, 1915.

Dozens of marvelous Mother Goose rhymes, stories, and songs are included in this classic collection, illustrated in soothing, old-fashioned colors featuring the familiar characters.

Tall Book of Mother Goose, illustrated by Feador Rojankovsky. [H] Harper Junior, 1942.

The novel format, old-fashioned illustrations, and familiar rhymes and songs all work together in this unusual book to read and sing together.

Tomie dePaola's Mother Goose, illustrated by Tomie dePaola. [H] Putnam, 1985.

More than two hundred well-known nursery rhymes are presented in this beautifully illustrated anthology featuring the familiar dePaola colors and characters.

Omerod, Jan. *Messy Baby.* [H] Lothrop, 1985.

Clothes on the floor! Books and toys all over the room! What a messy baby! What a patient daddy!

Oxenbury, Helen. *Beach Day.* [H] Dial Books for Young Readers, 1982.

The hot sun, the warm sand, the rushing waves, and the bright pail and shovel are all colorfully depicted in this nicely sized board book.

Also recommended: *Dressing; Shopping Trip.*

Rice, Eve. *Sam Who Never Forgets.* [H] Greenwillow, 1977. [P] Penguin/Puffin, 1980.

Sam is the most wonderful zookeeper! Portrayed in primary pastel colors, he goes from cage to cage every day, feeding the giraffe and the crocodile and the zebra and . . . But wait! Has Sam forgotten to feed the elephant?

Rockwell, Anne. *Planes.* [H] E. P. Dutton, 1985.

What toddler isn't mesmerized by the bigness and loudness of airplanes? The simple text and carefully defined illustrations show many different kinds of aircraft on the ground and in the air.

Rockwell, Harlow. *My Kitchen.* [H] Greenwillow, 1980.

Even the smallest detail of the kitchen is described *by* the smallest person *to* the smallest person through simple words and easy-to-follow pictures.

Scarry, Richard. *The Egg in the Hole Book.* [H] Western/Golden, 1964.

Nenny Hen has lost her egg! Only the reader can see—and touch it—as she runs frantically from Mr. Goat to Mrs. Goose trying to track it down. The cardboard pages, spiral binding, and hole-in-the-middle-to-put-your-finger-through format of this book make it special fun for young children.

Seuss, Dr. *The Foot Book.* [H] Random House/Books for Young Readers, 1968.

Look at all those feet! Left foot, right foot, high foot, low foot! Fuzzy fur feet, over-a-chair feet! In this rollicking rhyming book, "Oh how many feet you meet!"

Tafuri, Nancy. *Early Morning in the Barn.* [H] Greenwillow, 1983.

Oink, moo, cock-a-doodle-doo! Animal sounds are the only words you'll find in this colorful picture book about the chickens, geese, pigs, cows, and others who wake up on the farm.

Wadsworth, Olive A., pictures by Ezra Jack Keats. *Over in the Meadow.* [P] Scholastic/Blue Ribbon, 1985.

Called a "counting-out rhyme," this book introduces the reader to all kinds of wonderful animal families through intricate, tapestry-like illustrations: owls who tu-whoo; lizards who bask; beavers who beave.

Watanabe, Shigeo, pictures by Yasuo Ohtomo. *How Do I Put It On?* [H] Putnam/Philomel, 1980. [P] Putnam/Philomel, 1984.

"I can get dressed all by myself," says the young bear. But there is a right way—and many wrong ways—to get dressed, as this bear soon finds out.

Also recommended: *Where's My Daddy?*

Wells, Rosemary. *Max's First Word.* [H] Dial Books for Young Readers, 1979.

Max knows just one word—*Bang.* Big sister Ruby Rabbit tries to teach Max more words: *ball, cup, chair.* But the only response she gets: " 'Bang,' said Max." Until . . . Find out what Max finally says in this brightly colored, well-constructed board book with safe, rounded corners.

Also recommended: *Max's Toys: A Counting Book.*

Wildsmith, Brian. *Brian Wildsmith's ABC.* [H] Watts, 1962.

Spectacular, vividly colored drawings splash across the pages of this simple, elegant alphabet book whose outstanding illustrations from apple to zebra will be appreciated by parent and preschooler alike. Words are spelled in both upper- and lower-case, an unusual feature of this unusual book.

Wolde, Gunilla. *This Is Betsy.* [H] Random House, 1975.

The pages of this child-sized, comfortable, and comforting book follow young Betsy through her day, from washing and dressing herself in the morning to falling asleep at night.

THREE TO FIVE

Ahlberg, Janet and Allan. *Each Peach Pear Plum: An I-Spy Story.* [H] Viking, 1979. [P] Scholastic/Blue Ribbon, 1985.

This inventive book with full-color illustrations invites young children to find the hidden characters in each picture, who gather at the end for a final group shot.

Alexander, Martha G. *Bobo's Dream.* [H] Dial Books for Young Readers, 1970. [P] Dial Books for Young Readers, 1978.

Bobo is a little dachshund who dreams of being a hero in this adorable, miniature wordless book. And as it turns out, he gets his wish. Almost . . .

Anno, Mitsumassa. *Anno's Counting Book.* [H] Crowell Junior, 1977.

The fundamentals of counting are presented to the preschooler in dozens of ways through each intricate double-page spread. The same rural scenes are viewed during different hours of the day and months of the year, giving the child plenty of experience counting the number of flowers, trees, animals, and people from one to twelve.

Balian, Lorna. *Humbug Witch.* [H] Abingdon, 1965.

Once upon a time "there was this witch who was very witchy

[looking]," in a funny sort of way. But everything witchy that she tried to do backfired. So one day, this adorable witch in this charming book did a very surprising thing . . .

Also recommended: *The Aminal.*

Barton, Byron. *Airport.* [H] Crowell Junior, 1982.

Zoom! Vroom! Kaboom! All the sights and sounds of a busy airport are presented in simple, bold, primary colors.

Bemelmans, Ludwig. *Madeline.* [H] Viking, 1939. [P] Penguin/Puffin, 1977.

Madeline is one of twelve little girls "all in a row," who follow Madame quietly and obediently. At least eleven of them do. But one night, Madeline wakes up with a terrible stomachache . . .

Berenstain, Stan and Jan. *Inside, Outside, Upside Down.* [H] Random House/Books for Young Readers, 1968.

This amusing, colorful book featuring the Berenstain Bears illustrates simple concepts through a lively story.

Also recommended: *The Berenstain Bears; The Big Honey Hunt.*

Bridwell, Norman. *Clifford, the Big Red Dog.* [P] Scholastic, 1985.

Although he starts out small and red, Clifford soon becomes too big and red for his own good. The classic slapstick will keep young children laughing.

Bright, Robert. *Georgie.* [H] Doubleday, 1959.

Georgie is a ghost. But not your usual kind of ghost. Georgie is kind of shy, very friendly, and lives in Mr. and Mrs. McGovern's attic, appearing only when there's a good deed to be done.

Brown, Margaret Wise, pictures by Clement Hurd. *The Runaway Bunny.* [H] Harper Junior, 1972. [P] Harper/Trophy, 1977.

Hard as he tries to run away, Little Bunny's mother will run after him, because he is her "little bunny." If he becomes a sailboat, she will be the wind and blow him wherever he wants to go; if he becomes a trout, she will be the fisherman; and when he finally decides to stay where he is and be her "little bunny," she lovingly offers him a carrot!

Burningham, John. *Mr. Gumpy's Outing.* [H] Holt, Rinehart & Winston, 1971. [P] Penguin/Puffin, 1984.

Mr. G. is a real sport, taking all of his animals for a ride on the river. The simple, award-winning story is told in soothing pastel drawings with a comical twist.

Also recommended: *Mr. Gumpy's Motor Car.*

Burton, Virginia Lee. *Mike Mulligan and His Steam Shovel.* [H] Houghton Mifflin, 1939. [P] Houghton Mifflin, 1977.

People come from Bangerville and Bopperville, Kipperville and Kopperville to see Mike Mulligan and his steam shovel in Popperville! Young children will too, to watch the team in action as they explain in detail their many exciting jobs.

Also recommended: *Katy and the Big Snow; The Little House.*

Carle, Eric. *The Very Hungry Caterpillar.* [H] Putnam/Philomel, 1981.

My goodness, that caterpillar is hungry! And he can count, too! He eats his way through leaves and fruits and just about anything in his path, on each page leaving convenient little holes just the right size for a preschooler's eyes to look through or fingers to poke.

Also recommended: *Do You Want to Be My Friend?*

Cohen, Miriam, pictures by Lillian Hoban. *Will I Have a Friend?* [H] Macmillan, 1967. [P] Macmillan/Collier, 1971.

Going to school for the very first time is frightening for Jim. Young children will empathize with his concern over not knowing who his friend will be in this unintimidating book about a touchy subject.

Also recommended: *First Grade Takes a Test.*

Crews, Donald. *Truck.* [H] Greenwillow, 1980. [P] Penguin/Puffin, 1985.

One Way! Stop! Enter! Exit! Vivid highway signs in easy-to-read block letters, plus roads, tunnels, bridges, twists, and turns are encountered by a truck as it travels through fog and rain and dark of night on its appointed rounds.

de Brunhoff, Jean. *The Story of Babar.* [H] Random House/Books for Young Readers, 1937.

Babar the Elephant finds his way to Paris where he buys himself a stunning green suit, a handsome derby hat, and shoes with spats. Never has there been a more fashionable elephant! Yet in spite of his new clothes and new friends, Babar longs for home and heads back to live with his family happily ever after in Africa.

dePaola, Tomie. *Charlie Needs a Cloak.* [H] Prentice-Hall, 1974. [P] Prentice-Hall/Treehouse, 1982.

"Poor Charlie!" He must have a cloak to keep himself warm in winter. Only one thing to do—make one. And so he does in this interesting, entertaining, and educational story about how the cloak is made, from sheep to sewing.

Also recommended: *Pancakes for Breakfast*.

Duke, Kate. *Guinea Pigs Far and Near*. [H] E. P. Dutton, 1984.

Never has there been a bunch of sillier, funnier guinea pigs with so many problems that have so much fun. Children will delight in being taught concepts such as *above* and *below* and *inside out* by these natural clowns.

Emberley, Ed. *A Birthday Wish*. [H] Little, Brown, 1977.

Featuring wordplay without words, the colorful, hilarious, subtly connected comic episodes in this book remind us all that birthday wishes can come true.

Flack, Marjorie, illustrated by Kurt Weise. *The Story About Ping*. [H] Viking, 1933. [P] Penguin/Puffin, 1977.

All the ducks must return to the boat by sundown. The last to arrive gets a slap on the back—and it looks as if Ping will be the last one. Young children will share his adventures when he decides to stay out for the night, in this beloved old Chinese tale.

Freeman, Don. *Corduroy*. [H] Viking, 1968. [P] Penguin/Puffin, 1976.

Corduroy Bear, who lives in a department store, has always wanted a friend. In this warm, tender story, he gets one.

Also recommended: *Dandelion; Mop Top; A Pocket for Corduroy*.

Gàg, Wanda. *Millions of Cats*. [H] Coward, 1977. [P] Putnam/Coward, 1977.

Old-fashioned and hand-lettered, this amusing book tells the story of an old man who goes out to find one cat and returns with a million of them.

Also recommended: *The ABC Bunny*.

Galdone, Paul. *The Little Red Hen*. [H] Houghton Mifflin/Clarion, 1973. [P] Houghton Mifflin/Clarion, 1985.

No one will help Little Red Hen plant the wheat or take care of it or harvest it or bring it to the mill to be ground into flour or make bread with the flour. But just wait until it's time to eat it!

Also recommended: *The Three Bears; The Three Little Pigs*.

Goodall, John S. *The Adventures of Paddy Pork*. [H] Harcourt, 1968.

Without writing a word, this book proves that there's no place like home. Little Pig decides to leave Mom and join the circus. But he changes his mind quickly when he gets a true taste of life under the big top.

Also recommended: *Paddy Finds a Job.*

Heyward, DuBose, pictures by Marjorie Flack. *The Country Bunny and the Little Gold Shoes.* [H] Houghton Mifflin, 1939. [P] Houghton Mifflin/Sandpiper, 1974.

Did you know that there's not just one Easter bunny but five in all? And tiny Mrs. Cottontail, mother of twenty-one and an enterprising housekeeper, plans to be one of them.

Hoban, Tana. *Count and See.* [H] Macmillan, 1972. [P] Macmillan, 1972.

Numbers, numbers everywhere. From 1 to 15, then 20, 30, 40, 50, and 100, numbers are spectacularly illustrated in graphic, full-page, black-and-white photographs of the most unexpected models, from pigeons to bottlecaps to fish on ice to peas in pods. Opposite each photograph, the number is given, in numeral, in word, and in concept dot form.

Hughes, Shirley. *David and Dog.* [P] Prentice-Hall/Treehouse, 1981.

David and his stuffed pet, Dog, are inseparable. Until somehow Dog ends up on a bazaar table. And a little girl buys him. Preschoolers will anxiously await the suspenseful outcome in this terrific story of good friends—and sisters.

Hutchins, Pat. *Rosie's Walk.* [H] Macmillan, 1968. [P] Macmillan/Collier, 1971.

When Rosie the Hen goes out for a walk, the fox goes with her. Poor Fox! Rosie walks around the pond, but Fox falls in. Rosie walks by the sack of flour, but the sack falls on Fox. Rosie strolls by the beehive . . .

Also recommended: *Happy Birthday, Sam.*

Keats, Ezra Jack. *The Snowy Day.* [H] Viking, 1962.

Collage illustrations, made out of many types and textures of paper and fabric, shine in this award-winning book about a little boy and the fun he has in the snow.

Also recommended: *Whistle for Willie; Peter's Chair; Over in the Meadow.*

Kraus, Robert, pictures by Jose Aruego. *Leo the Late Bloomer.* [H] Crowell, 1971.

Leo can't do anything right—read, write, talk, or even eat right. Because Leo is a late bloomer. In fact, he turns out to be a late, late, late bloomer in this valuable story for frustrated children— and impatient parents.

Also recommended: *Whose Mouse Are You?*

Krauss, Ruth, pictures by Crockett Johnson. *The Carrot Seed.* [H] Harper Junior, 1945.

A wonderfully old, comforting picture book about a little boy who knows that the seed he planted will come up even though everyone else says it won't. This book teaches valuable lessons in a relaxed, nonthreatening way.

Lewin, Hugh, illustrated by Lisa Kopper. *Jafta.* [H] Carolrhoda, 1981.

An exuberant African child, Jafta describes his emotions in terms of animals: Jafta can "grumble like a warthog" and "skip like a spider." Sepia-tone drawings illustrate emotions.

Also recommended: others in *Jafta* series.

Lionni, Leo. *Swimmy.* [H] Pantheon, 1963.

All the other fish are red. Swimmy is black. But when the red fish are eaten by a hungry tuna, Swimmy saves the day by figuring out a clever way to save the rest of the fish in this magnificently illustrated, full-color story with a happy ending.

Also recommended: *Inch by Inch; Frederick.*

Lobel, Arnold. *Frog and Toad Are Friends.* [H] Harper Junior, 1970. [P] Harper/Trophy, 1979.

Frog and Toad are absolutely the best of friends, as preschoolers can see in these five beautifully illustrated stories about friendship, loyalty, and just having fun.

Also recommended: *Fables; Mouse Soup; Owl at Home.*

McCloskey, Robert. *Make Way for Ducklings.* [H] Viking, 1941. [P] Penguin/Puffin, 1976.

Jack, Kack, Lack, Mack, Nack, Quack, Pack, and Quack are Mr. and Mrs. Mallard's children. Fortunately, when the family in this ageless winner decides to go for a walk through downtown Boston, their friend Michael and other policemen are there to clear a path.

Also recommended: *Blueberries for Sal.*

McGovern, Ann, illustrated by Simms Taback. *Too Much Noise.* [H] Houghton Mifflin, 1967.

Amazing how you never appreciate something until it's gone. That's what happens to Peter, who lived in an old house that he thought was noisy—until the cow and the donkey and the sheep and the hen . . .

Also recommended: *Stone Soup.*

McPhail, David M. *The Bear's Toothache.* [H] Atlantic Monthly, 1972.
[P] Penguin/Puffin, 1978.

An irresistible fantasy about a little boy who dreams that a lovable, patient bear with a toothache comes to him for help. The ways that the little boy tries to help his friend are both ingenious and comical.

Mayer, Mercer. *Just for You.* [P] Western/Golden, 1975.

The almost fluorescently bright illustrations and simple words tell the story of how cuddly "little monster" tried soooooo hard all day to do things for his mother, but circumstances beyond his control kept getting in the way!

Also recommended: *A Boy, a Dog, and a Frog; There's a Nightmare in My Closet.*

Minarik, Else Holmelund, pictures by Maurice Sendak. *Little Bear.* [H] Harper Junior, 1957. [P] Harper/Trophy, 1978.

Little Bear is curious, adventurous, funny, and huggable. And fortunately for Little Bear, he has one of the most understanding mothers in all of children's literature, in these delightful easy-to-read stories.

Moore, Clement Clarke, illustrated by Anita Lobel. *The Night Before Christmas.* [H] Knopf, 1984.

Moore, Clement Clarke, illustrated by James Marshall. *The Night Before Christmas.* [H] Scholastic, 1985.

Whether illustrated in the elegantly subtle detail of Lobel or with Marshall's irreverent playfulness, this classic story still holds magic for readers and listeners.

Mosel, Arlene, illustrated by Blair Lent. *Tikki Tikki Tembo.* [H] Holt, Rinehart & Winston, 1968. [P] Scholastic/Blue Ribbon, 1984.

Have you ever wondered why the Chinese give their children such short names? This folktale, featuring childlike oriental-style drawings, will explain that it has to do with two boys, a well, and an old man with a ladder.

Noble, Trinka H., pictures by Steven Kellogg. *The Day Jimmy's Boa Ate the Wash.* [H] Dial Books for Young Readers/Pied Piper, 1980. [P] Dial Books for Young Readers/Pied Piper, 1980.

The class trip would have been boring if . . . the cow hadn't cried, the pigs hadn't got on the schoolbus, Jimmy's boa constrictor hadn't got into the henhouse and then gone after the wash, and . . . Children will appreciate the nonsensical humor in both story and pictures.

Payne, Emmy, pictures by H. A. Rey. *Katy No-Pocket.* [H] Houghton Mifflin, 1944. [P] Houghton Mifflin/Sandpiper, 1973.
All the other mother kangaroos have pockets for their babies. Poor Katy is pocketless! Where can she find a pocket?

Piper, Watty. *The Little Engine That Could.* [H] Several editions. [P] Scholastic, 1979.
The Little Blue Engine huffs and puffs, working hard all day. But when the big red engine conks out, Little Blue is called in to help. Can he make it up the hill?

Potter, Beatrix. *The Tale of Peter Rabbit.* [H] Several editions. [P] Several editions.
Peter is such a naughty little rabbit. While his brothers and sisters stay in their own yard as they're supposed to, Peter goes exploring—exactly where his mother told him not to.

Rey, H. A. *Curious George.* [H] Houghton Mifflin, 1941. [P] Houghton Mifflin/Sandpiper, 1973.
Preschoolers will understand George's uncanny ability to get into everything and will laugh at the funny predicaments he manages to get himself into.

Sendak, Maurice. *Where the Wild Things Are.* [H] Harper Junior, 1963. [P] Harper/Trophy, 1984.
When Max is sent up to bed for being a bad boy, that's when the trouble really starts! Max becomes a "wild thing"! The king of the "wild things"! And they're pretty wild in this award-winning modern classic.
Also recommended: *Chicken Soup with Rice; Alligators All Around.*

Shannon, George, illustrated by Jose Aruego and Ariane Dewey. *Lizard's Song.* [H] Greenwillow, 1981.
Where is your home? Rock is Lizard's home and he sings about it. Try as hard as he can, Bear just can't remember that song. Because it's Lizard's song. And Lizard's home. How about a song about Bear's home? And that's just what you get in this whimsical, bright picture book.

Sharmat, Mitchell, illustrated by Jose Aruego and Ariane Dewey. *Gregory, the Terrible Eater.* [H] Four Winds, 1980.
Gregory the Goat just won't eat "good food." He leaves all those yummy tin cans and all that delicious garbage on his plate and goes off looking for green vegetables and eggs! Young children will appreciate poking fun at food, as well as the colorful, comical illustrations.

Slobodkina, Esphyr. *Caps for Sale.* [P] Scholastic/Blue Ribbon, 1984.

"Monkey see, monkey do!" is what the peddler finds out when the monkeys take all of his hats while he's asleep. But how can he get them back? The peddler finds an unexpected way, and the gray hats, brown hats, blue hats, and red hats come showering down.

Spier, Peter. *Noah's Ark.* [H] Doubleday, 1977. [P] Doubleday/Zephyr, 1981.

Preschoolers will love seeing the animals march two by two in this spectacularly illustrated, intricately detailed, wordless version of the biblical story. Each page has its own format—some pages have one drawing, others two, three, four, etc.

Tresselt, Alvin R., illustrated by Yaroslava Mills. *The Mitten.* [H] Lothrop, 1964. [P] Scholastic/Blue Ribbon, 1985.

Do you know what happens if you lose your mitten in the snow? According to this gleeful retelling of an old Ukranian folktale, first a mouse crawls inside, then a frog jumps in with him, followed by an owl, then a rabbit, a fox, a wolf, a boar, and a bear. And, oh yes, a cricket!

Turkle, Brinton. *Deep in the Forest.* [H] E. P. Dutton, 1976.

Here is "Goldilocks and the Three Bears" revisited. Except for one thing—this time it's the bear who pays a visit on the people! No words are necessary in this amusing variation on the traditional tale.

Ungerer, Tomi. *Crictor.* [H] Harper Junior, 1958. [P] Harper/Trophy, 1983.

Crictor is not your run-of-the-mill snake. He lives with an old lady, whom he saves from burglars and who knits him a scarf. How's that for an unusual snake?

Waber, Bernard. *Ira Sleeps Over.* [H] Houghton Mifflin, 1972. [P] Houghton Mifflin/Sandpiper, 1975.

Ira's sleeping over at a friend's house for the very first time. He's sure they'll have a great time. Just one thing he's not sure about—should he bring his teddy bear?

Wells, Rosemary. *Stanley and Rhoda.* [H] Dial Books for Young Readers, 1978. [P] Dial Books for Young Readers, 1981.

In three colorful, large-format, easy-to-read stories, Stanley and Rhoda clean up Rhoda's room, treat Rhoda's bee sting, and get their preppy baby-sitter to take a bath with his clothes on!

Williams, Vera B. *A Chair for My Mother.* [H] Greenwillow, 1982. [P] Greenwillow, 1984.

When a terrible fire destroys all their furniture, a little girl's hardworking mother has nowhere to relax after a hard day. This is the beautiful, lavishly illustrated story of how the family puts all its pennies in a jar to save for that one perfect chair.

Wiseman, Bernard. *Morris the Moose.* [H] Harper, 1959.

Boy! Can life ever get confusing! First, the moose thinks the cow's a moose . . . then the deer thinks the moose is a deer . . . and then there's the horse . . . in this delightfully lively comedy of errors.

Zion, Gene, pictures by Margaret Bloy Graham. *Harry the Dirty Dog.* [H] Harper Junior, 1956. [P] Harper/Trophy, 1976.

Harry starts out as a white dog with black spots . . . until bath time. Then the clever, comical dog decides to disguise himself as a black dog with white spots. Young children will appreciate the simple story, enjoy the rollicking illustrations, and love Harry.

Zolotow, Charlotte, pictures by William Pene DuBois. *William's Doll.* [H] Harper Junior, 1972. [P] Harper/Trophy, 1985.

More than anything in the world, William wants a doll—to hold and bathe and dress and love. But his big brother calls him "creepy" and the kid next door says he's a "sissy." Doesn't anyone understand?

Also recommended: *My Grandson Lew.*

FIVE TO EIGHT

Aardema, Verna, pictures by Leo and Diane Dillon. *Why Mosquitoes Buzz in People's Ears.* [H] Dial Books for Young Readers, 1975. [P] Dial Books for Young Readers, 1978.

It's all the mosquito's fault! He annoyed the iguana, who frightened the python, who scared the rabbit, and so on, explains this dazzlingly illustrated, award-winning book of an African folktale about why Mother Owl won't wake the sun so that the day can come. If you were a mosquito, you'd buzz in people's ears, too!

Also recommended: *Who's in Rabbit's House?*

Allard, Harry, illustrated by James Marshall. *Miss Nelson Is Missing.* [H] Houghton Mifflin, 1977. [P] Scholastic, 1978.

Emergency! Emergency! Miss Nelson is missing—bad! Miss Viola Swamp is replacing her—worse! Where can Miss Nelson be? Her rowdy class looks everywhere—except the right place—in this cunning and very funny story.

Also recommended: *Miss Nelson Is Back.*

Anno, Mitsumasa. *Anno's Journey.* [H] Putnam/Philomel, 1981. [P] Putnam/Philomel, 1981.

Journey into the imagination with this wordless book full of delicately detailed people, places, things, children, countrysides, and cityscapes.

Atwater, Richard and Florence. *Mr. Popper's Penguins.* [H] Little, Brown, 1938. [P] Dell/Yearling, 1978.

It all goes back to Mr. P's fondness for penguins. And all of a sudden, penguins are popping out of everywhere! The rest is history—or calamity, in this wild and crazy adventure story.

Bang, Molly. *The Grey Lady and the Strawberry Snatcher.* [H] Four Winds, 1980.

The Grey Lady just loves strawberries. Unfortunately, so does the sneaky, creepy Strawberry Snatcher, who follows her everywhere —even on skateboard—and will stop at nothing to get the Grey Lady's berries. But little does he know that she can be pretty sneaky herself.

Also recommended: *Wiley and the Hairy Man.*

Barrett, Judith, pictures by Ron Barrett. *Cloudy with a Chance of Meatballs.* [H] Atheneum, 1978. [P] Macmillan/Aladdin, 1978.

Here is the funny, fanciful story of the land of Chewandswallow, where whatever the weather serves, the people eat. The weather comes three times a day, brings specials such as soup and juice rain, mashed potato snow, and hamburger storms. The Jell-O sets peacefully in the west until . . .

Baum, L. Frank. *The Wizard of Oz.* [H] Several editions. [P] Several editions.

The book is similar enough to the movie version to interest children, but just different enough to make them want to read it from cover to cover. Enter such unusual creatures as the Giant Humbug and the Quadlings.

Blume, Judy, illustrated by Sonia O. Lisker. *Freckle Juice.* [P] Dell/Yearling, 1978.

Andrew will go to drastic lengths to get freckles like his friend Nicky's. He buys a recipe—but gets a stomachache instead of freckles. He paints them on—and they won't come off! A funny book about a funny kid.

Also recommended: *The One in the Middle Is the Green Kangaroo; The Pain and the Great One.*

Bond, Michael, pictures by Peggy Fortnum. *A Bear Called Paddington.* [H] Houghton Mifflin, 1960. [P] Dell/Yearling, 1968.

That Paddington is one mischievous bear. And unusual, too. He comes from darkest Peru and loves marmalade. He also loves the Browns, who found him in London's Paddington Station, and gave him a name and a home. What did he give them? Lots of trouble—and fun!

Bonsall, Crosby. *Who's Afraid of the Dark?* [H] Harper Junior, 1980. [P] Harper/Trophy, 1985.

Stella the Dog is afraid of the dark. She trembles and shakes and hides when she sees scary shapes or hears creepy noises. Lucky for Stella, she has an understanding boy who hugs her tightly and soothes her so that they can both fall asleep.

Briggs, Raymond. *The Snowman.* [H] Random House/Books for Young Readers, 1978.

Through magical, wordless pictures, a snowman takes a little boy on an amazing flight.

Cleary, Beverly, illustrated by Louis Darling. *Ramona the Pest.* [H] Morrow, 1968. [P] Dell/Yearling, 1982.

Why does everyone call Ramona Quimby a pest? It's not her fault that she gets stuck in the mud and asks questions that make people laugh. And why is Ramona Quimby about to become the first kindergarten dropout in history?

Also recommended: others in the *Ramona* series; *The Mouse and the Motorcycle; Henry Huggins.*

Cole, Babette. *The Trouble with Mom.* [H] Putnam/Coward, 1984.

What do you do if your mom's a witch? How do you explain the bats and the cats and the broom and the buggy cupcakes to your friends? And what do you tell your friends' parents?

Cole, Joanna, pictures by Dirk Zimmer. *Bony-Legs.* [H] Four Winds, 1983.

How can a mirror and a comb help a young girl escape from Bony-Legs the Witch? Find out in this brightly illustrated retelling of a Russian folktale.

dePaola, Tomie. *Strega Nona.* [H] Prentice-Hall/Treehouse, 1975. [P] Prentice-Hall/Treehouse, 1975.

Strega Nona is one droll troll. When her dumb helper Anthony

uses her magical pasta pot without permission, he starts the spaghetti rolling—but he can't stop it. Help, Strega Nona!
Also recommended: *Nana Upstairs & Nana Downstairs.*

Estes, Eleanor, illustrated by Louis Slobodkin. *The Hundred Dresses.*
[H] Harcourt, 1974. [P] Harcourt, 1974.
How could Wanda with the funny last name have "a hundred dresses, all lined up in a row"? The strange girl with the foreign name wears the same blue dress to school every day. What is her secret? What is she hiding? And where has she suddenly disappeared to?

Flournoy, Valerie, pictures by Jerry Pinkney. *The Patchwork Quilt.*
[H] Dial Books for Young Readers, 1985.
Her grandmother's quilt is almost alive, made up of scraps of the family's old clothes and costumes from long ago. So when Grandma falls ill, Tanya knows that somehow she must finish the quilt made of memories.

Grahame, Kenneth. *The Wind in the Willows.* [H] Several editions.
[P] Several editions.
They're all here in the meadow on the riverbank. Mr. Badger, Mole, Rat, Mr. Toad, and the others have come back in great form, marvelously illustrated, to celebrate their seventy-fifth anniversary with you.

Greenfield, Eloise, pictures by Diane and Leo Dillon. *Honey, I Love: And Other Love Poems.* [H] Crowell Junior, 1978. [P] Harper/Trophy, 1986.
This unusual collection of "love poems" written in the voice of a child, tells the stories of everyday life—jumping rope, playing with a good friend, just being happy.

Guilfoile, Elizabeth, illustrated by Mary Stevens. *Nobody Listens to Andrew.* [P] Modern Curriculum, 1957.
Nobody ever listens to Andrew. Not his mother or his daddy or his sister or his brother or his neighbor or the housekeeper. Until he tells everyone what's upstairs in his bed. Then everyone listens!

Haley, Gail E. *A Story, A Story.* [H] Atheneum, 1970.
Many bold illustrations complement the retelling of this African "spider story" about Ananse, a small man who challenges the mighty Sky God and wins. Fascinating African words and a marvelous tribal rhythm add much to the enthralling tale.

Hoban, Russell, pictures by Lillian Hoban. *Bread and Jam for Frances.* [H] Harper Junior, 1964. [P] Harper/Trophy, 1986.

If there's one meal little Frances the Badger likes, it's bread and jam. In fact, it's the only meal she likes. Fortunately, Mother comes up with just the right cure for her picky eater

Also recommended: *Bedtime for Frances; A Baby Sister for Frances.*

Johnson, Crockett. *Harold and the Purple Crayon.* [H] Harper Junior, 1958. [P] Harper/Trophy, 1981.

Harold is a truly talented artist. He can make his drawings become real. And that's just what he does in this simple, charming little book, from taking a walk in the purple moonlight to falling asleep in the bed with the purple covers.

Jonas, Ann. *Round Trip.* [H] Greenwillow, 1983.

This graphically illustrated, black-and-white picture book will take you on an incredible round-trip. You'll start in the country at dawn, travel all the way to the city until it gets dark, and then return home as it becomes light.

Kellogg, Stephen. *The Mysterious Tadpole.* [H] Dial Books for Young Readers, 1977. [P] Dial Books for Young Readers, 1979.

Alphonse started out as no ordinary tadpole. Alphonse grew up to be no ordinary frog. Trust Uncle Allister to give his nephew a birthday present he—and everybody else—would never forget in this very funny, softly colored story about how Alphonse the lovable sea monster saved the day.

Also recommended: *The Island of the Skog.*

Leaf, Munro, illustrated by Robert Lawson. *The Story of Ferdinand.* [H] Viking, 1936. [P] Penguin/Puffin, 1977.

Ferdinand is an exceptional bull. He doesn't like to paw and snort and butt like the others. Instead, Ferdinand likes to sit peacefully and smell the flowers. Which, oddly enough, is how he gets into big trouble.

Lindgren, Astrid, translated by Florence Lamborn, illustrated by Louis S. Glanzman. *Pippi Longstocking.* [H] Viking, 1950. [P] Penguin/Puffin, 1977.

Who has bright red braids that stick straight out, wears shoes twice as long as her feet, is the daughter of a cannibal king, catches burglars, saves children from fires, is a "thing-finder," and lives with a monkey and a horse in Villa Villekulla? Pippi, who else!

Marshall, James. *George and Martha.* [H] Houghton Mifflin, 1972. [P] Houghton Mifflin/Sandpiper, 1974.

George and Martha are great friends. In these five stories they learn from each other how to be even better friends. Oh, by the way, George and Martha just happen to be hippopotamuses.

Miles, Miska, illustrated by Peter Parnall. *Annie and the Old One.* [H] Atlantic Monthly, 1971.

Annie's Navajo world comes alive in this beautiful, multidimensional story about a young girl's relationship with her aging grandmother and her Indian heritage. Annie learns that she must accept change, and the passing of old things, to make way for the growth of new ones.

Milne, A. A., illustrated by Ernest H. Shepard. *Winnie-the-Pooh.* [H] E. P. Dutton, 1961. [P] Dell/Yearling, 1970.

Open this venerable classic and join Pooh Bear, ever in search of honey, and his terrific friends: philosophical Piglet, pessimistic Eeyore, and faithful old Christopher Robin.

National Geographic Society. *Books for Young Explorers* (series).

Lavish full-color photographs, à la National Geographic Society, accompany the clear, factual text of books in the series, whose titles include: *Pandas, Spiders,* and *The Playful Dolphins.*

O'Neill, Mary, illustrated by Leonard Weisgard. *Hailstones and Halibut Bones.* [H] Doubleday, 1961. [P] Doubleday/Zephyr, 1973.

Using the five senses, this unusual book explores the nature of colors. The poems describe gold "as warm as a mitten," gray as "the bubbling of oatmeal mush, tiredness, and oysters," and yellow as "the color of happiness."

Parish, Peggy, illustrated by Fritz Siebel. *Amelia Bedelia.* [H] Harper Junior, 1963. [P] Harper/Trophy, 1983.

Amelia Bedelia, the mixed-up maid, strikes again! She has the endearing, hysterically funny habit of taking instructions literally. When reminded to put the lights out, Amelia actually places them outside and when asked to dress the turkey for dinner, she proudly displays him in a tuxedo! Amelia Bedelia creates chaos and produces shrieks of laughter wherever she goes.

Also recommended: *Teach Us, Amelia Bedelia.*

Prelutsky, Jack (editor), illustrated by Arnold Lobel. *The Random House Book of Poetry for Children.* [H] Random House, 1983.

Hundreds of poems—572 to be exact—literally tumble out of this overstuffed treasure chest of surprise, laughter, suspense, and adventure. Featuring more than four hundred festive illustrations, this compendium is divided into fourteen thematic sections: seasons, holidays, animals, etc., with poems by favorites such as Sandburg, Nash, and Ciardi.

Also recommended: *The New Kid on the Block.*

Seuss, Dr. *The Cat in the Hat.* [H] Random House/ Beginner, 1957. When mother's away, The Cat in the Hat will play! And play! This famous feline juggles with a fish and an umbrella and kites and books and cake. And don't forget Thing 1 and Thing 2. Is no one safe?

Also recommended: *Green Eggs and Ham; The Butter Battle Book; Horton Hatches the Egg; The 500 Hats of Bartholomew Cubbins.*

Sharmat, Marjorie, illustrated by Marc Simont. *Nate the Great.* [H] Putnam/Coward, 1972 [P] Dell/Yearling, 1977.

Introducing the greatest detective since Sergeant Joe Friday of "Dragnet." Nate is one cool customer, solving cases for friends with the intelligence of Sherlock Holmes, the daring of James Bond, and the wit of Maxwell Smart.

Also recommended: others in the *Nate the Great* series.

Silverstein, Shel. *Where the Sidewalk Ends.* [H] Harper Junior, 1974. There is only one place in the whole world where you'll find a kid who literally loses his head, a boy who actually turns into a TV set, and a girl who has "measles, mumps, a gash, a rash, and purple bumps" among other things! And that place is in this book, guaranteed to "ickle" your fancy!

Also recommended: *A Light in the Attic.*

Sobol, Donald, illustrated by Leonard Shortall. *Encyclopedia Brown, Boy Detective.* [H] Lodestar, 1963. [P] Bantam, 1978.

Come solve a whole bunch of short but mysterious cases with master boy detective Leroy "Encyclopedia" Brown. He's so good, he even works on hard-to-crack capers for his dad, the police chief! Solutions to each mystery are given at the back of the book.

Also recommended: others in the *Encyclopedia Brown* series.

Steig, William. *Sylvester and the Magic Pebble.* [P] Windmill, 1969. Woe is the day that poor Sylvester Duncan the Donkey found the magic pebble that made his every wish come true. He turns himself into a rock quite by accident, and now he can't turn himself back because everyone knows that a rock can't pick up a pebble!

Also recommended: *Doctor Desoto; The Amazing Bone.*

Van Allsburg, Chris. *Jumanji.* [H] Houghton Mifflin, 1981.

Have you ever heard of a game that has live lions and monkeys and rhinos in it? In one of the wildest, most elegant, and fascinating books ever, two bored children find an ordinary-looking game under a tree. But "Jumanji" turns out to be anything but ordinary!

Also recommended: *The Garden of Abdul Gasazi; The Polar Express.*

Viorst, Judith, illustrated by Ray Cruz. *Alexander and the Terrible, Horrible, No Good, Very Bad Day.* [H] Atheneum, 1972. [P] Macmillan/Aladdin, 1972.

It just couldn't be worse! Alexander wakes up with gum stuck in his hair, no dessert in his lunch bag, a cavity in his tooth, and ends up with plain white sneakers. Yeck! Haven't we all had days like that?

Ward, Lynd. *The Biggest Bear.* [H] Houghton Mifflin, 1952. [P] Houghton Mifflin/Sandpiper, 1973.

When Johnny goes hunting for the biggest bear, he gets a big surprise. The smallest bear. But soon the cub grows up—and up —and up—and Johnny and his big bear are in big trouble.

White, E. B., pictures by Garth Williams. *Charlotte's Web.* [H] Harper Junior, 1952. [P] Harper/Trophy, 1952.

"Salutations" is Charlotte the Spider's first word to Wilbur the Pig in this touching classic. This is the enchanting barnyard story of how clever Charlotte saves Wilbur and of Wilbur's gift to Charlotte.

Also recommended: *Stuart Little; The Trumpet of the Swan.*

Williams, Margery, illustrated by William Nicholson. *The Velveteen Rabbit.* [H] Several editions. [P] Several editions.

This favorite story proves that if you love a stuffed rabbit—really love it—and if you believe—really believe—then that stuffed rabbit can come to life!

Zemach, Margot. *It Could Always Be Worse.* [H] Farrar, Straus, & Giroux, 1977. [P] Scholastic, 1979.

The valuable lesson of being satisfied with what you have is offered in this colorful and beautifully illustrated retelling of an old Yiddish folktale. When a man complains to his rabbi about his noisy and crowded house, he is told to bring his cows, horse, chickens, and goats inside. Only when he's told to let them out again does he appreciate the peace and quiet.

EIGHT TO ELEVEN

Aiken, Joan, illustrated by Pat Marriott. *The Wolves of Willoughby Chase.* [H] Doubleday, 1962. [P] Dell/Yearling, 1962.

Funny and scary at the same time, this is the absorbing tale of Bonnie and her cousin Sylvia, trapped in the English country estate Willoughby Chase, left in the custody of the demented and wicked Miss Slightcarp. Older readers will thrill to Bonnie's daring, laugh at her mishaps, and always remain absorbed in her search for freedom and safety.

Alcott, Louisa May. *Little Women.* [H] Several editions. [P] Several editions.

Come into the March family parlor for an intimate look into the lives of four very different sisters—gentle Meg, tomboy Jo, fragile Beth, spoiled Amy. Join in as they cook up all kinds of wild schemes, from planning a secret society to attending an exclusive ball, remaining cheerful despite living with very little money during the difficult Civil War days.

Alexander, Lloyd. *Book of Three.* [H] Holt, Rinehart & Winston, 1964. [P] Dell, 1980.

Young Taran, the assistant pigkeeper, is brave, resourceful, and adventurous. In this colorful, thrilling fantasy, he is given the chance to fulfill his dream of herohood when charged with the task of defending his beloved homeland, Prydain, against evil forces seeking to destroy it.

Also recommended: sequels to the *Book of Three* in the "Prydain Chronicles" series.

Armstrong, William Howard, illustrated by James Barkley. *Sounder.* [H] Harper Junior, 1969. [P] Harper/Trophy, 1972.

His father is unjustly convicted of stealing a white man's ham and is thrown in jail. So begins a young black boy's series of hard lessons, paid for with humiliation, sweat, and tears.

Babbit, Natalie. *Tuck Everlasting.* [H] Farrar, Straus & Giroux, 1975. [P] Farrar, Straus & Giroux, 1975.

The Tuck family will live forever. A special spring is their secret for immortality—whether it's a curse or a blessing. The trouble starts when ten-year-old Winnie stumbles onto their secret, followed by an evil, mysterious stranger who plans to sell the springwater—whatever it costs!

Banks, Lynne, illustrated by Brock Cole. *The Indian in the Cupboard.* [H] Doubleday, 1981. [P] Avon/Camelot, 1982.
If your child believes in fantasy, in magic, in inanimate objects coming to life, your child should read this book. It all starts when Omri is given a secondhand plastic Indian for his birthday and brother Gillian gives him an old cabinet found in an alley. Omri puts the Indian in the cupboard and . . . magic!

Bellairs, John, pictures by Edward Gorey. *The House with a Clock in Its Walls.* [H] Dial Books for Young Readers, 1973. [P] Dell/Yearling, 1974.
Lewis's Uncle Jonathan has the most exciting, creepiest, haunted house ever! But the house's original owner was an evil sorcerer who devised a plan to end the world. In the walls of the house, he's hidden a clock, and each night Lewis and his uncle can hear it ticking . . . ticking away the minutes left until doomsday . . .

Blume, Judy. *Superfudge.* [H] E. P. Dutton, 1980. [P] Dell/Yearling, 1981.
Up to now, Peter's problem could be summed up in one word—Fudge—otherwise known as his little brother, Farley Drexel Hatcher. But Peter thought he had everything under control. Until his mom announced she was going to have a baby and his dad announced that they were moving. Is it any wonder that Peter wants to move out?
Also recommended: *Are You There, God? It's Me, Margaret; Blubber; Tales of a Fourth Grade Nothing.*

Brink, Carol R., illustrated by Trina Schart Hyman. *Caddie Woodlawn.* [H] Macmillan, 1970.
Hurrah for Caddie! Written by the granddaughter of the real Caddie Woodlawn, this warm, exciting, award-winning adventure story introduces the reader to a real pioneer heroine—with a dash of mischief thrown in for good measure. Children will enjoy the retelling of how Caddie tricks her city-slicker cousin and how she saves the entire town from an Indian attack.

Burnett, Frances H., pictures by Tasha Tudor. *The Secret Garden.* [H] Lippincott, 1985. [P] Dell/Yearling Books, 1971.
"The sweetest, most mysterious-looking place anyone could imagine." This describes the walled-in, locked-up haven found by a lonely little girl. This is the magical story of how this special place helps her find friends, health, and happiness.

Burnford, Sheila, illustrated by Carl Burger. *The Incredible Journey.* [H] Atlantic Monthly, 1961. [P] Bantam, 1977.

An old bull terrier, a bold labrador retriever, and a clever siamese cat make a most unlikely trio as they begin one of the most amazing journeys of all time. Together they combine their talents to travel over hundreds of miles of treacherous country in search of their lost master in this heartwarming tale of courage and loyalty.

Byars, Betsy C., illustrated by Ted CoConis. *The Summer of the Swans.* [H] Viking, 1970. [P] Penguin/Puffin, 1981.

Swans glide gracefully on the lake, their feathers unruffled. Sara was like that—until her fourteenth summer—when everything and everyone, including herself, started to go wrong. And then, suddenly and mysteriously, her little brother disappears and Sara is the only one who can find him.

Also recommended: *The Cybil War; The 18th Emergency; Midnight Fox; Trouble River.*

Cleary, Beverly, illustrated by Paul O. Zelinsky. *Dear Mr. Henshaw.* [H] Morrow, 1983. [P] Dell/Yearling, 1984.

Leigh Botts is lonely, in a new school in a different town. What starts out as an assignment to write to a favorite author turns into a revealing, personal diary of a boy who's feeling the way every child feels at one time or another.

Coerr, Eleanor, pictures by Ronald Himler. *Sadako & the Thousand Paper Cranes.* [H] Putnam, 1977. [P] Dell/Yearling, 1986.

Sadako was twelve when she died from leukemia, as a result of radiation from the Hiroshima bombing. She folded 644 paper cranes before she died, in the hope that "if a sick person folds a thousand paper cranes, the gods will grant her wish and make her well again."

Dahl, Roald, illustrated by Nancy Burkert. *James and the Giant Peach.* [H] Knopf, 1961. [P] Bantam/Skylark, 1981.

James accidentally plants seeds for a tree that grows with a tremendous hollow peach on top of it. Inside he meets three eccentric friends and together they soar to new heights and adventures inside the amazing flying peach.

Danziger, Paula. *The Cat Ate My Gymsuit.* [H] Delacorte, 1974. [P] Dell/Yearling, 1980.

Who would have thought that Marcy, thirteen-year-old "blimp with an impending case of acne," would lead a student revolt?

Certainly not Marcy. But when her favorite teacher is unfairly fired, Marcy springs into action, no holds barred.

DeClements, Barthe. *Nothing's Fair in Fifth Grade*. [H] Viking, 1981. [P] Scholastic/Apple, 1982.

Sometimes it seems like everyone's against you. That's the way it is in this compassionate, beautifully told story about overweight, neglected Elsie.

Eager, Edward, illustrated by N. M. Bodecker. *Half Magic*. [H] Harcourt, 1954. [P] Harcourt, 1985.

Four children discover a magic coin. Well, half magic. But it turns out to be twice as much fun! And leads to three times as much danger!

Farley, Walter, illustrated by Keith Ward. *The Black Stallion*. [H] Random House, 1982.

Shipwrecked on a deserted island, a young boy discovers a superlative horse. Together, the boy and this "wildest of all wild creatures" explore distant lands and meet challenge after challenge in this exciting, easy-to-read story.

Fitzgerald, John D., illustrated by Mercer Mayer. *The Great Brain*. [H] Dial Books for Young Readers, 1967. [P] Dell/Yearling, 1971.

Not every kid has "The Great Brain" for a big brother—Tom D. Fitzgerald, ten-year-old genius. Tom solves many exciting and adventurous cases: He finds the Jensen kids in Skeleton Cave, shows Basil how to fight back, and teaches Andy that a peg leg can come in handy!

Also recommended: others in the *Great Brain* series.

Fitzhugh, Louise. *Harriet the Spy*. [H] Harper Junior, 1964. [P] Dell/Yearling, 1984.

"Maybe when I grow up I can have an office. . . . On the door it can say 'HARRIET THE SPY' in gold letters. . . . I guess I won't put the price on the door. They'll have to come in and ask me." It's Harriet's spy work that gets her in trouble. When her friends find out what she's written about them in her secret spy notebook, watch out!

Also recommended: *Sport*.

Fritz, Jean, pictures by Margot Tomes. *Homesick: My Own Story*. [H] Putnam, 1982. [P] Dell/Yearling, 1984.

Her parents' memories and letters from the States always made young Jean feel that she was American. Here is the compelling, semiautobiographical story of what it was like for a girl who had picnicked on China's Great Wall and been called a "foreign devil" in China on the eve of the revolution to come to the United States she had only seen in her heart.

Gardiner, John Reynolds, illustrated by Marcia Sewall. *Stone Fox.* [H] Crowell Junior, 1980. [P] Harper/Trophy, 1983.

The National Dogsled Race means everything to ten-year-old Willy. Winning it will give his grandfather the will to live and save the farm from bankruptcy. Only one man stands between Willy and his dog Searchlight winning the race—Stone Fox.

George, Jean C., pictures by John Schoenherr. *Julie of the Wolves.* [H] Harper Junior, 1972. [P] Harper/Trophy, 1974.

Alone. Lost. Dying. Miyax/Julie is deep in the Alaskan wilderness with only one hope for survival—the wolves. She must ask them for food, for warmth, for love, for her life. But in the end, only she can make the final choice . . .

Also recommended: *My Side of the Mountain.*

Gipson, Fred. *Old Yeller.* [H] Harper, 1956. [P] Harper, 1964.

Travis couldn't possibly have done it alone—protect his mother and little brother and do all the farming and the hunting, too. It took teamwork—a fourteen-year-old boy and his big, yellow dog, who helped the boy become a man on the hard Texas frontier.

Greene, Bette, pictures by Charles Lilly. *Philip Hall Likes Me, I Reckon Maybe.* [H] Dial Books for Young Readers, 1974. [P] Dell/Yearling, 1975.

Competitiveness comes naturally to Beth. She has always won. So why is Philip Hall, the smartest and cutest boy in the class, suddenly beating her at just about everything? Could it be that Beth is letting him win?

Hahn, Mary D. *Daphne's Book.* [H] Houghton Mifflin/Clarion, 1983.

Popular Jessica and Daphne the misfit are assigned to work together on a class project. Slowly Jessica learns of Daphne's exceptional talents. But she also learns her terrible secret.

Hamilton, Virginia, et al., illustrated by Leo and Diane Dillon. *The People Could Fly: American Black Folktales.* [H] Knopf, 1985. [P] Knopf, 1985.

Forty spectacular graphics and twenty-four selections of the best black folklore make the oral tradition come alive in thrilling detail. The stories provoke laughter, terror, and reflection on the plight of American slaves' desperate fight for personal freedom.

Henry, Marguerite, illustrated by Wesley Dennis. *Misty of Chinco-teague* [H] Rand McNally, 1947. [P] Rand McNally, 1947.

Misty is the most beautiful colt in the world. That's why Paul and Maureen must catch her and her strange wild mare in this thrilling tale.

Also recommended: *King of the Wind.*

Holling, Holling C. *Paddle-to-the-Sea.* [H] Houghton Mifflin, 1941. [P] Houghton Mifflin, 1980.

Do you believe that the small, wooden canoe carved by an Indian boy can possibly make the treacherous journey from Lake Superior all the way to the Atlantic Ocean? How can the little wooden Indian inside the canoe possibly survive the torrential rains, the bustling lumber camps, the violent waterfalls to become a true Paddle Person—a Paddle-to-the-Sea?

Howe, Deborah and James, illustrated by Alan Daniel. *Bunnicula: A Rabbit Tale of Mystery.* [H] Atheneum, 1979. [P] Avon/Camelot, 1980.

Chester the Cat knew right off that there was something very wrong with that rabbit. I, Harold the Dog, had to agree. Our worst fears were confirmed when we saw Bunnicula's fangs and found all those white, dried-up veggies. We definitely had a vampire bunny on our hands.

Also recommended: *Celery Stalks at Midnight; Howliday Inn.*

Konigsburg, E. L. *From the Mixed-Up Files of Mrs. Basil E. Frankweiler.* [H] Atheneum, 1967. [P] Dell/Yearling, 1977.

If you're going to run away from home, the Metropolitan Museum of Art is as good a place as any to run to. That's what Claudia and Jaime think. And while they're at it, the zany pair track down eccentric Mrs. Frankweiler, owner of a mysterious statue, who helps them find the way to go home.

Lawson, Robert. *Ben & Me.* [H] Little, Brown, 1939. [P] Dell/Yearling, 1973.

"Ben" just happens to be the world-famous Benjamin Franklin. And the "Me" is Amos the Mouse who, with marginal humility, herein announces in his own charming and inimitable way that he was, in fact, largely responsible for Franklin's inventions.

L'Engle, Madeleine. *A Wrinkle in Time.* [H] Farrar, Straus & Giroux, 1962. [P] Dell/Yearling, 1973.

Everyone knows that the shortest distance between two points is a straight line—right? Wrong. In this award-winning fantasy, Meg

and her little brother Charles Wallace discover a tesseract—a
wrinkle in time—that leads them to a strange trio of witches, much
danger, darkness, and wickedness, and gives them the only
chance in the universe of finding their father who's hopelessly
trapped in time.

Lewis, C. S., illustrated by Michael Hague. *The Lion, the Witch, and
the Wardrobe.* [H] Macmillan, 1968. [P] Macmillan/Collier, 1970.
Lucy finds it first. Then all four children enter the world of the
wardrobe and take off on an enchanted and enchanting journey
through space, through time, and through Narnia.

Lowry, Lois. *Anastasia Krupnik.* [H] Houghton Mifflin, 1979. [P]
Bantam, 1981.
It's hard to be ten! Good thing Anastasia has her secret notebook
complete with fickle "Things I Love" and "Things I Hate" lists.
Can you believe it—her parents are even going to have a baby!
And at their age!
Also recommended: others in the *Anastasia* series.

McCloskey, Robert. *Homer Price.* [H] Viking, 1943. [P] Penguin/
Puffin, 1976.
"Homer Price has the world well under control." The heartland
Midwest has never been viewed with more homegrown humor,
gentle teasing, and affection than through the eyes of gawky,
lovable Homer Price.

MacLachlan, Patricia. *Sarah, Plain and Tall.* [H] Harper Junior,
1985.
The most beautiful stories are simple and don't use one more
word than they have to—this is just such a story. Sarah answers a
newspaper ad for a wife, coming halfway across the country to the
hostile frontier to be a mother to Caleb and Sarah. She wouldn't
have it any other way—neither would they.

Montgomery, L. M., illustrated by Jody Lee. *Anne of Green Gables.*
[H] Putnam/Grosset & Dunlap, 1983. [P] Bantam, 1976.
When the Cuthberts decide to adopt an orphan to help with the
chores, they expect a nice, quiet, sturdy boy. Are they in for a
surprise! What they get is Anne Shirley—impish, unpredictable,
and so full of life that it just wouldn't be Green Gables without
her.

North, Sterling, illustrated by John Schoenherr. *Rascal: A Memoir of
a Better Era.* [H] E. P. Dutton, 1984. [P] Avon/Flare, 1976.
Introducing one of the most engaging, adorable, and uproari-

ously funny characters ever to grace the pages of a book. Rascal the raccoon finds his way into everything—and everyone's heart —in this great family story.

Norton, Mary, illustrated by Beth and Joe Krush. *The Borrowers.* [H] Harcourt, 1953. [P] Harcourt, 1965.

For such tiny people, the Borrowers lead very exciting lives! Although they try to live quietly in their apartment under the old grandfather clock, disaster strikes more than once in this amusing and suspenseful story.

O'Brien, Robert C., illustrated by Zena Bernstein. *Mrs. Frisby and the Rats of NIMH.* [H] Atheneum, 1971. [P] Macmillan/Aladdin, 1971.

Can the rats save Mrs. Frisby and her field mouse family from being crushed to death? Can she help the "rats race" to escape from NIMH? And what does NIMH stand for anyway?

O'Dell, Scott. *Island of the Blue Dolphins.* [H] Houghton Mifflin, 1960. [P] Dell, 1978.

Karana is abandoned on the deserted island, left behind by her people, left to eat alone, sleep alone. Be totally alone. Will they ever return? Will Karana be alive to see them?

Paterson, Katherine, illustrated by Donna Diamond. *Bridge to Terabithia.* [H] Crowell Junior, 1977. [P] Avon/Camelot, 1979.

Terabithia is a secret place, where Leslie and Jess are protected from domineering teachers, bullying classmates, Jess's fears, and Leslie's imaginary enemies. And it is what Jess learns from Leslie during their time together in Terabithia that helps him survive the unexpected tragedy of Leslie's sudden, senseless death in this sensitive, beautifully crafted award winner.

Also recommended: *Come Sing, Jimmy Jo; The Great Gilly Hopkins.*

Peck, Robert N., illustrated by Charles Gehm. *Soup.* [H] Knopf, 1974. [P] Dell/Yearling, 1979.

If there were an award for getting into the most trouble the most times, Soup would win it, hands down. If there's something mischievous going on, you can bet Soup is right in the middle, in this fun, easy-to-read story about boyhood pals.

Rawls, Wilson. *Where the Red Fern Grows.* [H] Doubleday, 1961. [P] Bantam, 1974.

Old Dan had the brawn, Little Ann the brains, and Billy the will to train the dogs into the best hunting team around. A complex book about glory and sadness, victory and defeat, staying young and growing old, this story shows us the magical strength you'll find only "where the red fern grows."

Robinson, Barbara, illustrated by Judith Gwyn Brown. *The Best Christmas Pageant Ever.* [H] Harper Junior, 1979. [P] Several editions.

This outrageous, gently irreverent story about the worst kids in history, who "lied and stole and smoked cigars (even the girls) and talked dirty and hit little kids and . . ." brings new meaning —and chaos—to the Christmas story.

Rockwell, Thomas, pictures by Emily McCully. *How to Eat Fried Worms.* [H] Watts, 1973. [P] Dell/Yearling, 1975.

"I'll bet you fifty dollars you can't eat fifteen worms." That's how this "innocent" story, whose table of contents alone will make you choke, starts out. Where it—and the worms—end up, well that's another story.

Rodgers, Mary. *Freaky Friday.* [H] Harper Junior, 1972. [P] Harper/Trophy, 1973.

. . . Or what happens when a thirteen-year-old girl wakes up one morning in curlers—and in her mother's body? And vice versa, in this wacky collection of calamities that prove that the grass is always greener.

Selden, George, illustrated by Garth Williams. *The Cricket in Times Square.* [H] Farrar, Straus & Giroux, 1960. [P] Dell/Yearling, 1970.

Chester Cricket arrives rather unceremoniously in Bellinis's Times Square subway station newsstand via a rerouted picnic basket from his native Connecticut. In this amazing fantasy, Chester, pals Harry the Cat, Tucker Mouse, and others manage to create true chaos while saving the newsstand from bankruptcy.

Smith, Doris, illustrated by Charles Robinson. *A Taste of Blackberries.* [H] Crowell Junior, 1973. [P] Scholastic/Apple, 1976.

Jamie is a daredevil, a joker, a tease. No one is more full of life. That's why it's so hard for a young boy to believe that Jamie's dead, in this realistic, touching portrayal of the beginning, and end, and beginning of a friendship.

Speare, Elizabeth G. *The Witch of Blackbird Pond.* [H] Houghton Mifflin, 1958. [P] Dell/Yearling, 1972.

"Witch!" is what the townspeople shout at Kit Tyler. Coming from the gentle Caribbean, Kit has never fit into bleak pre-Revolutionary War Connecticut life. Only when Kit is with the mysterious "Witch of Blackbird Pond" does she feel at peace. And every minute they're together, Kit risks her life . . .

Sperry, Armstrong. *Call It Courage.* [H] Macmillan, 1968. [P] Macmillan/Collier, 1971.

Mafatu, "stout hearted one," fears the sea that claimed his mother and almost killed him as an infant. Now it is time for Mafatu to prove his courage—to his father the Chief, to his people, to the evil Sea God, to himself. Mafatu paddles a canoe far out into the sea, toward a cannibal-infested island, toward uncertain dangers, toward death.

Taylor, Mildred, illustrated by Jerry Pinkney. *Roll of Thunder, Hear My Cry.* [H] Dial Books for Young Readers, 1976.

Cassie Logan is strong and good. But Cassie Logan may have met her match. Because she has come up against one of the worst enemies that a person can have in this eloquent story of black survival in the face of racism.

Also recommended: *Let the Circle Be Unbroken.*

Twain, Mark. *The Adventures of Tom Sawyer.* [H] Several editions. [P] Several editions.

Tom is one-in-a-million, an imp whose charismatic personality lets him breeze through almost anything. Even his own death!

Wagner, Jane, photographs by Gordon Parks, Jr. *J.T.* [P] Dell/Yearling, 1971.

J.T. is one tough customer. He steals, cheats, lies, and fights. And he brags about it. J.T. doesn't know how to live any other way. Until he finds a half-dead alley cat that changes everything forever.

Wilder, Laura Ingalls, illustrated by Garth Williams. *Little House on the Prairie.* [H] Harper Junior, 1953. [P] Harper/Perennial, 1975.

Laura will never forget the day that she, Ma, Pa, Mary, and baby Carrie moved west. Neither will any child who reads this classic story. In this second of eight books, the pioneer family will have to deal with Indians, bears, fevers, and wolves as well as enjoy the unspoiled wilderness.

Also recommended: others in the *Little House* series; *Farmer Boy.*

FURTHER RESOURCES FOR PARENTS AND CHILDREN

Resources to aid parents in encouraging their children's reading are rich and diverse. To show what is available, we have compiled a sampling of books for parents, inexpensive book lists, children's book clubs, children's magazines, and organizations concerned with children's reading and learning. We regret that space doesn't permit us to include all of the publications, services, and groups that exist. Check with your local librarian, bookseller, or your child's teacher for additional suggestions.

BOOKS FOR PARENTS

The following books are written especially for parents and offer a wide range of helpful information and suggestions. Check with your local librarian or bookseller for these titles and for other recommendations.

Butler, Dorothy. *Babies Need Books.* [H] Atheneum, 1982. [P] Atheneum, 1985.
> Long before children can read independently or speak sentences, writes Dorothy Butler, they will feast on picture books, traditional rhymes, and simple stories. Chapters like "When I Was One, I Had Just Begun" and "When I Was Three, I Was Hardly Me" explore the child's changing appetite for books.

Butler, Dorothy, and Mary Clay. *Reading Begins at Home.* [P] Heinemann Educational Books, 1982.
> According to Butler and Clay, parents can best instill a love of books in their children by providing a reading environment in which stories are read aloud, word games are played, and draw-

ings are described. A helpful reading list progresses from easier to harder books.

Dreyer, Sharon Spredemann. *The Bookfinder: When Kids Need Books.* [H] [P] American Guidance Service, Inc., 1985.

Bookfinder III, which reviews 725 books published between 1979 and 1982, is the companion volume to Bookfinder I (books published through 1974) and Bookfinder II (books published between 1975 and 1978). Helps match books to children's interests and concerns through subject, author, and title indexes.

Gross, Jacquelyn. *Make Your Child a Lifelong Reader.* [P] Tarcher, 1986.

Jacquelyn Gross believes that parents are naturally equipped to make reading an emotionally and intellectually involving experience for their children. Chapters feature single-sentence "suggestions" in bold print which lend discussions a practical flavor. A reading list follows each major section.

Hearne, Betsy. *Choosing Books for Children.* [H] Delacorte, 1981. [P] Dell, 1982.

Offers parents insights about matching books with children and developing their confidence in evaluating children's books. Each chapter examines a different genre of contemporary children's literature, followed by a short list of recommended titles.

Kimmel, Margaret Mary, and Elizabeth Segel. *For Reading Out Loud.* [P] Dell, 1984.

Underscores the importance of reading aloud to older children who have already begun reading independently. Describes noteworthy literature for children (ages five to fifteen) and suggests approaches to discussing challenging books and themes.

Larrick, Nancy. *A Parent's Guide to Children's Reading.* [P] Bantam, 1982.

A comprehensive and well-organized guide to stimulating children to read and learn. Suggests reading activities and strategies through which parents can reach children of different ages and interests, and includes suggested titles for children as well as a list of other helpful books for parents.

Lee, Barbara, and Masha Kabakow Rudman. *Leading to Reading.* [P] Berkley, 1985.

Describes activities that employ television, comic books, and video games to make reading fun. Appendices include a briefly annotated book list for children, selections for parents, and a list of book clubs and other reading organizations.

Russell, William. *Classics to Read Aloud to Your Children.* [H] Crown, 1984.

An anthology of classic stories and poems to read aloud to school-aged children. Selections are divided into three reading levels (five and up, eight and up, and eleven and up). Introductions to each selection include approximate reading time and a "vocabulary and pronunciation guide."

Trelease, Jim. *The Read-Aloud Handbook.* [P] Penguin, 1985.

This bestselling guide demonstrates how faithfully reading aloud to children fosters the *desire* to read. Trelease's "Treasury of Read-Alouds" offers an annotated selection of good read-alouds.

PERIODICALS FOR PARENTS

Bulletin. Reviews more than seventy children's books per issue. Published by the Center for Children's Books. To subscribe, write to: The University of Chicago Press, P.O. Box 37005, Chicago, Ill. 60637.

The Horn Book Magazine. A bimonthly journal about books for children and young adults featuring articles, columns, and an extensive book review section. To subscribe, write to: The Horn Book, Inc., 31 St. James Avenue, Boston, Mass. 02116.

Parents' Choice. A quarterly review of children's media including children's books, movies, television programs, toys, games, records, videos, and computer software. An introductory copy can be obtained for $1.50 by writing to: Parents' Choice Foundation, P.O. Box 185, Newton, Mass. 02168.

Why Children's Books? A quarterly newsletter for parents discussing good children's books grouped under topical headings. For ordering information, see *The Horn Book Magazine,* above.

BOOK LISTS

The following organizations publish lists of recommended books for children. Some are comprehensive lists of favorites, marked (C) below; others include only books published in the previous year, marked (A).

AMERICAN LIBRARY ASSOCIATION (ALA), 50 East Huron Street, Chicago, Ill. 60611. Enclose SASE (self-addressed, stamped 4¼" × 9½" envelope) with 2 oz. postage *for each copy ordered.*

- *Books for Everychild* (C). Titles with short descriptions. 25¢ with SASE.
- *Randolph Caldecott Medal Winners* (C). Current and previous recipients. 30¢ with SASE.
- *John Newbery Medal Winners* (C). Current and previous recipients. 30¢ with SASE.
- *Notable Children's Books* (A). Titles with short descriptions. 30¢ with SASE.
- *Poetry for Children* (C). Titles with short descriptions. Free with SASE.
- *U.S.A. Through Children's Books* (A). Books representing America's cultural diversity. Free with SASE.

CHILD STUDY CHILDREN'S BOOK COMMITTEE (CSCBC), Bank Street College, 610 W. 112 Street, New York, N.Y. 10025.

- *Books to Read Aloud to Children through Age 8* (C). Titles with short descriptions. $4.
- *Children's Books of the Year* (A). Describes over five hundred titles. $4.
- *Paperback Books for Children: A Selected List Through Age 12* (C). Titles with short descriptions. $3.

THE HORN BOOK, INC., 31 St. James Avenue, Boston, Mass. 02116.

- *Children's Classics* (C). A sixteen-page annotated and illustrated book-selection aid for parents of infant-to-adolescent-age children. $3.

INTERNATIONAL READING ASSOCIATION, 800 Barksdale Road, P.O. Box 8139, Newark, Del. 19714-8139.

- *Children's Choices* (A). Titles with descriptions. Free with a 6½" × 9½" SASE and 2 oz. postage. Include title of publication in mailing address.
- *Sixty Favorite Paperbacks* (A). Fiction, poetry, and riddles with descriptions. Free with SASE and 1 oz. postage. Include title of publication in mailing address.

LIBRARY OF CONGRESS, CHILDREN'S LITERATURE CENTER, Washington, D.C. 20540.

- *Books for Children* (A). Titles with short descriptions. $1 from the Superintendent of Documents, U.S. Government Printing Office, Washington, D.C. 20402.

NEW YORK PUBLIC LIBRARY OFFICE OF CHILDREN'S SERVICES, Office of Branch Libraries, 455 Fifth Avenue, New York, N.Y. 10016.

- *The Black Experience in Children's Books* (C). Titles with short descriptions. $4.
- *Children's Books, 1985* (A). Recommends one hundred titles. $2.50.
- *Children's Books, 1911 1986.* (C). Retrospective list with descriptions, grouped by decade. Free with SASE and 1 oz. postage.
- *Libros en Espanol* (C). Books in Spanish for children and bilingual books. Free with SASE and 1 oz. postage.
- *Stories: Folklore & Fairytales* (C). Titles with short descriptions. $4.

READING IS FUNDAMENTAL, INC. (RIF), P.O. Box 23444, Washington, D.C. 20026.

- *Children's Bookshelf* (C). Titles with short descriptions. $1.

MAGAZINES FOR CHILDREN

The following periodicals offer subscriptions to the home. For prices and terms, please write to the address provided.

Baseball Digest. Focuses on major league baseball—the history of the game and today's players and pennant races. Twelve issues per year. Ages "8–80."
   Century Publication Company, 1020 Church Street, Evanston, Ill. 60201

Boys' Life. Articles on sports, recreation, outdoor life, and hobbies, as well as fiction. Features the jokes and cartoons of subscribers. Also available in braille from Volunteer Services for the Blind (919 Walnut Street, Philadelphia, Pa. 19107). Twelve issues per year. Ages 8–17.
   Boy Scouts of America, 1325 Walnut Hill Lane, Irving, Tex. 75038-3096

Chickadee. Short articles, stories, word hunts, and other puzzles that explore the world of animals. Color photographs and drawings. Ten issues per year. Up to age 9.

Young Naturalist Foundation, 59 Front Street East, Toronto, Ontario M53 1B3, Canada

Child Life. One of six health magazines from the Children's Better Health Institute, emphasizing nutrition, exercise, and safety. Includes stories, games, puzzles, and nonfiction articles. Eight issues per year. Ages 7–9.

Children's Better Health Institute, Box 567 B, 1100 Waterway Boulevard, Indianapolis, Ind. 46206

Children's Digest. A health magazine for children aged 8–10. For additional information and publisher's address, see *Child Life,* just above.

Children's Playmate. A health magazine for children aged 5–7. Same address as for *Child Life.*

Classical Calliope. Each issue examines a single topic from ancient history. Contains puzzles and subscribers' letters as well as regular features on word origins, abbreviations, and usage. Four issues per year. Ages 10–16.

Cobblestone Publishing, Inc., 20 Grove Street, Peterborough, N.H. 03458

Cobblestone. Introduces significant people and events in American history, presented through informative articles, biographical sketches, and fictional pieces. Regular departments include a column of readers' contributions and a calendar of the month's important historical events. Twelve issues per year. Ages 8–14. See *Classical Calliope,* above, for publisher's address.

Cricket: The Literary Magazine for Children. Showcases children's literature by internationally known authors and illustrators—usually never-before published. Also features games, puzzles, crafts, and readers' contributions. Twelve issues per year. Ages 6–12.

Open Court Publishing Company, 315 Fifth Street, Peru, Ill. 61354

Dolphin Log. Vibrant color photographs illustrate articles on plants, fish, and birds of the sea. Four issues per year. Ages 7–15.

Cousteau Society, 930 West 21 Street, Norfolk, Va. 23517

The Electric Company Magazine. A lively mix of humor and information, including games, puzzles, fiction, feature articles, book re-

views, and contributions from children. Cartoons cover over half the pages; many photographs. Ten issues per year. Ages 6–10.
Children's Television Workshop, 1 Lincoln Plaza, New York, N.Y. 10023

Faces. Each issue features a single international theme through which cultural similarities and differences are explored. Ten issues per year. Published in cooperation with the American Museum of Natural History (New York, N.Y.). Ages 8–14.
See *Classical Calliope* for publisher's address.

Highlights for Children. Stories, poems, crafts, projects, puzzles, hidden pictures, and word games with a strong emphasis on values and high ideals. Also presents contributions from children. Graphs indicating the reading difficulty for different features appear on the contents page. Eleven issues per year. Ages 2–12.
2300 West Fifth Avenue, P.O. Box 269, Columbus, Ohio 43216

Humpty-Dumpty. A health magazine for children aged 4–6.
Children's Better Health Institute, Box 567 B, 1100 Waterway Boulevard, Indianapolis, Ind. 46206

Jack & Jill. A health magazine for children aged 6–8. Same address as for *Humpty-Dumpty.*

Muppet Magazine. Features interviews with media and sports celebrities. Regular departments include Miss Piggy's advice and reviews of recent films, records, and books. Ages 6–9.
Lorimar-Telepictures Publications, Inc., 300 Madison Avenue, New York, N.Y. 10017

National Geographic World. Articles on history, science, travel, and special events to enrapture the young adventurer, with captivating photographs and drawings. Twelve issues per year. Ages 8–12.
National Geographic Society, P.O. Box 2330, Washington, D.C. 20013-9865

Odyssey. Clearly written articles examine astronomy and outer space. Illustrated with photographs from observatories and government agencies, including NASA. Also offers games, puzzles, crafts, and readers' contributions. Twelve issues per year. Ages 8–14.
Kalmac Publishing, 1027 North 7th Street, Milwaukee, Wis. 53233

Owl. A colorful collection of stories and activities to inspire interest in the environment. With striking photographs and drawings. Ten issues per year. Ages 8 and up.

Young Naturalist Foundation, 59 Front Street East, Toronto, Ontario M53 1B3, Canada

Play. Debuts about eight plays in each issue, some for middle and lower grades. Production notes accompany every play. A subject index of earlier titles allows youngsters to find plays concerning holidays and other special events. Seven issues per year. Ages 8–18.

120 Boylston Street, Boston, Mass. 02116

Ranger Rick's Nature Magazine. Thoughtfully photographed nature articles, as well as indoor and outdoor activities that encourage children to protect the environment while they enjoy its beauty. Twelve issues per year. Ages 6–12.

National Wildlife Federation, 1412 Sixteenth Street, N.W., Washington, D.C. 20036

Sesame Street Magazine. Each issue features stories, poems, games, and activities relating to a theme (e.g., exploring America), followed by regular departments for children on counting and writing, plus a special section devoted to parenting. Ten issues per year. Ages 2–6.

Children's Television Workshop, 1 Lincoln Plaza, New York, N.Y. 10023

Short Story International (Seedling Series). Tales from all over the world introduce children to other cultures. Every issue offers about eight stories, each with a one-page illustration. Four issues per year. Grades 4–7.

International Cultural Exchange, 6 Sheffield Road, Great Neck, N.Y. 11021

Stamp Fun. Short articles exploring the artistic and historic value of the postage stamp. Six issues per year. Ages 6 and up.

U.S. Postal Service, Washington, D.C. 20265-9997

Stone Soup. Features the poems, stories, book reviews, and artwork of children. Cover and end page feature full-color reproductions of children's art from around the world. Ages 7–13.

Children's Art Foundation, P.O. Box 83, Santa Cruz, Calif. 95063

3-2-1 Contact. Projects, experiments, puzzles, and questions and answers—designed to link scientific inquiry with human progress. Regular features include "Factoids" (fun facts) and "TNT: Tomorrow's News Today," and "The Blood Hound Gang" (a science mystery series). Ten issues per year. Ages 10–14.

Same address as for *Sesame Street Magazine.*

Turtle. A health magazine for children aged 2–5.
Children's Better Health Institute, Box 567 B, 1100 Waterway
Boulevard, Indianapolis, Ind. 46206

Your Big Backyard. A generously illustrated, large-print introduction
to the wonders of nature. Twelve issues per year. Ages 3–5.
National Wildlife Federation, 1412 Sixteenth Street, N.W., Washington, D.C. 20036

CHILDREN'S BOOK CLUBS

The following book clubs send books and/or information to members' homes. For prices and terms, write to the address listed.

B. DALTON BOOKSELLER BOOK CLUBS
P.O. Box 10480
Minneapolis, Minn. 55440
• *Kids Book Club:* Discounts on books, audio and videocassettes, and
other items, plus membership button and "Fun Pages" newsletter. Sign up in any B. Dalton store. Ages 4–8.
• *Young Readers Club:* Discounts on club selections, plus "Young
Reader" newsletter. Sign up in any B. Dalton store. Ages 8–12.

CHILDREN'S BRAILLE BOOK-OF-THE-MONTH CLUB
National Braille Press, Inc.
88 Saint Stephen Street
Boston, Mass. 02115
New children's books from major publishers, rebound with
braille inserts for the shared enjoyment of blind and sighted
readers. Preschool–Grade 3.

CHILDREN'S CHOICE BOOK CLUB
P.O. Box 984
Hicksville, N.Y. 11802
Features hardcover children's classics and award winners from
major publishers. Ages 2–7.

CLUB DEL LIBROS, NINON Y JUVENTAD
AIMS International Books, Inc.
3216 Montana Avenue
P.O. Box 11496
Cincinnati, Ohio 45211
Club members may order from a catalog of Spanish children's
books at a discount. Preschool–Grade 6.

FIELD PUBLICATIONS BOOK CLUBS
245 Long Hill Road
Middletown, Conn.   06457
- *Weekly Reader Children's Book Club:* Hardcover fiction and nonfiction. Three grade levels: primary, intermediate, senior.
- *I Can Read Book Club:* Features Harper *I Can Read* books: hardcover fiction, animal stories, read-alouds, etc. Ages 4–8.
- *Fraggle Rock Book Club:* Stories with characters from Jim Hensen's muppets (from the HBO show "Fraggle Rock.") Ages 3–7.
- *Especially for Girls:* Fiction with themes of special interest to girls. Ages 10–14.

GROLIER BOOK CLUBS
Grolier Enterprises Inc.
Sherman Turnpike
Danbury, Conn.   06816
- *Beginning Readers Program:* Picture books and beginning stories from Random House, such as the Dr. Seuss series. Ages 4–6.
- *Disney's Wonderful World of Reading:* Stories such as Pinnochio and Snow White are part of this collection of more than eighty Disney classics from Random House. Ages 6–8.

MARCUS BOOK CLUB
1712 Fillmore Street
San Francisco, Calif.   94115
Fiction and nonfiction focusing on black culture and experience, reviewed in the *Marcus Book Club Review Catalog.* A price list and order form are included, from which club members may order books at discount.

PARENTS MAGAZINE READ-ALOUD BOOK CLUB
685 Third Avenue
New York, N.Y.   10017
Original hardcover picture books from Parents Magazine Press. Ages 2–7.

TROLL BOOK CLUBS
Troll Associates
320 Route 17
Mahwah, N.J.   07430
- *Troll At-Home:* Bookbags sent each month include a paperback, a cassette, and a list of activities. Three age groups.
- *ABC Adventures:* Hardcovers with cassettes tell stories through the alphabet. Ages 2–6.

- *American Story Library:* American history hardcovers which explore Colonial and Frontier America. Ages 10–14.
- *First Start:* Hardcover beginning readers, with cassettes. Ages 2–6.
- *Happy Time Adventures:* Paperbacks and cassettes featuring stories. Ages 6–8.
- *Heroes of America:* Hardcover biographies of significant Americans in various fields (government, science, sports, etc.). Ages 7–11.
- *Learn-About Library:* Hardcover nonfiction books exploring topics in science and nature. Ages 5–9.
- *Legends of Ancient Greece:* Hardcover collection of Greek myths in simple language. Ages 8–12.
- *Question and Answer Library:* Hardcover books about science and nature in a question-and-answer format. Ages 6–10.
- *Read-Along Classics:* Paperbacks and cassettes featuring classic fairy tales. Ages 6–10.
- *Read-Along Mysteries:* Paperback mystery stories, with cassettes. Ages 7–10.
- *Talking Picture Dictionary:* Paperbacks, with cassettes, which present every letter of the alphabet. Ages 3–8.
- *Venture:* Nonfiction paperbacks and cassettes on a variety of topics (science, geography, history, etc.). Ages 5–9.

WALDENBOOKS CLUBS
P.O. Box 10218
201 High Ridge Road
Stamford, Conn.   06904

- *Kids Club:* 10 percent discount on hardcover and paperback children's books sold at Waldenbooks stores, plus a membership kit and a discount on *Kids Club Magazine.* Up to age 12.
- *Happy Birthday Club:* Children receive a birthday card and a $1-off Birthday Bonus Coupon that may be redeemed at any Waldenbooks store. Up to age 14.

The following book clubs are operated through schools and/or libraries. Check with your children's teachers or librarians to see about joining.

- Field Publications *(Buddy Books, Goodtime Books, Discovering Books)*
- Doubleday & Company *(Junior Literary Guild)*
- Scholastic Book Clubs *(See-Saw, Lucky, Arrow)*

- Troll Book Clubs (Grades K–1, 2–3, 4–6)
- Dell Publishing Co. *(Trumpet)*

ORGANIZATIONS

The following organizations offer information and inexpensive publications on a wide range of topics related to children's reading and learning.

ACTION FOR CHILDREN'S TELEVISION (ACT)
   20 University Road
   Cambridge, Mass.   02138
   A nonprofit organization working to encourage diversity in children's TV. Offers a number of handbooks and other materials for parents and educators, including *A Look at Books for Children's TV.* For an order form and list of materials, write to the address above.
ASSOCIATION FOR CHILDHOOD EDUCATION INTERNATIONAL (ACEI)
   11141 Georgia Avenue, Suite 200
   Wheaton, Md.   20902
   A professional membership organization that works to promote the quality and availability of educational programs for children. Low-cost publications, available to nonmembers, include a *Bibliography of Books for Children, Functions of Folk and Fairy Tales,* and an annotated bibliography of *Excellent Paperbacks for Children.* For a catalog and order form, write to the address above.
ASSOCIATION FOR CHILDREN WITH LEARNING DISABILITIES (ACLD)
   4156 Library Road
   Pittsburgh, Pa.   15234
   A nonprofit organization devoted to advancing the education and welfare of children who have learning disabilities. Low-cost materials cover a range of learning disabilities, including dyslexia, and include many pamphlets for parents. For a catalog and order form, write to the address above.
CHILDREN'S BOOK COUNCIL, INC. (CBC)
   67 Irving Place
   New York, N.Y.   10003
   A nonprofit organization encouraging the reading and enjoyment of children's books. Sponsors National Children's Book Week each November, and prepares and sells posters and other materi-

als to promote year-round reading. For more information, write to the address above.

CHILDREN'S RADIO THEATRE
1314 14 Street, N.W.
Washington, D.C.   20005
Sponsors the Henny Penny Playwrighting Contest for youngsters. Open to any child, aged 8–15, who wants to participate. Winning scripts and honorable mentions are used on the show. The Children's Radio Theatre has a catalog of cassettes of the shows it airs. For a catalog or rules for the contest, write to the address above.

CONTACT LITERACY CENTER
c/o Contact Center, Inc.
P.O. Box 81826
Lincoln, Neb.   68501-1826
A nonprofit organization that brings people and resources together to implement new ideas and programs involving literacy. Maintains a National Literacy Hotline (1-800-228-8813). For more information, write to the address above.

FOUNDATION FOR CHILDREN WITH LEARNING DISABILITIES
99 Park Avenue, 6th Floor
New York, N.Y.   10016
Promotes awareness of learning disabilities and funds programs which assist the learning disabled and their families. Publishes *The FCLD Learning Disabilities Resource Guide,* a state-by-state review of organizations and programs, and *Their World,* an annual magazine featuring the stories of learning-disabled individuals. For more information, write to the address above.

INTERNATIONAL READING ASSOCIATION (IRA)
800 Barksdale Road
P.O. Box 8139
Newark, Del.   19714-8139
A nonprofit organization dedicated to the improvement of reading instruction and the promotion of a lifetime reading habit. Offers a number of free or low-cost publications like *Good Books Make Reading Fun for Your Child* that help parents motivate their children to read. For a publications catalog and a free parents brochure, send a self-addressed, stamped envelope (1 oz. postage) to the address above.

Orton Dyslexia Society
724 York Road
Baltimore, Md. 21204

An international nonprofit organization concerned with specific language difficulty or developmental dyslexia. Offers a number of reprints and inexpensive books that discuss dyslexia and other reading problems. For a catalog of materials, an order form, or more information, write to the address above.

Acknowledgments

This book was made possible by the creative contributions of hundreds of individuals, many of them volunteers who devote time to Reading Is Fundamental projects nationwide. We are deeply grateful to the many friends of RIF who have joined us in developing the guide. We extend special thanks to:

- Bonnie Bernstein for synthesizing thousands of ideas from RIF files and survey questionnaires and developing the activities. Her insight as a parent is evident throughout the activities.
- E. A. Hass for writing annotations for "Books to Grow On" that will entice parents and children.
- Maria Salvadore and Margaret Coughlan for helping to shape "Books to Grow On" through their wide knowledge of children and children's books.
- Loretta Barrett, Anne Sweeney, and Karen Van Westering of Doubleday & Company for supporting the idea that RIF's expertise in encouraging children to read should be shared with a wider audience.
- The John D. and Catherine T. MacArthur Foundation for a generous grant in 1982 that allowed RIF to research parents' informational needs and establish a program of services for parents.
- James Wendorf, RIF's director of parent services, for managing the entire project, for his creative editorial contributions, and for his invaluable assistance in shaping this book to respond to the needs parents have expressed to RIF.
- Victoria Heland for her perceptive editorial assistance and to Gail Oerke for her careful and extensive research.
- The entire staff of Reading Is Fundamental for contributing ideas and lending enthusiastic support to this guide and to the ongoing

work of RIF. Special thanks to: Barbara Atkinson, Catherine Burt, Jeffrey Campbell, Heather Campbell, Mary Chor, Jennifer Cutting, Barbara Feldman, Stacey Ficerai, Jolie Kelly, Jessie Lacy, Christina Mead, Paul Morenberg, Donna Ormiston, Krystal Patrick, Susan Ryan, Nancy Sullivan, and Ruth Walton.

• And to the millions of children served by Reading Is Fundamental for replenishing our spirits with their adventures in reading.

CONTRIBUTORS TO ACTIVITIES

We wish to thank the following people and organizations for suggesting activity ideas for the guide. All of the ideas reflect our contributors' creativity and their dedication to children and reading. Due to space limitations, we selected some ideas, combined others, and reserved still others for future use. Additional activities derive from RIF's years of experience and from RIF project reports too numerous to list.

ALABAMA
Pam Billings
ALASKA
Susan Hanson
Michael Opitz
Phyllis Wahl
ARIZONA
Leta Farmer
Our Lady of Lourdes Academy (Nogales)
ARKANSAS
Bennie J. Corrigan
Gerry Koons
Nancy Mason
CALIFORNIA
Clarice Berantz
Aleatha Bond
Mary K. Chartier
Genevieve Gunis
Katherine Elementary School (Simi)
Joyce Lanferman

Jacqueline Polley
Harriet Siegel
Edwin B. Swanson
Helen Wright
COLORADO
Denver General Hospital
Meg Edmonds
Janice Fellner
Ruth Lent
Janice Lund
Berniece McClure
CONNECTICUT
Barbara Lisio
Dominick M. Lonardo
DELAWARE
Alexis Gordon
FLORIDA
Lillian Boula
Eloise Cerny
Mary Beth Ewart
Eve Gualtieri

Lee County School Board
Larry A. Powell
GEORGIA
Brenda Kingery
IDAHO
Janise Kerner
ILLINOIS
Jane Blackmon
Board of Education, School District #169 (East Chicago Heights)
Mary Jo Diamond
Catherine Fansher
Barbara Golden
Camille Kramer
Gail Helen Lamothe
Cindy Mathiesen
Charlotte Sprengel
Shari Stromberger
INDIANA
Jack Humphrey
Maxine Pearman
Tom Whitaker
IOWA
Jan Arends
Janet Christensen
Judith Fixsel
George William Holland
Lou Kuempel
Jan Lautner
Geraldine McCarthy
Linda Mentzer
Barbara Nelson
Sue Rusk
Tri-Center Elementary School (Neola)
KANSAS
Pam Bergkamp
Joan Butts

Beth Jantz
Connie M. Kennedy
Marion Elementary School
KENTUCKY
Dishman-McGinnis School (Bowling Green)
Patricia Milner
LOUISIANA
Marilyn Payne
Katherine Weigel
MAINE
Paulette Borja
Paulette Clapp
E. M. Curtis School (West Enfield)
Louise Keegan
Beverly J. Osborn
JoAnn Pritchard
MASSACHUSETTS
Jamaica Plain High School
Mattahunt Community School
Marie-Elizabeth Pimental
Barbara Planton
Anne Seymour Schiraga
Eleanor S. Snelgrove
MICHIGAN
David Bosio
Barbara Brower
Jean Dalton
Ruth Doggett
Fennville District Library
Fisher School Staff (Marquette)
Janet Grames
Rebecca Jennings
Mary A. Kessler
Mayville Community Schools
Janet Swartzendruber
Walkerville RIF Project
Carolyn Willobee

MINNESOTA
Dorothy McCoy
Carol Orvis
Lylah Rosa
Verda Tschritter

MISSOURI
Joan Campbell
Phyllis Dannar
Betty Lohraff
Jan Powell
Norma Vavra
Julie Wayman

MONTANA
Gwen Taylor

NEVADA
Charlyne Arosio
Winnemucca Grammar School

NEW HAMPSHIRE
Delphine Rogers

NEW JERSEY
Grace Conway
M. K. Drury
Margaret Ehrenfeld
Mrs. J. Engelbart
Rosalie Hamilton
Mrs. L. Hayes
Maureen Lake
John Reed
Ellen Singer

NEW MEXICO
Elizabeth A. Casaus
Janet Romero

NEW YORK
Gail Bryant
E. Cooper
Camille Coulborn
Bea Graney
Marilyn Mines
North Tonawanda Public
    Library

Beth Pettit
Judi Purcell
Mehar M. Safvi
Gladys Slentz
James Weik

NORTH CAROLINA
Marilyn Z. Campbell
Sally A. Collier
Leonorah H. Dover
Durham County Library
Charlotte Elliott
Lillian Morgan
Ronnie Sams

NORTH DAKOTA
Lenora Jensen
Carl Morken
Beverly Quamme
Standing Rock Community
    High School Student
    Council (Fort Yates)

OHIO
Anita Ankerman
Susan Barlow
Cambridge City Schools
Carroll Community RIF
    (Carrollton)
Jean Close
Gloria Davis
Mary K. Howard
Ruth Patterson
Susie Quesinberry
Connie Schneider
Shreve Elementary School
Rita Wesseling
Dona J. White
Mrs. Yuri Wilcox
Joyce Zilles

OKLAHOMA
Westville Elementary School

OREGON
North Santiam School District #126 (Aumsville)
Waterloo School (Lebanon)
PENNSYLVANIA
Dorothy M. Beazley
Marlene Branton
Bernadette Bria
Sandra Camacho
Canton Area Elementary School Teachers
Genevieve D. Coale, Ph.D.
Pamela Dubell
M. Hart
Joan Ide
Carol Klinger
Margaret Kovaleski
JoAnn Lim
Deborah Martin
Cathy Mazur
Virginia B. Modla, Ph.D.
Mrs. C. Mosimann
New Hanover-Upper Frederick School (Frederick)
Marjorie M. Shaner
Mr. Richard Shepps
Darrell L. Smith
Debbie Smith
Deborah Troy
Daniel E. Waters
Jean Whitenight
RHODE ISLAND
Tara Anderson
Central Falls Free Public Library
Cumberland School Volunteers, Inc.
Robert E. Hargraves
Virginia M. Mello
Mebba Underdown

SOUTH CAROLINA
Sam Cason
Lynne Hamilton
Beverly Harris
Peggy Hunter
Linda Janetta
Sheila Pawlyk
Lee Strait
York Road Elementary School (Rock Hill)
TENNESSEE
Boys Clubs of Memphis
Oak Ridge Schools
TEXAS
Jane Browning
Nelda Burson
Cheryl DelSignore
Oralia Gonzalez
Debbie Marcak
Pam McCombs
Carolyn Reagan
San Marcos CISD Migrant Program
Joann Voight
Peggy Wilkerson
VERMONT
Ursula Bass
Phyllis Billings
Carol Craft
Anza Myers
Anne L. Olufsen
Southeast School PTA (Rutland)
Jean Tinney
VIRGINIA
B. J. Bowdler
Rachael DeHaven
WASHINGTON
Laurie Sherburne

BOOK SELECTION COMMITTEE

We are grateful to the following people for serving on the book selection committee:

Barbara Foree
Winnemucca, Nevada
Donna Frey
Bozeman, Montana
Ilene George
Winnemucca, Nevada
Phillis Gershator
St. Thomas, Virgin Islands
Rosanne E. Goble
Newton, Kansas
James A. Gollata
Ladysmith, Wisconsin
Bea Graney
Syracuse, New York
Elizabeth Gregory
Columbia, South Carolina
Bessie K. Grossman
Lindenhurst, New York
Judith Hankes
Ladysmith, Wisconsin
Claire Harrison
San Francisco, California
David Hartle-Schutte
Fort Defiance, Arizona
Cindy Heath-Mizell
Dufur, Oregon
Susan Young Hoffman
DeForest, Wisconsin
Donna Hymel
Monroe, Louisiana
Thelma H. Jones
Oklahoma City, Oklahoma
Carolyn Jordan
Dallas, Texas
Martha Jordan
Monroe, Louisiana
Patricia J. Karsch
Homer, New York
Virginia Kitts
Knoxville, Tennessee

Marie Kunkle
Kokomo, Indiana
Patty Lockett
Freedom, California
Ann Logue
Okeechobee, Florida
Pat Mansfield
Winnemucca, Nevada
Cynthia McCarty
Monroe, Louisiana
Norma J. McShane
Bennington, Vermont
Maureen Melvin
Okeechobee, Florida
Mary Jane Mowle
West Lafayette, Indiana
William L. Oswald
Dallas, Texas
Sylvia L. Parks
Columbia, South Carolina
Kathy Pattee
Bozeman, Montana
Deborah Sovyrda Pawelchak
Ladysmith, Wisconsin
Irene R. Pieper
Milwaukee, Wisconsin
Janet M. Porte
Greenfield, Wisconsin
Bernice Portis
Dallas, Texas
Sister Janet Provost, I.H.M.
St. Stephen, Wyoming
Lois A. Rainis
Woodbury, New Jersey
Don Reese
Weaverville, California
Zoe A. Reznick
Yonkers, New York
Emily S. Rodgers
Soddy, Tennessee

Evangelina C. de Rodriguez
  Rio Piedras, Puerto Rico
Nancy Flanders Rose
  White River Junction,
  Vermont
Mary F. Roussel
  Westwego, Louisiana
Mary Roybal
  Winnemucca, Nevada
Jane D. Sack
  Statesboro, Georgia
Diana Sauceda
  Dallas, Texas
Patricia L. Scott-Baumgarten
  Leavenworth, Kansas
Barbara Shepard
  Rainier, Oregon
Jean Sherrill
  Orlando, Florida
Marie Shimp
  Cambridge, Ohio
Louise Smith
  Columbia, South Carolina

Phyllis A. Smith
  Statesboro, Georgia
Lena Mae Sparkman
  Prairie Grove, Arkansas
Jane A. Steele
  Vancouver, Washington
Marian Thompson
  Wilkinsburg, Pennsylvania
Virginia Towne
  Lake Forest, Illinois
Beverley Triber
  Columbia, South Carolina
Helen G. Walls
  Bear, Delaware
Arla Bolton Weaver
  Haslett, Michigan
Susanne L. Woodford
  Federal Way, Washington
Elaine Yamashita
  Kahului, Hawaii
M. Patricia Youngman
  Ellensbury, Washington

About Reading Is Fundamental . . .

Reading is Fundamental, Inc. (RIF) is a national nonprofit organization that works for a literate America by inspiring young people to read and to aspire through reading. RIF works through a network of local projects spanning all fifty states, Washington, D.C., Puerto Rico, the Virgin Islands, and Guam. This grassroots network makes it possible for millions of children to choose and to own books that interest them without cost to them or their families. With the help of more than ninety thousand volunteers—nearly 40 percent of whom are parents—RIF conducts imaginative activities that bring books alive and make reading a meaningful experience for children. RIF also works directly with parents to help them encourage reading in the home.

Founded in 1966 by Mrs. Robert S. McNamara, RIF is now the largest reading-motivation program in America. Since its founding, it has brought more than seventy-eight million books to America's children. RIF is affiliated with the Smithsonian Institution.